D1274300

A History
of the

INDIANA
HISTORICAL
SOCIETY

1830-1980

A History
of the

INDIANA
HISTORICAL
SOCIETY

1830-1980

Lana Ruegamer

Indianapolis: Indiana Historical Society 1980

PREFACE

In February, 1979, Gayle Thornbrough invited me to write a sesquicentennial history of the Indiana Historical Society. It was explained to me that what was wanted was the assessment of a nonparticipant, hence my primary qualification for the task was that I was, by Society standards, a newcomer and an outsider, since my own association with the organization had begun only in the fall of 1975. I have been granted full access to the Society's records and have not been censored at any turn. The views represented are my own and do not represent an official point of view—hence the title is "*A History of the Indiana Historical Society,*" not "*The* History. . . ."

Many people have contributed to this project. Lisa Nowak, Indiana Historical Society editorial assistant, was a stalwart and imaginative researcher, running down the answers to hundreds of obscure queries, assembling dozens of brief biographies, and generally performing whatever research tasks she was asked to do. It would have been impossible to complete the research for this study within the time allotted without her dedicated and efficient assistance.

Thanks are also due to the staffs of various research libraries: in the Indiana State Library, the Indiana Division (especially Anne Altemose), the Newspaper section, the Genealogy, Reference and Loan divisions; the Archives division of the Commission on Public Records; Saundra Taylor, head of manuscripts, and Carole Coady of the Lilly Library, Indiana University, Bloomington; Elizabeth Stege Teleky, the Joseph Regenstein Library, University of Chicago; the Rutherford B. Hayes Memorial Library; and the staff of the Stevens Museum Genealogy Library, Washington County Historical Society, Salem, Indiana. Thanks also to the staff of the Indiana Historical Bureau, who assisted the project on several occasions. Thomas Rumer, head librarian, and the staff of the Indiana Historical Society Library were unfailingly helpful when confronted with an apparently endless series of requests. Eric Pumroy, manuscripts librarian, was a major source of information on the contents and history of the library itself, contributing much fugitive information. Alice M. Johnston, Indiana Historical Society financial secretary, was a helpful guide to the Society's filing system, past and present.

Thanks also are due to Society photographer Dan Kiernan for substantial aid in preparing illustrations and to those individuals and institutions that permitted the Society to use illustrative material from their collections. A special thanks to Charles Griffo, Indianapolis *Star-News*, for permission to reprint news photographs from those publications.

I am grateful for information provided by the following persons: Gayle Thornbrough, Dorothy L. Riker, Hubert H. Hawkins, Caroline Dunn, and James H. Kellar all granted long interviews on one or more occasions; Cleta Robinson responded to questions in a telephone interview; and Howard H. Peckham provided a thoughtful letter reviewing his tenure as secretary. They were generous eyewitness commentators on various aspects of the Society's history, and whatever seems vivid and real in this presentation is mainly attributable to their testimony.

The manuscript benefited from the comments of numerous readers. Within the Society Gayle Thornbrough, Dorothy Riker, and Paula Corpuz read and criticized all drafts. Mrs. Corpuz also took time from her research duties to act as chief copy editor. The outside reader was Martin Ridge of the Huntington Library, San Marino, California, who generously read all drafts, raising important questions about organization and interpretation and challenging errors of style and syntax at every turn. All the readers have improved this book; its inperfections are attributable to the author alone.

Most of all I want to thank Gayle Thornbrough for the opportunity to write the book and for the serene patience and confidence she demonstrated while waiting for me to deliver it.

Lana Ruegamer, *Editor*
Indiana Historical Society

TABLE OF CONTENTS

A History
of the

INDIANA
HISTORICAL
SOCIETY

1830-1980

I

An
Introduction

John Hay Farnham
(1792-1833)

Founder and corresponding secretary

I

"This meeting is fully impressed with the importance and necessity of collecting and preserving the materials for a comprehensive and accurate history of our country, natural, civil and political, many of which are of an ephemeral and transitory nature, and in the absence of well directed efforts to preserve them are rapidly passing into oblivion. . . ."

John H. Farnham
December 11, 1830

Western historical societies tended to leap prematurely into the world in the 1820s and 1830s and then be rewarded for their impertinence by widespread neglect and indifference, leading almost invariably to early death. For reasons not easily discerned, this did not quite happen to the Indiana Historical Society. It was, to be sure, neglected, and for the first fifty-six years of its history it usually seemed more dead than alive; but then every four or five years the Society would rise from its deathbed, acquire a transfusion of new members, and make enthusiastic new plans before sinking back, a few months later, into its usual torpor. It would be pleasing to report that when the Society finally achieved regular annual meetings after 1886, it was rewarded for its extraordinary tenacity by generous legislative appropriations and widespread popular support; but this was not the case. Though the Society was no longer on the verge of death after 1886, it was small, modest, and virtually impoverished for many years to come.

Only in the wake of Progressivism and the state centennial, supported by a new state agency and the rise of professionalism in history, did the Society take on a more vigorous aspect. Between 1924 and 1944, under the leadership of a respected professional historian and administrator, the Society became an effective institution. Under later secretaries between 1945 and 1976 it became a large society, and since 1977, buoyed by dramatic new prosperity, the Society has emerged as the peer of the more distinguished state historical societies.

In its 150-year history, the Indiana Historical Society has been somewhat anomalous: it did not die when expected, nor did it flourish when other, later societies flourished. It did not acquire the normal state support at the normal time. Its lengthy relationships with the state historical agency and, independently, with the State Library are at least unusual and probably unique. It seemed such an oddity to Walter Muir Whitehill in 1962 when he published *Independent Historical Societies* that he described it in a chapter entitled "State Archival Agencies," apparently questioning that it belonged with the historical societies at all.[1]

And yet, anomaly or not, the Indiana Historical Society has been an institution of real consequence to Indiana history during most of its one hundred and fifty years, and within the past fifty years it has made occasional noteworthy contributions to the national historical community. Certainly the Society's history has demonstrated the flexibility of the historical society form as it is adapted to the peculiar and complex conditions that prevailed in Indiana.

The Society's history also reveals how rare and valuable were the persons who concerned themselves about state and local his-

---

[1] The standard history of American historical societies is Walter Muir Whitehill, *Independent Historical Societies* (Boston: Boston Athenaeum, 1962). For his discussion of the Indiana Historical Society see pp. 495-97.

tory. Though in recent years professionally trained historians have newly turned to local history to study patterns of social and geographic mobility in the United States, most local history still depends upon the concerned observer and participant in his or her community—someone who feels a responsibility to remember, record, and preserve as carefully and fully as possible the persons, institutions, events, and ways of life in danger of being forgotten.

It is this task—making sense of the individual communities in this large national republic by affording them the dignity of a special investigation and discovering their individuality—that falls essentially to historical societies. The role is an important one both because it is critical in providing the material for an accurate national history and because it is crucial in linking people to a community. A sense of the specificity of a place is nowadays often difficult to acquire in a highly mobile national society, with ubiquitous restaurant "chains," national communications networks, undistinguishable interstate highways, and all the trappings of a mass production economy. Local historians rescue communities, states, and regions from anonymity—as family historians and other biographers rescue individuals—revealing and explaining the special nature of places, institutions, and persons of local significance.

Historical societies are not, of course, uniquely American phenomena any more than the need for a special sense of being linked to a community is American. Societies first appeared in Europe, springing up in the eighteenth and nineteenth centuries. Historical consciousness was, of course, an important facet of the Enlightenment. The Massachusetts Historical Society, founded in 1791, is among the world's older historical societies, and it led the way in America. All the early societies seem to have been prompted by the same urge: to save rapidly disappearing records. They were always formed by learned men. In

Europe the societies, chartered and subsidized by ruling princes, hastened to protect documents and artifacts that were often already many hundreds of years old; in America early historical societies were chartered by states and founded by individuals concerned about preserving material from the much more recent past.[2]

From a European point of view there may have been something faintly amusing about the formation of historical societies in America around the beginning of the nineteenth century. Even Massachusetts, after all, was less than two hundred years old when its society was founded, and in European terms that is scarcely a history at all. But if the Massachusetts society might have seemed amusing, the formation of societies in western states within a decade or two of their admission to statehood might, from the same view, have seemed downright absurd. Nevertheless, among the earliest American state historical societies were four from western states: Tennessee (1820), Illinois (1827), Michigan (1828), and Indiana (1830).[3]

One need not find these societies absurd to find them at least surprising. Frontiers are not places where one expects to find people with the leisure to read, write, and collect historical material. Frontiers are places whose history lies ahead, not behind them.

Yet American frontiers were populated in large part by persons from older and established communities, some of whom brought with them a sense of responsibility for history, an historical conscience. To these persons the point was not that there was only a brief history to record in a new state like Indiana, but

---

[2] For the international historical society movement see J. Franklin Jameson, *The History of Historical Societies* (Savannah, Ga.: Morning News, [1914]); Julian P. Boyd, "State and Local Historical Societies," in *American Historical Review*, XL (1934), 10-37.

[3] For early societies see Leslie W. Dunlap, *American Historical Societies, 1790-1860* (Madison, Wis.: [Cantwell Printing Co.], 1944).

that what little history there was seemed in peril of being lost. Perhaps for persons in a frontier community, looking for some special sense of identity in new and apparently undistinguishable villages, even a brief history was especially valuable. Moreover, Americans in the early nineteenth century were highly conscious of their past. Tocqueville reported in the 1820s the Americans' heady awareness of their special role in the world, their historic importance as a new country with a new form of government. Americans were making history, and nowhere was this more apparent than on the frontier, where farms and villages were being created out of a wilderness.[4]

Such a place was Indiana in December, 1830, when the Indiana Historical Society was founded by a "large and respectable" meeting of legislators and other citizens in Indianapolis. Organized as a territory only thirty years before, Indiana was still a rapidly growing frontier state. Its white population had increased from around 2,500 in 1800 to 343,000 in 1830. The state had been admitted to the union only fourteen years before, in December, 1816. The federal census described Indiana in 1830 as 100 percent rural, though dozens of villages dotted the countryside and contested noisily for pre-eminence. Even the capital city, Indianapolis, a mere grandiose plan in 1821, boasted not many more than a thousand inhabitants a decade later. There were, in fact, larger and also otherwise more impressive Indiana towns than Indianapolis in 1830: Vincennes, Madison, New Albany, Richmond, Lafayette, Salem, and Lawrenceburg all either rivaled or surpassed the capital in population, and most were either Wabash or Ohio River towns, hence more accessible

---

[4] Tocqueville was usually annoyed by this awareness, which he saw as rude conceit and excessive national pride. Alexis de Tocqueville, *Democracy in America* (2 volumes. Cambridge: Sever and Francis, 1863), I, 141-42, 408, II, 275-76. Howard Mumford Jones comments extensively on American republican self-consciousness in the early national period. Howard Mumford Jones, *O Strange New World: American Culture: The Formative Years* (New York: Viking, 1964), pp. 312-50.

than Indianapolis. But even the largest towns, New Albany and Madison, were only rough frontier villages in comparison with eastern cities and towns.[5]

The census report that Indiana was 100 percent rural in 1830 was euphemistic. "Rural" suggests agriculture, farms, cleared land, whereas, though there were also prairie lands and meadows, much of Indiana was a primeval forest. Unlike the present-day well-cared-for state and national forests, filled mostly with young trees and with dead timber cleared out regularly, the Indiana forest of 1830—especially in the southern part of the state where most pioneers settled—was dense and ominous. There were enormous trees, both standing and fallen, and, though the timber was an essential resource for building and for fuel and though woodlands promised fertile soil, the forest itself was simply an obstacle to the pioneers. The trees harbored dangerous animals and hostile Indians; they were maddeningly difficult to remove, especially the stumps and roots of ancient trees; and at night they created an eerie atmosphere, as a British traveler to Indiana in 1830 reported:

> The gloom and pitchy darkness of an American forest at night, cannot be conceived by the inhabitants of an open country, and the traversing a narrow path interspersed with stumps and logs is both fatiguing and dangerous. Our horse seemed so well aware of this danger, that whenever the night set in, he could not be induced to move, unless one of us walked a little in advance before him, when he would rest his nose on our arm and then proceed.[6]

---

[5] For Indiana towns ca. 1830 see *The Indiana Gazetteer or Topographical Dictionary* (2d ed. Indianapolis: Douglass and Maguire, 1833). The directory lists the following as the ten largest towns in Indiana: Terre Haute, 600; Jeffersonville, 700; Salem, 1000; Lawrenceburg, 1000; Indianapolis, 1085; Lafayette, 1200; Vincennes, 1600; Richmond, 1740; Madison, 2500; New Albany, 2500.

[6] S. A. Ferrall, *A Ramble of Six Thousand Miles through the United States of America* (London: Effingham Wilson, 1832), pp. 91-92.

Besides the difficulties created by the forest, there were other
perils for the pioneers. Much of Indiana was marshy, breeding
grounds for mosquitoes and malaria that killed hundreds during
the "sickly" season in August and September. Cholera epidemics
were also regular visitors.

But of course Indiana was filled with more than trees and dan-
gers; to the thousands of settlers who made their way into the
state every year in the 1820s and 1830s, it was filled with splendid opportunities. Land was cheap; the soil beneath the trees
was wonderfully fertile; and each new town meant profit and
hope for its founders. Timothy Flint, a geographer and traveler
well acquainted with western bravura, was especially struck
by Indiana's vigorous town promoters. "None of the western
states have shown a greater propensity for town making than
this," he commented in 1828, adding that the founding of so
many towns detracted from the importance of any one of them.
"In no part of the world," Flint went on, "has the art of trumpet-
ing, and lauding the advantages, conveniences and future
prospects, of the town to be sold, been carried to greater
perfection."[7]

The exhilaration of the pioneer lawyer and businessman
watching immigrants flood into the state was as heady as the
pioneer farmer's response to the virgin land. A clever, hardworking man could build a fortune, a town, a reputation, perhaps a
dynasty in this new place. The National Road coming west from
Ohio was under construction in Wayne County, and the Michigan Road, designed to go from the Ohio River to Lake Michigan,
with the partial aim of expediting the removal of the Indians
from their territory in northern Indiana, was also begun in 1830.

---

[7] Timothy Flint, *Condensed geography and history of the Western States . . .*
(1828), reprinted in Harlow Lindley (ed.), *Indiana as Seen by Early Travelers*
(*Indiana Historical Collections*, III, Indianapolis: Indiana Historical Commission, 1916), p. 447.

Since the railroad was still only a novelty—the first section of the first American railroad was completed by the Baltimore and Ohio company in 1830—, Hoosier businessmen and legislators were planning to open up the interior of the state by linking canals to extensive natural streams.[8]

The depression of the 1820s had ended; the West was booming and western interests had shared in the triumph of Tennessee's Andrew Jackson in 1828. Jackson's victory in the Battle of New Orleans fifteen years earlier was still celebrated annually as a reflection of both national pride and western self-confidence. However, the state political scene in 1830 was not all that a conscientious citizen might have hoped. Organized political parties were beginning to make their influence felt, and Governor James Brown Ray, the last Hoosier governor to run as a nonpartisan candidate, was not accepting the changed political climate gracefully. Throughout 1830 he was engaged in lengthy, bad-tempered altercations with his opponents on petty subjects. The new parties' rallying calls to voters to support "Measures, not Men" reflected rejection of personal politics as exemplified by Ray.[9]

Fortunately, the growth of partisanship did not prevent the simultaneous growth of nonpartisan concern about the moral and intellectual development of the new state. Many of the ambitious young leaders in politics and business were also

---

[8] R. Carlyle Buley, *The Old Northwest: Pioneer Period, 1815-1840* (2 volumes. Indianapolis: Indiana Historical Society, 1950), I, 500-502, 511; Lee Burns, *The National Road in Indiana* (Indiana Historical Society *Publications*, VII, No. 4, Indianapolis, 1919), p. 220.

[9] For Battle of New Orleans celebration see Gayle Thornbrough, Dorothy Riker, and Paula Corpuz (eds.), *Diary of Calvin Fletcher* (7 volumes to date. Indianapolis: Indiana Historical Society, 1971-1980), I, 188. For the political scene see Dorothy Riker and Gayle Thornbrough (eds.), *Messages and Papers of James Brown Ray* (*Indiana Historical Collections*, XXXIV, Indianapolis: Indiana Historical Bureau, 1954).

anxious to shape Indiana's social life and conscience. In most instances this concern was expressed in local religious and reform groups, advocating programs ranging from free public education and Sunday schools to temperance and African colonization of free Negroes.[10]

The frequent hostility or indifference of a large majority of the population did not significantly deter these would-be community leaders, who were an elite group of educated professional men. John Hay Farnham, the principal founder of the Indiana Historical Society, was an excellent representative of this group.

Farnham was born in 1791 in Newburyport, Massachusetts, to a distinguished family. His grandfather, Daniel Farnham (1719-1776), was a Harvard graduate, the first lawyer in Newburyport, and a prosperous public official during the colonial period.[11] His father, William Farnham, was a cultured and elegant man, admired by John Quincy Adams for his "science of politeness." He was headmaster of a grammar school for some years and held various minor federal offices during John Adams's presidency. William Farnham married one of the Emersons of Concord in 1790 and fathered a large family, of whom John Hay Farnham was the oldest child.[12] William Farnham apparently suffered some financial reverses by the time John was ready to prepare for Harvard—perhaps it was just the strain of supporting seven children—, for John Farnham was

---

[10] Thornbrough, Riker, and Corpuz (eds.), *Diary of Calvin Fletcher*, I, 153n, 186; Jacob Piatt Dunn, *History of Greater Indianapolis* (2 volumes. Chicago: Lewis Publishing Co., 1910), I, 87, 510-11. Most modern historians find it impossible to accept the early nineteenth-century characterization of the African colonization movement as a genuine reform movement and place it instead with reactionary movements.

[11] *Sibley's Harvard Graduates* (16 volumes. Boston: Massachusetts Historical Society, 1958), X, 364-66.

[12] John J. Currier, *History of Newburyport, Massachusetts, 1764-1909* (2 volumes. Newburyport: John J. Currier, 1909), II, 229.

Western Guide, August, 1873

left, Indianapolis in 1820, showing an auction of town lots; *below,* state treasurer Samuel Merrill moving the state archives to Indianapolis, 1825

opposite, **founding officers of the Society:**
above, Benjamin Parke, president; Isaac Blackford, 1st vice-president; *below,* Jesse Holman, 2d vice-president; James Scott, 3d vice-president

Indiana State Library

Society Library

Society Library

Society Library

Indiana University

Indiana University

Indiana State Museum

Jameson Woollen

Indiana University

Founding officers of the Society:
opposite, above, Bethuel F. Morris,
recording secretary; James Blake,
treasurer; *below,* Samuel Merrill,
executive committee; George H. Dunn,
executive committee

right, James Whitcomb, executive
committee; *below,* John Law, executive
committee; Isaac Howk, executive
committee

Indiana Historical Bureau

Mary Gilbert

Society Library

obliged to meet most of his own expenses at an academy and, beginning in 1807, at Harvard. At some point "in early life," John Farnham was injured and probably crippled by "a severe accident" that made him thereafter "constantly subject to much inconvenience and suffering. . . ."[13] It did not, however, prevent him from working his way through college. He was graduated in 1811. By 1818 Farnham was in Frankfort, Kentucky, editing a newspaper.[14] By 1819, he had moved to Jeffersonville, Indiana, and by 1820 was practicing law. In 1819 he was also appointed a Kentucky-based receiving officer of the American Antiquarian Society, of Worcester, Massachusetts, and contributed a description of Kentucky's Mammoth Cave for the society.[15]

Farnham spent his winters at the state capital (Corydon, until 1824, when the capital moved to Indianapolis), offering his considerable skills as speechwriter, bill-drafter, and polemicist to members of the state legislature. In 1821 he married Evelyn Marie Leonard, a fellow New Englander whose family then lived in Corydon. For nine legislative sessions between 1822 and 1833, Farnham was elected as a senate clerk. He also built a successful law practice and accumulated a small fortune.[16]

[13] This information about John H. Farnham comes from Samuel Merrill's unpublished "Eulogium on the Death of the Honorable John H. Farnham" [ca. 1833], mss. in Indiana Historical Society Library.

[14] Clarence S. Brigham, *History and Bibliography of American Newspapers, 1690-1820* (2 volumes. Worcester, Mass.: American Antiquarian Society, 1947), I, 152.

[15] Dwight L. Smith, "One Small Candle," June 24, 1972 (Bound typescript. Stevens Museum Genealogical Library, Salem, Indiana); "Extract of a Letter from John H. Farnham, Esq. a Member of the American Antiquarian Society, describing the Mammoth Cave, in Kentucky," in American Antiquarian Society *Transactions*, I (1820), 355-61; James Flint, *Letters from America* (Edinburgh: W. & C. Tait, 1822), "Addenda," p. 309.

[16] Warder W. Stevens, *Centennial History of Washington County, Indiana* (Indianapolis: B. F. Bowen & Co., 1916), p. 616; Herman Rave, article, Indianapolis *News*, September 16, 1898.

Some time around 1824 Farnham and his young family moved to Salem, Indiana. Farnham was immediately recognized as an important figure in the community. An artist depicted him as bright-eyed and intelligent, with the rather supercilious expression of a man who thinks well of himself and feels an amused contempt for the rest of the world. He was unpopular, tactless, opinionated, and tremendously industrious. His fellow citizens did not like him, but they did respect him. In Salem he was asked to deliver the Fourth of July address in 1826, the fiftieth anniversary of the Declaration of Independence. It was an important public event. (That same day Robert Owen announced a new moral order to the citizens of New Harmony.) Farnham chose the occasion to urge his neighbors to obey the sections of the Indiana constitution of 1816 calling for the establishment of free public schools. The speech profoundly offended the community and although he was not physically assaulted, perhaps in deference to his physical infirmity, he and his family were socially ostracized for a time.[17]

So far were his Salem neighbors from accepting the justice and desirability of free public schools that many denied the Indiana constitution of 1816 even allowed for such a policy. Farnham, like his unpopular Tory grandfather, was undaunted by his persecution ("the narrow circle of prejudice in which I unhappily got caught"), and simply wrote away to John Badollet, one of the authors of the education section of the constitution, for confirmation of the correctness of Farnham's own interpretation.[18]

---

[17] John Hay Farnham, "The Necessity of the Public School System in Indiana," pamphlet, July 4, 1826, Indiana Historical Society Library; Elizabeth Tucker Cauble, "John Hay Farnham," in *Indiana Magazine of History*, XX (1924), 154-59.

[18] John Hay Farnham to John Badollet, July 12, 1827, John Badollet Papers, microfilm in Indiana Historical Society Library.

John Farnham also supported temperance laws, female education, and the "humane guardianship of the poor." Naturally, he was an Adams man in politics.[19] In all of these views, Farnham was far from the opinions of the ordinary Hoosier of his day, but by virtue of his talents and his inclination to speak his mind, he was in a position to secure a hearing. Moreover, he was joined in the expression of highminded, though often unpopular views, by a number of other prominent public men in the state, many of whom were also founders of the Indiana Historical Society.

The first officers of the Society were among the most prominent men in the state. In addition to Farnham, they included Benjamin Parke, a highly respected federal district court judge and member of the Indiana constitutional convention of 1816; the three judges of the Indiana supreme court, Isaac Blackford, Jesse L. Holman, and James Scott; the distinguished judge and reformer Bethuel F. Morris; James Blake, a private citizen with an unusual public conscience, described in later years as "The Grand Old Man of Indianapolis"; Samuel Merrill, Indiana state treasurer, later a banker; George H. Dunn, a popular legislator and later also state treasurer; James Whitcomb, just beginning his political career in 1830, later to serve two terms as governor and as United States senator; John Law, a judge and historian of Vincennes; and Isaac Howk, speaker of the Indiana House of Representatives. Though only half of these men were to remain active in the Society for more than five years (three died within five years—Farnham, Howk, and Parke), all were involved in civic enterprises throughout their lives. Bethuel Morris (1792–1864), for instance, was a devoted Presbyterian, active in the Sunday school, the temperance society, the Indianapolis Board of Health, and was a trustee of Indiana University.[20] Similarly Jesse

---

[19] [John Hay Farnham], *Inaugural Address of His Excellency John H. Farnham to the Indianapolis Legislature, Friday Evening, January 4th, 1833* ([Indianapolis]: N. Bolton, 1833).

[20] Dunn, *Greater Indianapolis*, I, 87, 112, 135, 239, 342, 447, 556, 582.

Holman, who lost his supreme court seat at the end of December, 1830, and did not maintain a connection with the Society, became a Baptist minister and a founder of Franklin College.[21]

Benjamin Parke (1777-1835), like Farnham a resident of Salem, was an obviously appropriate choice for first president of the Society. For one thing, though only in his early fifties he was an historic figure in Indiana. Son of a New Jersey farmer, Parke had left home at age twenty and studied law at Lexington, Kentucky, with the eminent attorney James Brown. In 1801 the amiable and dignified Parke moved to Vincennes, struck up a friendship with William Henry Harrison, and quickly moved into a position of influence in the territory. He was attorney general, congressman, territorial judge, and he fought in the Battle of Tippecanoe as captain of a horse company.[22]

Parke was an honest man as well as a prominent one. He suffered severe financial hardships from his association with the Vincennes Steam Mill Company. The organizers of the company named him agent in 1821 to capitalize on his prestige, and when the mill burned down mysteriously in February, 1822, taking with it most of the paper assets of the Vincennes State Bank, Parke alone among the officers of the company and of the bank accepted responsibility for the company's indebtedness. He sold all of his property in Vincennes to satisfy the mill's creditors, moved to a modest house in Salem, and spent the rest of his life repaying the balance of the debt from his salary as a United States district court judge.[23]

Parke was also a cultural leader. He founded the Vincennes

---

[21] *Representative Men of Indiana* (2 volumes. Cincinnati: Western Biographical Publishing Company, 1880), 4th District, pp. 34-35.

[22] Charles Dewey, *An Eulogium upon the Life and Character of the Hon. Benjamin Parke: Delivered at Indianapolis, on the 1st day of June, 1836, at the request of the members of the Bar* (Indianapolis: Bolton & Livingston, Printers, 1836).

[23] Jacob Piatt Dunn, *Indiana and Indianans* (5 volumes. Chicago: The American Historical Society, 1919), I, 330-31.

Public Library, the Indianapolis Law Library, and the Salem
Female Academy. His was to be the first signature on the Indiana
Historical Society's constitution, and he would preside at several
meetings of the Society before his death in 1835.[24]

Six of the twelve founding officers of the Society served for
many years, and it would fall upon their shoulders to prevent
the organization's demise. Fortunately, most of these founders
were relatively young (only Blackford among the six was over
forty), and their faithful, though intermittent, interest would
help to maintain the Society's existence throughout the long
struggle to establish the organization on a regular, active basis.

John Law (1796-1873) of Vincennes held office for the longest
period of all the founders. He served in different offices for
thirty-six years. Like all the other founders except James Blake,
Law was a lawyer. Like Farnham, he came from a distinguished
Yankee family, the Laws of Connecticut, and enjoyed an excellent education (he was graduated from Yale in 1814, at age
eighteen).[25]

Isaac Blackford (1786-1859) served twenty-nine years. A
Princeton graduate, Blackford was most known for his lengthy
service on the Indiana supreme court and his punctilious report-
age of supreme court decisions. He was also active, however, in
organizations supporting improved education and in the Indiana
Colonization Society. Saddened by the early deaths of his wife
and only child, the learned and conscientious Blackford lived
quietly in rooms in the otherwise deserted governor's mansion

---

[24] Dewey, *Eulogium . . . of the Hon. Benjamin Parke*; *Proceedings of the Indiana Historical Society, 1830-1886* (Indiana Historical Society *Publications*, I,
No. 1, Indianapolis, 1897).

[25] James A. Woodburn, "The Indiana Historical Society: A Hundred Years,"
in *Centennial Handbook, Indiana Historical Society, 1830-1930*, edited by
Christopher B. Coleman (Indiana Historical Society *Publications*, X, No. 1, Indianapolis, 1930), pp. 20-23.

on the Circle. He attended the Society's meetings regularly and presided more often than any other officer during those years.

Jimmy Blake (1791-1870)—afterwards "Uncle Jimmy"—served the Society for twenty-three years. A businessman who undertook a wide variety of enterprises with only occasional success, Blake was at different times ginseng trader, tavernkeeper, railroad builder, rolling mill operator, manufacturer of corn molasses, bank director, and fire insurance company president. Above all, Blake was a bon homme.[26] He came to Indianapolis in 1821 and was a founder not only of the town but also of nearly all its good works. Large, brawny, and enthusiastic, Blake was Fourth of July parade marshal every year for many years and Calvin Fletcher called him the "unofficial host of Indianapolis." For thirty-five years he was president of the Indianapolis Benevolent Society. He was active in Sunday schools, temperance, the fire department, the militia, and the movement to reform the treatment of the insane. He greeted trains full of returning soldiers during the Mexican War and the Civil War, comforted the sick, attended funerals, and served continually on committees.[27] The range of his benevolences was staggering and took a toll on his pocketbook. Fortunately, his wife was independently wealthy.[28] Blake had no political ambitions, never held public office. The Society for Blake, as for most of the other founders, was one among many other interests.

---

[26] *Representative Men of Indiana*, 7th District, pp. 102-103; Dunn, *Greater Indianapolis*, I, 92, 96, 98, 128, 330, 360.

[27] John H. Holliday, *Indianapolis and the Civil War* (Indiana Historical Society *Publications*, IV, No. 9, Indianapolis, 1911), p. 527; Thornbrough, Riker, and Corpuz (eds.), *Diary of Calvin Fletcher*, I, 43.

[28] James H. Madison, "Businessmen and the Business Community in Indianapolis, 1820-1860" (Ph.D. dissertation, Indiana University, 1972), p. 136. Calvin Fletcher wrote on December 29, 1840, "[James Blake] owes $14000 fourteen thousand dollars   all been expended in building benevolent societies   lost debts on merchandize &c." Thornbrough, Riker, and Corpuz (eds.), *Diary of Calvin Fletcher*, II, 262.

George H. Dunn (1797-1854) and Samuel Merrill (1792-1855) served as Indiana Historical Society officers for eighteen years each. Dunn, a native New Yorker who migrated to Lawrenceburg, Indiana, participated actively at meetings and was often called upon to act as recording secretary *pro tem.* "Solid, undemonstrative," he was a successful businessman and a responsible Presbyterian layman.[29] Merrill, a Vermont Yankee educated at Dartmouth College, served actively both on the Society's executive committee and as the second president of the Society. He, too, was a prominent Presbyterian, to be credited with bringing Henry Ward Beecher to Indianapolis, and he was a solid supporter of public education.[30]

James Whitcomb (1791-1852), another Vermonter, served as a Society officer for only nine years in two widely separated terms on the executive committee, but whenever he served he was full of ideas and active in meetings. Whitcomb was educated at Transylvania University. A successful politician and respected lawyer, Whitcomb as governor secured the passage of laws providing for a state hospital for the insane and state schools for the blind and for the deaf and mute.[31]

This group of civic-minded men—all lawyers except for Jimmy Blake—came to Indianapolis from various parts of the state during the legislative session in the winter of 1830–1831,

---

[29] *History of Dearborn and Ohio Counties, Indiana* (Chicago: F. E. Weakley & Co., 1885), pp. 153-54, 227, 272, 299; Leander J. Monks, Logan Esarey, and Ernest V. Shockley (eds.), *Courts and Lawyers of Indiana* (3 volumes. Indianapolis: Federal Publishing Co., 1916), I, 88.

[30] Dunn, *Indiana and Indianans,* I, 368, 470, II, 873, 886; Jane Shaffer Elsmere, *Henry Ward Beecher: The Indiana Years, 1837-1847* (Indianapolis: Indiana Historical Society, 1973), pp. 79-80.

[31] William Wesley Woollen, *Biographical and Historical Sketches of Early Indiana* (Indianapolis: Hammond & Co., 1883), pp. 82-93; *Proceedings of the Indiana Historical Society, 1830-1886,* pp. 10, 13, 17, 18, 19, 22, 23, 27, 28, 34, 35, 36.

when Governor James Brown Ray announced on December 7 the arrival of four boxes of public documents from the Secretary of State of the United States. Two of the boxes, Ray told the legislature, were to be presented to the state college at Bloomington, and two boxes of duplicate material were to go to "the first established historical society in Indiana."[32] The Congress had passed a law the preceding summer authorizing the distribution of the printed copies of the diplomatic correspondence of the American Revolution and copies also of the House and Senate journals to various state and federal offices and repositories around the country, and including "each incorporated university, college, historical or antiquarian society and athenaeum...."[33] Hence, two unsolicited boxes of historical material appeared in Indianapolis earmarked for a nonexistent historical society.

John H. Farnham needed no more stimulus to action than this. He quickly published notice of a public meeting to consider the formation of a state historical society, and four days later, December 11, 1830, on the fourteenth anniversary of Indiana's admission to the Union, the Indiana Historical Society was founded.[34]

Since historical societies were founded in Ohio (February, 1831) and Virginia (December, 1831) after the boxes were, presumably, sent out to them, it may be that those societies were also founded at the prompting of the Federal Congress. Since other states were to lack historical societies for many years to come, one must assume that their boxes were either misappropriated or unclaimed in 1830. The earliest western societies, however, did not thrive—boxes or no boxes. Tennessee's society

---

[32] Riker and Thornbrough (eds.), *Messages and Papers of Governor James Brown Ray*, p. 583.

[33] United States Congress, *Statutes at Large*, Sess. I (May 26, 1830), p. 407.

[34] *Proceedings of the Indiana Historical Society, 1830-1886*, p. 10.

failed in 1822, only two years after it began. Illinois's ambitious young society could not endure the strain of its self-imposed research assignments and quietly dissolved in the mid-1830s after its founder, James Hall, left the state. Michigan's society lived only in widely separated fits and starts until its termination in 1861.[35]

The Indiana Historical Society also did not thrive for many years, but unlike its western predecessors it never altogether vanished. For 150 years Farnham's society of civic-minded men continued to exist. Its history reflects the surprising tenacity of that small group and their ability to recruit successors.

---

[35] Dunlap, *American Historical Societies,* pp. 149-50, 173-74, 209-10; Randolph C. Randall, *James Hall: Spokesman of the New West* (Columbus: Ohio State University Press, 1964), pp. 159-60.

II

Many Beginnings

1830-1886

Society Library

Signatures on Society constitution,
the first page

II

"The Indiana Historical Society came into existence on December 11, 1830. Its existence has been very quiet. So quiet at times as to suggest death."
Jacob Piatt Dunn, 1897

It began very well. John Farnham put notices in the Indianapolis newspaper, and a few days later on December 11, 1830, a Saturday night, more than half the members of the Indiana General Assembly and a number of other interested men met at the Marion County Courthouse "at candle lighting" to form an historical society.[1]

Farnham invited William Graham of Brownstown, a rugged Jackson County pioneer and a former speaker of the house, to chair the meeting and appointed the elegant Henry P. Thornton, representative from Salem, secretary.[2] Farnham then spoke briefly on the need for an historical society and presented resolutions to form one:

Whereas, This meeting is fully impressed with the importance and necessity of collecting and preserving the materials for a compre-

---

[1] Indianapolis *Indiana Journal,* December 11, 1830; John B. Dillon's remarks in *ibid.,* October 8, 1873.

[2] For Graham see Monks *et al., Courts and Lawyers of Indiana,* I, 83-84, 88. For Thornton see *History of Lawrence, Orange and Washington Counties, Indiana* (Chicago: Goodspeed Brothers & Co., 1884), p. 112. Both men were Clay supporters, like Farnham. *Proceedings of the Indiana Historical Society, 1830-1886,* pp. 9-10.

hensive and accurate history of our country, natural, civil and political, many of which are of an ephemeral and transitory nature, and in the absence of well directed efforts to preserve them are rapidly passing into oblivion; and whereas, the establishment of safe depositories for the keeping of natural curiosities, manuscripts, public documents, etc., in the custody of intelligent guardians interested in their accumulation and preservation, has ever been found promotive of the public good and auxiliary to the advancement of science and literature; therefore,

Resolved, As the sense of this meeting, that it is expedient to form ourselves into a society to be known and designated by the name of the "HISTORICAL SOCIETY OF INDIANA."

Farnham then presented a constitution, which was duly adopted and signed by approximately ninety of the men present. The signatures on the Society's constitution of 1830 attest to the presence at that meeting of many of the most distinguished figures in Indiana history: in addition to the founding officers, there were Calvin Fletcher, William Polke, Milton Stapp, Noah Noble, Albert S. White, Charles Dewey, James M. Ray, Obed Foote, Tilghman A. Howard, William Conner, David Wallace, Samuel Judah, John Tipton, Isaac Coe, and John De Pauw, to mention a few of the more conspicuous names. It was initially as impressive a show of public support for an historical society as the movement had yet inspired in America.[3]

Even so, during the ensuing fifty-six years the Indiana Historical Society was to endure a discouraging series of lapses and reorganizations. The Society would meet in only twelve of the fifty-six years between 1830 and 1886 and only once in the decade of the 1860s. Before 1886 it would accumulate and then lose a valuable collection of books and manuscripts. The ques-

---

[3] *Proceedings of the Indiana Historical Society, 1830-1886*, pp. 10-13. The figure "ninety" was acquired by evaluating the manuscript of the original constitution, which indicates dates when dues were collected, hence when signers joined, since they signed in order of joining.

tion arises, how could the Society survive these repeated disappointments? The answer seems to lie in the nature of the Society's leadership in this period.

The Farnham Years, 1830-1833

John Farnham was both an industrious and a well-educated man. As a member of the American Antiquarian Society he was acquainted with the workings of historical societies. The Indiana Historical Society was essentially shaped by his hand. He called the first meeting and wrote the constitution. The Society's constitution bound its members to co-operate to collect materials on "the natural, civil, and political history of Indiana." Unlike most of the earlier societies, Indiana's constitution omitted mention of ecclesiastical history, and the Indiana society's inclusion of political history as a field for collection was an innovation. The Society's other goals were "the promotion of useful knowledge, and the friendly and profitable intercourse of such citizens of the state as are disposed to promote the aforesaid objects." The fellowship of persons interested in history, then, was an important object for Farnham.[4]

The Society's original constitution provided for two meetings a year, both during times when many of the lawyer-legislator founders were likely to be in Indianapolis: the first during the supreme court sessions in May and the second during the annual legislative session in December and January. The organization was to be led by a president, three vice-presidents, a treasurer, a corresponding secretary, a recording secretary, and five executive committee members, all twelve of whom were charged with

---

[4] For discussion of the usual characteristics of early societies see Dunlap, *American Historical Societies*, pp. 18-20, and throughout.

responsibility to arrange lectures, publish appropriate materials, keep the Society's possessions safe, and report yearly on their proceedings. Unlike most of the other early societies, Indiana's did not provide for a librarian and cabinet keeper. The constitution also omitted mention of regular committees to help with the work of the Society. All of the Society's responsibilities, then, were entrusted to its twelve officers, no one of whom would have a special duty to oversee its collections.

The membership requirements, as Farnham originally wrote them, were simply that a candidate sign the constitution and pay a dollar a year in dues. This policy was first amended in the organizational meeting to provide for election by ballot; it was then restored at the second meeting, when Farnham persuaded the Society to eliminate the election requirement. The issue would crop up again in future years. The early Society, in any event, aimed to be a popular society, open to all interested persons, though in practice this was limited to all interested men.[5]

Perhaps the structure of the organization made little difference as long as there was at least one person who was willing to do all the work and a few others interested enough to attend executive committee meetings and comprise a quorum. The sine qua non was the one person willing both to do all the work himself and to spur his fellow members to support the work at least by their presence at meetings.

Farnham's new Society met again on December 15, 1830, to elect officers and plan a program of action. Farnham nominated Benjamin Parke, his fellow townsman and a widely admired jurist, to be president. This was a promising strategy, since Parke was civic-minded, popular, and readily accessible to Farnham.

---

[5] For the constitution and changes see Minutes of the Indiana Historical Society, 1830-1877 (Bound mss., Indiana Historical Society Library), pp. 1-4, 16-18. Hereafter this manuscript material will be cited as Minutes of IHS.

The election of the three supreme court judges Blackford, Holman, and Scott, to the three vice-presidencies may have been primarily a gesture to add dignity to the new society, but one of the justices, Isaac Blackford, was to prove a loyal member. The other offices were filled by men who showed an interest in the Society's work: Bethuel F. Morris, recording secretary; James Blake, treasurer; Samuel Merrill, George H. Dunn, Isaac Howk, James Whitcomb, and John Law, executive committee. Farnham chose the most demanding office, that of corresponding secretary, for himself.[6]

At the suggestion of Jeremiah Sullivan (1794-1870), a vigorous politician and Presbyterian reformer known also as the man who named Indianapolis, the constitution was amended at the second meeting to provide for the election of honorary members to the Society. Eight honorary members were elected that evening, all western men, most of them interested either in historical societies or education. They included William Henry Harrison, former territorial governor and the hero of Tippecanoe; Governor Lewis Cass of Michigan Territory, president of the Historical Society of Michigan; Governor Edward Coles of Illinois; President Andrew Wylie of Indiana College, the struggling young school at Bloomington; educational innovator William Maclure of New Harmony; James Hall, president of the Illinois Historical Society; John Badollet of Vincennes, friend of Secretary of the Treasury Albert Gallatin and the putative author of the education article in the Indiana constitution; and Francis Vigo, the elderly fur trader who had advised George Rogers Clark more than fifty years earlier about the famous trek from Kaskaskia to Vincennes. The point of electing honorary members was to "solicit such information and assistance in further-

---

[6] *Proceedings of the Indiana Historical Society, 1830-1886*, pp. 15-16. For a complete list of officers since 1830 see Appendix.

ance of the objects of the society as it may be in their power to
make."[7]

The meeting also considered the question of appropriate subjects for the Society's attention. Their choices described the only
history the new state could look back upon: the Indian tribes,
the territorial period, ancient artifacts, and the primeval
environment.

Before adjournment on December 15, James Morrison re-
minded the group to claim the two boxes of books addressed to
the Indiana Historical Society in the governor's offices and urged
the executive committee to apply to the legislature for an act of
incorporation and also to request copies of all printed public documents. Such a bill was presented to the Indiana senate by one
of the original signers of the Society's constitution, William C.
Linton (1795-1835), a Terre Haute merchant, on December 28.
The charter conferring corporate status to the Society was
granted January 10, 1831, and continues to be the Society's legal
basis for existence in 1980. A joint resolution of the General
Assembly ordered the boxes to be delivered to the Indiana
Historical Society.[8]

On December 18, the officers and executive committee met,
eight of the twelve being present. It was the third Society meeting within the space of a week. On the subject of speakers for
the coming meetings, John Law proposed that Parke be asked to
speak at the May meeting "on the civil and political history of
this state from its earliest settlement." Farnham suggested that
Isaac McCoy, the Baptist missionary to Indians in Michigan

---

[7] *Ibid.*, p. 18. For Sullivan see *Representative Men of Indiana,* 4th District, pp.
62-64.

[8] Indiana *Senate Journal,* 1830-1831, pp. 168, 233; Indiana *House Journal,*
1830-1831, pp. 150-51, 169; *Laws of Indiana,* 1830-1831, p. 62. For Linton see
Biographical Directory of the Indiana General Assembly. Vol. I: *1816-1899*
(Indianapolis: Indiana Historical Bureau, 1980). For the text of the charter see
below, pp. 352-53.

Territory, and Benjamin Adams, Farnham's old neighbor from
Newburyport, Massachusetts, then living in Indiana, address
the next December meeting on "the ancient remains of the aborigines and natural curiosities in the state," reflecting an early
interest in prehistory that was to continue through the Society's
history.[9] Farnham also proposed that Andrew Wylie be asked
to speak at the same meeting on "the value and importance of
historical societies."

The officers authorized Farnham to undertake an extensive
letter-writing campaign to solicit help from fellow historical
societies and from "the most distinguished friends of science in
this and our sister states." Farnham was also asked to write to
the Indiana congressional delegation, the states, and the territories requesting "such aid and patronage as it has been customary
for them to give similar societies." To secure information about
Hoosier pioneers, Farnham was instructed to find volunteers
from each county to write histories of local settlers.

Armed with this mandate and driven by his own rather fero-
cious energy, Farnham set out to tell the country about his new
Society. He instructed Treasurer Jimmy Blake to have printed
four hundred copies of a circular with extracts from the constitution and the minutes of the meetings just held and also including a brief letter requesting the addressee's assistance in the
work of the Society. These circulars Farnham sent off to at least
some of those whom he had been instructed to address. Farnham
also wrote personal letters to some of the honorary members and
perhaps to some old friends in Massachusetts, too. The letter he
wrote to Francis Vigo is probably representative:

---

[9] For Adams see George R. Wilson (ed.), "Hindostan, Greenwich and Mt.
Pleasant. The Pioneer Towns of Martin County.—Memoirs of Thomas Jefferson Brooks," in *Indiana Magazine of History*, XVI (1920), 287. Adams and
Farnham had explored caves together in Jeffersonville and wrote accounts of
their findings for the American Antiquarian Society.

INDIANAPOLIS, December 20, 1830

COL. FRANCIS VIGO,
DEAR SIR,

I have the honor to inform you that the first Historical Society ever established in the State of Indiana was organized at this place on Wednesday Even last the 15th inst that Benjamin Parke was elected President, Judge Blackford, Holman & Scott Vice Presidents, J. H. Farnham Corresponding Secretary Judge Morris Recording Secretary, & James Blake Treasurer.—Judge Law, Samuel Merrill, Isaac Houk, Judge Dunn and James Whitcomb were elected the Executive Committee of said Society. One of the cardinal objects of the Society is to rescue from oblivion events of an interesting character that transpired at an early period of the settlement of what is now Indiana, and to collect all interesting information respecting the aborigines, and the remains of antiquity natural curiosities, habits and manners customs & curiosities of the native inhabitants etc—Believing that you could materially contribute to this important object of the society, and impressed with respect & gratitude for your patriotic services in the early settlement of Indiana, especially in pioneering the brave & gallant Clark & his intrepid soldiers thro' the wilderness from Kaskaskia to St. Vincents, in consequence of which the British Commander Hamilton & his men were captured, the Historical Society of Indiana have elected you an Honorary Member of the same and have directed me to communicate to you information of the fact, and to request of you thro' Judge Law, or Judge Blackford Officers of the Society to communicate to them any interesting information respecting the early settlement & history of Indiana that may be in your possession, assuring you that the same will be gratefully received   Any communication addressed to me at Salem Washington County Indiana will be safely received. Your acceptance of the within appointment will gratify the public and your obt servant

JOHN H FARNHAM
Corresponding Secretary of the Historical Society of Indiana[10]

Farnham had no responses to his work before the May, 1831, meeting. In fact the only recorded business of that meeting was

---

[10] Quoted in Woodburn, "The Indiana Historical Society: A Hundred Years," in Coleman (ed.), *Centennial Handbook*, p. 14n.

Jimmy Blake's report that Dr. Isaac Heylin, a former Philadelphian and one of the Society's founding members, had contributed a copy of *Annals of Philadelphia*. By November, however, Farnham had accumulated a number of treasures, and he called a special meeting to report to the Society about its new collection. They included a long letter from Massachusetts statesman Nathan Dane, confirming his own authorship of the slavery exclusion article of the Ordinance of 1787 governing the Northwest Territory, and a number of printed volumes. The books included all nine volumes of Dane's *General Abridgement of American Law*, copies of several speeches of Congressman Edward Everett—the famous orator, clergyman, and Farnham's former classmate at Harvard—, and from Jonathan Jennings, the former Indiana governor and congressman, four volumes of journals of Congress, and the journal of the Federal Convention of 1787.[11]

The members were pleased. The group authorized the executive committee to publish "such correspondence as they may deem of sufficient importance," the Nathan Dane letter, for example, which was, in fact, published, along with Farnham's original inquiry to Dane, in 1831.[12] The executive committee instructed Jimmy Blake to purchase a bookcase to accommodate its books, which were then stored in Henry P. Coburn's office. Coburn, like Farnham a Harvard graduate and Massachusetts na-

---

[11] Nathan Dane was also an officer of the Massachusetts Historical Society and may have prompted Farnham's election to that body as a corresponding member in August, 1831. *Proceedings of the Massachusetts Historical Society, 1791-1835*, I, 446-47; *Journal, acts and proceedings of the convention, assembled at Philadelphia, Monday, May 14, and dissolved Monday, September 17, 1787, which formed the Constitution of the United States* . . . (Boston: T. B. Wait, 1819); Nathan Dane, *A General Abridgement and Digest of American Law* (9 volumes. Boston: Cummings, Hilliard & Co., 1823-1829).

[12] A month later Samuel Merrill moved that the Society have 500 copies printed and distributed to members. Indianapolis *Indiana Journal*, December 14, 1831. The letter was subsequently reprinted by the Society in 1897.

tive, was both clerk of the Indiana supreme court and officer of the Society from 1835 to 1854, and his office was in a building near the courthouse on the circle.[13]

Since by the time of the November meeting Farnham had apparently not been able to persuade either Benjamin Adams or Isaac McCoy to agree to address the Society at the December meeting, the executive committee requested that he, Farnham, and James Whitcomb speak instead "upon such subjects as they may severally select."

Fortunately, the Rev. Andrew Wylie of the state college at Bloomington, a zealous Presbyterian clergyman, did not let the Society down. Out of the five men invited at different times to address the first annual meeting of the Indiana Historical Society in December, 1831, only Wylie accepted the honor. He addressed a small crowd at the hall of the Indiana House of Representatives at the courthouse on a severely cold Saturday evening, December 11, on the value and importance, not of historical societies, but of history.[14] In a discourse that ran to thirty-six pages when printed, Wylie (comparing Moses and George Washington in the course of his speech) argued that history had a salutary moral influence on the world, but he conceded that it had other uses as well, from that of amusement to inspiring poetry. Reverend Wylie then spent twenty pages reviewing the history of the West since B.C. 200, ending with a spirited defense of Protestantism.[15]

Wylie placed the concerns of the historical society in Indian-

---

[13] For Coburn see Dunn, *Greater Indianapolis*, II, 1235-37. The information that the books were kept in Coburn's office is verified by several sources: Berry R. Sulgrove, *History of Indianapolis and Marion County, Indiana* (Philadelphia: L. H. Everts & Co., 1884), pp. 105-106, and John Coburn, "What the Indiana Historical Society Has Done," in *Indianian*, IV (1899), 299.

[14] Indianapolis *Indiana Journal*, December 14, 1831.

[15] Andrew Wylie, *A Discourse Delivered before the Indiana Historical Society* . . . (Indianapolis: A. F. Morrison, 1831).

apolis squarely in the context of great historical forces spanning centuries and continents. This richly erudite production must have been received with pleasure and nostalgia by most of the Society's members, who were generally educated men with their college years a decade or two behind them. The Indianapolis *Indiana Journal* praised "the Reverend Orator" and noted especially that "The intimate connection of historical studies with the duties of life, more especially in relation to individuals engaged in a public career, was exhibited with much force and felicity."[16]

Certainly this was a connection the Society wished to draw for prominent figures in Indiana history, and especially for those who were still available to contribute their memoirs to the Indiana Historical Society. Apparently none of the first lot of honorary members had responded to Farnham's requests for information on early Indiana. The second group of honorary members was composed of distinguished citizens of other states (nine of them were from Massachusetts!), hence not in a position to write on Indiana's early history.[17] But Farnham took it upon himself to urge Indiana men like William Polke and John Tipton to contribute memoirs and documents to the Society. To former Judge Polke, the Michigan Road commissioner and close associate of Harrison, Farnham wrote in January, 1832, requesting "a memoir of your personal history." Polke was an especially interesting figure because he had been captured by Indians in his early childhood. Farnham warned that "The time is rapidly drawing near when the living actors in those interesting and

---

[16] Indianapolis *Indiana Journal*, December 14, 1831.

[17] This group included Nathan Dane, Joseph Story, Daniel A. White, Edward Everett, Thomas L. Winthrop, Orville Dewey, Jared Sparks, John Quincy Adams, Francis C. Gray, Nathan Guilford, Timothy Flint, Samuel Gilman, Rowland Heylin, William Gibbs Hunt, James Kent, and Edward Livingston. *Proceedings of the Indiana Historical Society, 1830-1886*, p. 29.

eventful scenes will be able to speak only in the Records they may chuse to leave behind them," then softened his warning with the benediction "God preserve you a thousand years."[18] Farnham apparently also approached the newly elected United States Senator John Tipton of Logansport, asking for copies of correspondence and other documents in the Virginia archives related to the George Rogers Clark expedition in 1779. Tipton in turn wrote to Governor Cass of Michigan for copies of documents on the Battle of Tippecanoe.[19]

Meanwhile, at John Law's request President Benjamin Parke wrote to Roman Catholic Bishop Benedict Joseph Flaget of Bardstown, Kentucky, in late December, 1831, or early January, 1832, requesting the gift of a specific document in the church archives at Vincennes over which Flaget had authority. The document was a manuscript Indian grammar and dictionary. Fortunately Flaget's response to that letter survives because it was printed in a newspaper in 1843, on the occasion of one of the Society's later revivals.

January 30, 1832

DEAR SIR:
The day before I received your friendly letter, I had a long conversation with a Father Jesuit lately from Europe, concerning the Grammar and Dictionary you mention; telling him it had been written formerly by a member of his society who, about 150 years ago, preached the gospel to the Indian nations, who lived between Lake Michigan and Ohio River. He expressed an uncommon desire of having the book in his possession, at least for a while, that he might draw a copy of it. My surprise was not small when next day came your letter, in which, acting in the name of the Historical Society of Indiana, whose president you are, you manifested the laudable desire of possessing the

---

[18] John H. Farnham to William Polke, January 30, 1832, Polke Papers, Lilly Library, Indiana University, Bloomington.

[19] Thomas W. Gilmer to John Tipton, May 3, 1832, [John Tipton to Lewis Cass], June 5, 1832, John Tipton Papers, Indiana Division, Indiana State Library.

said manuscript. I wish indeed to gratify both parties: and if the manuscript can be found, it will be possible for me to do so.

I have already sent word to Rev. Mr. Picot, who has succeeded to Rev. Mr. Chempomier, to look for the book and send it to me by the first opportunity. If ever I receive it I will give a chance to the Father Jesuit, who lives with me to copy it, if it be in his power; and this once done, with pleasure I would enrich the Library of the Historical Society with this precious monument of piety, learning and zeal; for very few individuals feel more than I do for the State of Indiana, where I went sent by Archbishop CARROLL in 1792, that is to say, exactly 40 years ago.

(Accept my good wishes etc)

BENEDICT JOSEPH FLAGET
Bishop of Bardstown[20]

There is no record of what, if anything, resulted from this activity. The Society's minutes are silent about 1832 and 1833. Farnham was a busy man in the winter of 1832-1833. He was re-elected secretary of the senate for that session, and he was also elected governor of the Indianapolis legislature, a popular mock legislature that met weekly on Saturday nights in the senate chamber of the courthouse to discuss all the important issues of the day. Farnham's "inaugural address" delivered January 4, 1833, is a document that combined a rather sly wit with a real statement of his political ideals.[21] However, Farnham was not neglecting the Society altogether. On January 17, 1833, Indianapolis was the scene of a large public dinner in honor of William Henry Harrison during the South Carolina nullification crisis. Farnham was present and announced at the end of the evening that General Harrison

---

[20] Law had requested Parke to write to the appropriate Roman Catholic authorities for copies of records in November, 1831. *Proceedings of the Indiana Historical Society, 1830-1886*, p. 28. The letter from Flaget was printed in the Indianapolis *Indiana Journal*, March 7, 1843.

[21] For the Indianapolis Legislature see Dunn, *Greater Indianapolis*, I, 81. See also [Farnham], *Inaugural Address*.

had presented to the Historical Society of this State, to be deposited in its archives the original correspondence of the Territorial Executive with the Government of the U. States, and that of the individual states, together with other interesting and valuable papers relating to the Territorial History of Indiana. . . .

Little wonder that Farnham hailed Harrison "as the friend and patron of the *Indiana Historical Society*"![22]

Farnham continued to be busy through the winter and spring as the mainstay of the Washington County Temperance Society and a sought-after public speaker. (He delivered the Washington's Birthday address in Salem in 1833, for example.) Benjamin Parke was also occupied during this time preparing an address to be delivered in Indianapolis on the feasibility of a statewide lyceum movement as a major tool for adult education.[23]

The Indiana Historical Society lost the services of both of these men in the summer of 1833. Cholera, a regular visitor to Indiana in the early part of the nineteenth century, arrived in Salem on June 25. Within two weeks more than a hundred persons had died, about 10 percent of the population, putting a cloud over the village that effectively stopped its growth for a generation.[24] Farnham's brother-in-law and friend Dr. Charles Hay (later the father of John Milton Hay) was swamped with patients, and Farnham helped him to attend to them, attempting at the same time to study the disease. The epidemic was all but over when Farnham became ill and died on July 10, twelve days before his forty-second birthday. His wife and infant child also perished in the epidemic. They were survived by two children,

---

[22] Indianapolis *Indiana Journal*, January 23, 1833. Unfortunately nothing more is known about Harrison's supposed gift to the Society. See also below, Chapter VII.

[23] Salem (Ind.) *Phoenix*, February 27, March 13, April 10, 1833; Dewey, *Eulogium . . . of the Hon. Benjamin Parke*, p. 10.

[24] Stevens, *Centennial History of Washington County, Indiana*, pp. 199-202.

Catherine Hay Farnham and William Sawyer Farnham, the latter around seven years old.[25]

The epidemic also killed Benjamin Parke's only heirs—his young son Barton, preparing for college, and his grandson, the only child of Parke's daughter, who had died not long before. Parke, a rather frail man, never recovered from the blow. He set aside his public work and plans for a statewide address, and he died of grief and consumption two years later, at age fifty-eight.[26]

The Society met some time after Farnham's death to hear a eulogy prepared by Samuel Merrill. The manuscript of the Merrill eulogy, given to the Society by his descendant Katharine Merrill Graydon in 1930, is a curious document, riddled with defensive references to Farnham's faults, as though Merrill were addressing, not Farnham's friends, but men who found him deeply annoying. "There are few whose characters are so likely to be misunderstood," Merrill wrote,

> as those who find pleasure and perform what they think duty in being constantly engaged. They value time and conceive that no part of it should be wasted. Interruptions may disturb and vex them, and their avocations may be so pressing as often to induce them to make hasty

[25] Letter from Dr. A. W. King, Redlands, California, in Salem (Ind.) *Democrat*, January 16, 1900. Farnham apparently saw the epidemic coming; his will is dated June 18, 1833. Probate Court Minute Book, B, pp. 121-22, Washington County Courthouse, Salem, Indiana. The surviving children's names appear in "An Act for the benefit of the heirs of John H. Farnham . . ." in *Laws of Indiana*, 1834-1835, pp. 148-49. These children lived for several years with the Charles Hay family until their guardian, Farnham's sister Charlotte, a thirty-seven-year-old spinster from Boston, came to Indiana to claim the children. She married one of Farnham's executors, George W. Leonard of Madison, Evelyn Farnham's uncle, and they lived the rest of their lives in Madison, Indiana. Both the Farnham children died young. The son, William Sawyer Farnham, died March 21, 1847, in Madison, aged twenty-one. *Items From Early Indiana Newspapers of Jefferson County, Indiana, 1817-1886*, compiled by Mary Hill (Madison, Ind., 1945), pp. 19, 34, 199.

[26] Woollen, *Biographical and Historical Sketches*, pp. 388-89; Dewey, *Eulogium . . . of the Hon. Benjamin Parke*, p. 10; John L. Campbell, "Benjamin Parke," in *Indianian*, VII (1901), 15-17.

conclusions. The system and order requisite to employ time to advantage may conflict with the pleasure and convenience of the idle, and it is not uncommon that those who are merely *busy* should be hastily pronounced proud, petulant and selfish.

Merrill went on to praise Farnham:

> In the extensive correspondence on behalf of this Society conducted solely by him, in the donations to it made by him and through his instrumentality, in his readiness and facility as an officer of the Senate to make suggestions in the best language, in his untiring efforts to extend the benefits of common schools, and to elevate the literary character of the State, and in the force, freedom and honesty with which he expressed his opinions on all important measures, it must be long before his place will be filled.

Farnham had been the man who had done "all the work" for the Society. Apparently he had not always been gracious about this with his fellow members.[27]

Perhaps the wonder is that the Society did not die once and for all after Farnham's death. Parke was in mourning, the other founders had been drawn in by Farnham's energy. It would have been understandable at this point if the Society had simply faded away. Certainly it appeared likely that this would happen. The Society met only briefly in 1835 after Parke's death to elect new officers. Samuel Merrill, who was elected president, was an extremely busy man. He was president of the State Bank of Indiana, and he was an officer in a wide variety of civic organizations. Though public spirited and capable, he was claimed more urgently by other responsibilities than those of the historical society. Supreme Court Judge Isaac Blackford, elected corresponding secretary, was similarly preoccupied with other causes.

Yet there were at least a few positive counterweights in the Society's overall prospects: for one thing, thanks to Farnham's

---

[27] Merrill, "Eulogium on the Death of the Honorable John H. Farnham."

industry and his own gifts, the Society owned some property—
a bookcase full of valuable books in a book-starved time and
place. Henry P. Coburn kept the bookcase in his office until
1848; his son later recalled having read many of the Society's
books as a boy.[28] But in addition to the books and their loyal
preserver Coburn, there were at least two Society members who
were actively engaged in writing Indiana history in the years
after Farnham's death. John Law, a Society founder and resident
of Vincennes for more than thirty years, wrote a brief colonial
history of Indiana delivered as an address before the Vincennes
Historical and Antiquarian Society in 1839. Law continued his
interest in history; he corresponded for more than twenty years
with Lyman Draper of the Wisconsin Historical Society on various aspects of the Old Northwest.[29] The other historian member—he appears to have joined the Society in 1835—was John
B. Dillon, usually described, despite Law's apparent priority, as
Indiana's first historian.[30] These men—Henry Coburn, his son
John Coburn, Law, and Dillon—together preserved the Society
through the leaderless years from 1835 to 1886.

The Society Adrift, 1835-1886

The Indiana Historical Society did not meet between 1836 and
1842. This was a trying time in Indiana's history, the period of

---

[28] Indianapolis *Daily Sentinel*, October 8, 1873. Farnham, who had a large
personal library, gave some of his books to the Society. There are a few volumes yet in the Society's collection with "Indiana Historical Society, Presented
by John H. Farnham" written in Farnham's hand on the flyleaf.

[29] See letters from John Law to Draper, 1844-1868, in Lyman Draper Collec-
tion, Wisconsin State Historical Society Library (microfilm copy in Indiana
Division, Indiana State Library); John Law, *Address Delivered before the
Vincennes Historical and Antiquarian Society, February 22, 1839* (Louisville:
Prentice and Weissinger, 1839).

[30] John Dillon's name appears among those of members with annotations
"paid 1835." Minutes of IHS, 1830-1877, p. 6.

the boom and rapid bust of a massive internal improvements program, an economic disaster exacerbated by the nationwide depression following the Panic of 1837. The fact that the Society's president, Samuel Merrill, was also president of the State Bank of Indiana during this difficult period may have tended to diminish the Society's chances for an early revival. It was not Merrill but John Law who took the lead in reorganizing the Society in the winter of 1842-1843.[31]

Meeting on December 30, 1842, in the supreme court room, the Society again elected three supreme court justices (Blackford, Jeremiah Sullivan, and Farnham's and Parke's close friend Charles Dewey) as vice-presidents. Merrill was re-elected president, Law was made corresponding secretary, and most of the executive committee were also former officers: Henry Coburn, James M. Ray, and George H. Dunn. The new faces at the executive committee meeting were those of young Henry Ward Beecher, the new Presbyterian preacher brought from Lawrenceburg to the capital by Merrill's efforts, and Douglass Maguire, the Indianapolis publisher. Honorary members were elected, including the historians George Bancroft of Boston and John B. Dillon of Logansport. Dillon had just moved to Indianapolis to find subscribers for his widely anticipated history of Indiana, not yet published. Law was asked to deliver the annual address in 1843.[32]

In what was to prove a familiar pattern, the Society sent out an urgent circular pleading for money and support. The 1843 circular was unusual only in that the Society was offering a "bargain" membership, since dues were reduced to fifty cents a year and all arrears were canceled. "If every citizen of moderate

---

[31] Editorial, Indianapolis *Indiana Journal*, March 7, 1843.

[32] *Proceedings of the Indiana Historical Society, 1830-1886*, pp. 30-31; Indianapolis *Indiana State Sentinel*, January 10, 1843.

means would contribute his half-dollar fee for membership," the circular's author Charles Cady asked, "how much could be done in a few years for the honor, interest and good repute of the state?" The state's newspapers enthusiastically printed the circular and urged their readers to support the Society, but once again it lapsed into inactivity.[33]

The historical interests of the state, fortunately, did not depend altogether on the Indiana Historical Society. Although the state did not sustain an effective historical society in this period, it did produce a capable historian in John B. Dillon.

Dillon was born ca. 1807 in Wellsburg, Brooke County, Virginia. Though his family moved to Ohio when Dillon was a young child, after his father's death he was sent back to Virginia when he was nine years old to be apprenticed to a printer in Charleston. Dillon set off in 1824 at age seventeen for Cincinnati, where he published poetry and worked for ten years as a compositor. At some point in his youth Dillon suffered an injury or disease in one of his eyes, and by the time he moved to Logansport, Indiana, in 1834, he wore peculiar dark green spectacles, designed as much to shield his bad eye from onlookers as to aid his vision. Obviously reticent and shy about personal matters, he apparently neither discussed the condition of his eyes, even with close lifelong friends, nor removed the glasses in anyone's presence. Dillon edited the Logansport *Canal-Telegraph* from 1834 to 1842. He also read law and was admitted to the Cass County bar in 1840, but it was clear to his friends from the outset that the scholarly and literate Dillon, like Indiana Supreme Court Judge Isaac Blackford, did not have the makings of a successful practicing attorney. Even in frontier Indiana, which was filled with unusual characters, Dillon was a striking person. As a longtime friend put it, "His quiet ways, shrinking

---

[33] *Proceedings of the Indiana Historical Society, 1830-1886*, pp. 31-34.

left, Marion County Courthouse, sketch by Christian Schrader; *below*, first Indiana Historical Society circular

Indiana State Library

opposite, John H. Farnham letter to William Polke

CIRCULAR.

INDIANAPOLIS, JANUARY   1831.

MY DEAR SIR:

The preceding abstract from the Constitution and proceedings of the "Indiana Historical Society," exhibits an index of its character, and will, it is hoped, attract your favorable regard. In pursuance of the general objects of the Society, and in obedience to its resolutions, the Corresponding Secretary has the honor to address you, respectfully soliciting such aid, information, and patronage, as it may be in your power to afford. All communications, addressed to the undersigned at Salem, Washington county, Indiana, will be gratefully received, and, whenever necessary, promptly acknowledged.

I have the honor to remain,
With sentiments of respect,
Your ob't. servant,

John Farnham

Cor Sec'y

Society Library

Indianapolis, Jan: 30, 1832.

Hon William Polke,

My dear Sir,

Having been favored in one or two conversations that I have had the honor to hold with you with a brief sketch of your capture by the Indians in early infancy under circumstances peculiarly interesting & impressive, & of several occurrences in your eventful life, a correct knowledge of which would reflect much light on the early history of the western country in general, and on that of Indiana in particular — I beg the liberty of respectfully requesting you on behalf of the Indiana Historical Society to compose a memoir of your personal history, from the highly eventful capture alluded to down to your late & present acquaintance with the various tribes of Indians in and about this State: — If you can find time to blend in the narrative such observations as will throw light on the early civil & political history of the Territory & State of Indiana, in which you have been a conspicuous actor, we shall feel ourselves so much the more indebted to your kindness. The time is rapidly drawing near when the living actors in these interesting & eventful scenes will be able to speak only in the Records they may chuse to leave behind them. That this time, so far as regards yourself may be extended to the utmost limit of your wishes. I beg leave to close this communication by invoking in your favor the Spanish Benediction. — God preserve you a thousand years!

· John H Farnham Corr. Sec'y
of the Indiana Histl: Soc'y

49

Indiana Historical Society
presented by
John H. Farnham;
May 1852

Society Library

Indiana State Library

left, John B. Dillon; *above,* John Farnham gave the Society volumes from his own large library. This inscription appears in Samuel Bayard, *Abstract of Laws . . .* (1804).

opposite, above, first Indiana State Capitol, where the Society's library was housed from 1848 to 1859; *below,* old State Bank, Kentucky Avenue and Illinois Street, home of the Society's library throughout the Civil War

Society Library

Indiana State Library

Society Library

opposite, above, Bishop George Upfold; Calvin Fletcher; *below,* James M. Ray; Charles H. Test

right, John B. Dillon; *below,* Henry P. Coburn, clerk of the Supreme Court and guardian of the Society's books, 1831-1848; John Coburn, mainstay of the Society in the 1870s and 1880s

Indiana Magazine of History

Indiana State Library

manners, hesitation of speech, nervous sensibility and proud
reserve kept him from the familiar contact of the people. . . ."
Though Dillon was kind and gentlemanly, he also suffered
from unpredictable outbursts of temper. Certainly he was no
hail fellow, well met.[34]

Dillon, however, attracted devoted friends: his fine sensibil-
ities, high moral character, shy delight in intellectual companionship, and obvious unfitness for the hurly-burly of business on
the frontier drew to him the sympathetic interest of more rugged
men. In Logansport Dillon was befriended by Horace Biddle, the
Lasselle family, and Senator John Tipton. Tipton, an old Indian
fighter with an interest in history, had joined the Society in 1832
and even undertook to gather copies of documents for the
Society.[35]

By 1838 Dillon had begun "to collect materials for the purpose of writing a History of the early settlement of Indiana."
Tipton opened his own historic journals to him and tried to aid
Dillon from Washington, writing to John Tyler in Williams-
burg, Virginia, for copies of George Rogers Clark's official correspondence with Governor Patrick Henry.[36] Unfortunately,
Tipton died in 1839, but Dillon persevered. In 1841 he wrote to
William Polke, a relative of Tipton's, requesting Polke's memoirs
of the early settlement of the state (as Farnham had done nearly

---

[34] For John B. Dillon see John Coburn, *The Life and Services of John B. Dillon,
with a Sketch by Judge Horace P. Biddle* (Indiana Historical Society *Publica-
tions*, II, No. 2, Indianapolis, 1886), pp. 39-62; Dunn, *Indiana and Indianans*,
III, 1269-70; obituary notices, Indianapolis *Saturday Herald*, March 4, 1879;
Indianapolis *News*, January 28, 1879; Indianapolis *Journal*, January 28, 1879;
Indianapolis *Daily Sentinel*, January 28, 1879.

[35] See above, note 19.

[36] John B. Dillon to William Polke, February 2, 1841, Polke Papers; John Tipton
to John Tylor [sic], May 29, 1838, Tipton Papers; Nathaniel Bolton, *A Lecture
Delivered before the Indiana Historical Society on the Early History of Indianapolis and Central Indiana . . .* (Indianapolis: Austin H. Brown, 1853), reprinted in Indiana Historical Society *Publications*, I, No. 5, Indianapolis, 1897,
p. 154.

a decade before), and by September, 1842, Dillon reported that he was almost finished with the manuscript of the first volume (to 1800) of "The History of Indiana, from its earliest exploration by Europeans, to the close of the Territorial Government in 1816: with an Introduction containing Historical Notes of the Discovery and Settlement of the Territory Northwest of the River Ohio."[37]

In his research Dillon had "travelled much throughout the state, and had access to the state library, the records of the several departments, and many valuable private manuscripts."[38] But Dillon in a prepublication description stressed the incomplete nature of his work, its preliminary quality, and bemoaned that

> Many interesting facts, connected with the early settlement of Indiana, have been perverted, or lost forever, because they were never recorded, and the stream of tradition seldom bears to the present, faithfully, the history of the past.[39]

Dillon gave up editing the Logansport *Canal-Telegraph* in 1842 and moved to Indianapolis to raise money to publish his history. He spent some time at least early in 1844 traveling in the East doing research for the second volume of his history, which he planned to publish in the summer. Though that volume did not appear, the General Assembly elected him state li-

---

[37] Dillon to Polke, February 2, 1841, September 1, 1842, Polke Papers. A letter Polke wrote not long after Harrison's death in 1841 testifies that Polke was not impervious to these pleas for his memoirs. He wrote to Senator Albert White offering to tell White about the early days, "as now is the time to rescue from oblivion many interesting facts connected with the History of In[diana]. . . ." Polke to [Albert S. White], May 18, 1841, William Polke Letterbook, *ibid.*

[38] Logansport (Ind.) *Wabash Gazette*, March 16, 1844. Dillon's research efforts may also have prompted the Indiana law of January 6, 1842, directing the secretary of state to preserve the manuscript journals of the house and senate. *Laws of Indiana*, 1841-1842, p. 126.

[39] Quoted in Buley, *Old Northwest*, II, 556n.

brarian in January, 1845, a post he held until 1851, serving two three-year terms.[40]

With a bona fide Indiana historian and Indiana Historical Society member ensconced as state librarian in Indianapolis as of January, 1845, one might reasonably have hoped for a rapid and vigorous recovery for the Society. Dillon did take an active part in the Society's brief revival in 1848. He was elected to the executive committee, appointed librarian, made a member of the committee to publicize the Society, and asked to prepare an address for the following meeting.[41]

There were several interesting features about the 1848 revival: for one thing, the Society for the first time replaced a living president. (Samuel Merrill, who had failed to be re-elected president of the State Bank in 1844 and had become president of the Madison and Indianapolis Railroad, was replaced as Society president by Judge Blackford—like Merrill a mainstay of the movement to improve education and of nearly every other "good work" proposed in Indianapolis.) Another novel feature of the 1848 meetings was the active participation of a working governor of the state, James Whitcomb, who was in the last year of his six years as governor. Whitcomb was responsible for acquiring legislative permission to move the Society's library from Henry Coburn's office on the Circle to a committee room in the statehouse.[42]

---

[40] Samuel Merrill to Jane Merrill, March 5, 1844, Merrill Papers, Indiana Historical Society Library; Indianapolis *Indiana State Journal*, January 8, 1844. Someone—probably not John Dillon, perhaps it was Law or another Society member—persuaded the Indiana General Assembly in January, 1843, to authorize each county seminary to subscribe to Dillon's book. *Laws of Indiana*, 1842-1843, p. 145. The book cost $3,000 to publish. Indianapolis *Indiana State Journal*, January 3, 1844.

[41] *Proceedings of the Indiana Historical Society, 1830-1886*, pp. 35-36.

[42] *Ibid.*, p. 34; see also memorial from Whitcomb and Ray dated January 24, 1848, in Indiana *House Journal*, 1848, p. 327.

The library that Dillon was chosen to preside over was described in the 1848 circular as "quite large and valuable. . . ."[43]
The move to the statehouse was presumably prompted partly
by the hope that the Society's presence in the capitol would remind the legislature to nurture it with appropriations. Further,
since the State Library, over which Dillon had charge, was also
located in a room in the statehouse in 1848, Dillon's responsibilities toward the Society library could more easily be dis-
charged when it was placed in the same building.

Unfortunately there is nothing to indicate that this new home
for the Society and the appointment of a librarian in any way
alleviated its moribund condition. Dillon did deliver his promised lecture, on the decline of the Miami Indians, in May, 1848—
the first Society lecture in nearly seventeen years—, and it was
published. Five years later, Dillon's successor as state librarian,
Nathaniel Bolton, delivered another public lecture under the Society's auspices, on the subject of early days in Indianapolis.
These small results were all that the Society achieved until
1859.[44]

Since John Dillon, as Indiana's historian and the Society's librarian, seems the person one would most have expected to work
at keeping the Society active during the years he was in Indianapolis, the question arises why he did not.

The answer is assuredly *not* that he was too busy earning a
living. Dillon was famous for his indifference to money and for
his extremely modest lifestyle. He dressed in a plain, gentlemanly fashion—a silk hat and a black frock coat "which he

---

[43] Indianapolis *Indiana State Sentinel*, February 3, 1848.

[44] John B. Dillon, *The National Decline of the Miami Indians* (Indiana Historical Society *Publications*, I, No. 4, Indianapolis, 1897); Bolton, *Early History of
Indianapolis*, reprinted in Indiana Historical Society *Publications*, I, No. 5,
Indianapolis, 1897. Dillon's address was originally published in the Cincinnati *Gazette*, August 28, 1849.

always wore buttoned"—,[45] collected a library when he had an income, and otherwise lived a simple, abstemious life. His public career consisted of a series of minor offices for which he was overqualified and which were secured for him by his friends' efforts, not by his own requests.

Dillon was employed, for example, as state librarian until 1851, when the Democratic legislature replaced him with Nathaniel Bolton. Dillon's friend Judge Charles Test, Indiana secretary of state in 1851, immediately appointed him assistant secretary of state, an office Dillon held until 1853. In 1853 and 1854 Dillon published a semimonthly agricultural magazine *Farm and Shop*. After 1854, except for a very small salary as secretary of the State Board of Agriculture, John Dillon apparently had no regular income until he left for Washington, D.C., in the summer of 1862, but his *History of Indiana* went through three editions (1843, 1850, 1854) before he issued a revised and enlarged edition in 1859, and he probably received some income from sales of this book.

One explanation for the Society's neglect is simply that the other social needs of a rapidly growing, economically distressed community obviously took precedence over an organization to preserve its history, even in the estimation of a contemporary historian like Dillon. Dillon was active in many other public causes during his years in Indianapolis: he served on a committee with Calvin Fletcher, Henry Coburn, and Jimmy Blake to raise money for Irish famine relief early in 1847; he worked with the State Board of Agriculture from 1851 to 1859; he was active in the temperance movement and was even nominated to run for mayor as a temperance candidate in April, 1854; he was a member of both the new Board of Trade in 1853 and the Mar-

---

[45] William Watson Woollen, *Reminiscences of the Early Marion County Bar* (Indiana Historical Society *Publications*, VII, No. 3, Indianapolis, 1917), p. 201.

ion County Library Board; and, along with Coburn and Fletcher, he was a trustee of the Indianapolis schools for several terms in the 1850s, diligently examining students in order to evaluate the schools.[46]

Dillon did continue historical work while he lived in Indianapolis. He assembled a book of documents and reports on *Internal Improvements and State Debts, 1828-1840*, published by the state. He also worked to revise and expand his Indiana history to cover the period to 1816. In addition Dillon wrote at least two addresses on historical subjects: one on the decline of the Miami Indians delivered before the Society in 1848 and one on the history of education in Indiana in 1856.[47] And, in addition to his own work, Dillon continued to look after the Society's library, the only visible sign of an otherwise moribund Society through most of the 1850s.

Even the presence of so historic an event as the Indiana constitutional convention of 1850 did not provoke a revival of the Society, but the absence of an active historical awareness was occasionally noted and brought to public attention. When the old Marion County Courthouse was razed in the spring of 1857, Berry Sulgrove, editor of the Indianapolis *Journal*, spoke out critically about the state's neglect of historical documents. He reported that in 1825 the territorial records at Vincennes had been packed "in two large dry goods boxes, and stored away in an old frame Building, which was liable to be destroyed by fire at any time." Sulgrove said that the secretary of state, William W. Wick, had been notified of their existence but had never claimed them, and now "these have all been lost or destroyed. . . ." Likewise in the present day (1857), Sulgrove complained, when the courthouse was razed

---

[46] Thornbrough, Riker, and Corpuz (eds.), *Diary of Calvin Fletcher*, III, 352, IV, 291n, 306, V, 288n, 334n, VI, 291n.
[47] *Ibid.*, V, 615.

There was a large number of old papers of an official nature, bearing dates prior to the formation of the Indiana Territory into a State. They were thrown on the ground, and scattered to the four winds. A few were saved by several persons who had curiosity enough to cull from the heap those of the most interesting character.[48]

In 1859 Dillon's new *History of Indiana*, an expanded and revised version of his 1843 work brought down to 1816 and with two chapters on the period from 1816 to 1859, was published. And, probably coincidentally, the Indiana Historical Society was reorganized in February, 1859. The leading actors in this event appear to have been John Law, who had moved to Evansville a few years before, and a pair of state legislators, Senator Aaron B. Line of Franklin and Senator Hamilton Smith of Perry County. This revival was notable in several ways. First, in response to a Society memorial, the Indiana General Assembly voted a $500 appropriation, the second largest sum the state was ever to appropriate directly to the Society. Second, the Society elected John B. Dillon its secretary and provided him with a special room, one that did not have to be shared with legislators, in which to keep the Society's collections safe.

The reorganization meeting in February, 1859, began with a brief stocktaking, in which the company noted that only thirty-nine of the original ninety-one members of 1830 were still alive, and fewer than a half dozen of those were present, including Calvin Fletcher, John Law, Allen Hamilton, James M. Ray, and James P. Drake. Officers were elected: John Law, president; the legislators Line and Smith were made vice-presidents along with Bishop George Upfold; James M. Ray was named treasurer and Dillon, secretary. Fletcher along with Henry P. Coburn's son John, Dr. George Mears, Addison L. Roache, and Henry Smith Lane of Crawfordsville composed the executive commit-

---

[48] Indianapolis *Daily Journal*, May 4, 1857.

tee.[49] Except for Law, who declared himself a Democrat in 1858, the members of this Whiggish group of officers were in the process of becoming Republicans.

President Law urged the group to revive and support the state historical society. To entertain his listeners and demonstrate the kind of document the Society should find and preserve, Law pulled out the original letter from Patrick Henry to George Rogers Clark in 1778, giving Clark secret orders to capture Kaskaskia. Law read this dramatic document aloud to his audience.[50] Impressed, the group began to cast around for ways to promote the Society, and someone suggested asking for an appropriation from the legislature. Most thought this was a hopeless idea, but Senator Line "came boldly forward and appealed to the pride of Indiana, and charged some of them with old fogeyism. . . ."[51] Line's energy carried the day. An appropriation of $500 was requested and received, earmarked "to aid the Indiana Historical Society in the purchase of the different kinds of transcripts, documents, etc., as are calculated to shed light on the early civil, social, and political history of the state. . . ," with a proviso that the Society should report fully on its status and how the money was spent to the next Assembly.[52]

The new executive committee, meeting several times that winter, again appointed Dillon to be the Society's librarian and

[49] *Ibid.*, February 17, 1859.

[50] Law left his audience with the impression that they were seeing the original document. *Ibid.*; Thornbrough, Riker, and Corpuz (eds.), *Diary of Calvin Fletcher*, VI, 310-11. A facsimile was lithographed and exchanged with other societies. Law explained to Lyman Draper in 1867 that the document was an autograph copy of the original. Law to Draper, September 12, 1867, Draper Collection.

[51] James Sutherland, *Biographical Sketches of the Members of the 61st General Assembly of the State of Indiana* (Indianapolis: Indianapolis Journal Co., 1861), pp. 61-63.

[52] *Proceedings of the Indiana Historical Society, 1830-1886*, pp. 40-41.

agreed to furnish a room for the Society's exclusive use in the building formerly used by the old State Bank of Indiana, located at the "point" between Kentucky Avenue and Illinois Street. The building was owned in 1859 by the new Bank of the State of Indiana, whose cashier, James M. Ray, was also the Society's treasurer. The Indianapolis *Locomotive* reported in July that the room was "very handsomely and conveniently fitted up and furnished with carpet, chairs, tables, Bookcases, &c, in the first story of the State Bank building. . . ."[53]

Meanwhile in March, Dillon sent out the news of the appropriation and the new headquarters in a circular notable for its confident tone. The Society was seeking donations (or deposits, or material to purchase) and for the first time described in detail exactly what was wanted:

> any kind of rare, interesting or valuable materials of western history— such as books, pamphlets, autograph letters, manuscripts, maps, paintings or daguerreotypes of soldiers, legislators, jurists, or pioneer settlers of Indiana, authentic drawings or engravings of Indiana scenery —drawings and descriptions of old forts, blockhouses, Indian mounds, old dwelling-houses, and old public edifices—plans of towns and

---

[53] Indianapolis *Locomotive*, July 2, 1859. There is conflicting evidence on the question of the location of the Society's room. Fletcher, a member of the executive committee, reported in his diary on March 10, 1859, that the group had agreed "to fix up the room at the Branch Bank." Thornbrough, Riker, and Corpuz (eds.), *Diary of Calvin Fletcher*, VI, 320. The Indianapolis branch of the State Bank was located at the point between Pennsylvania Street and Virginia Avenue in a building that resembled the State Bank building at Kentucky Avenue and Illinois Street. (In 1858 the building at Pennsylvania and Virginia was purchased by the Sinking Fund Commission.) The Indianapolis *Daily Journal* reported on March 15, 1859, that the Society had accepted the offer of a room in the State Bank building on Illinois Street. Although there are many references to the Society's room in "the old State Bank," these alone did not confirm the location at Kentucky and Illinois, since it is possible that the branch bank was also called the old State Bank. However, the combination of the *Journal* item in March, 1859, with its specific reference to Illinois Street and the letter written by James M. Ray in 1873 (see below, p. 68) make the weight of the available evidence come down on the Kentucky and Illinois side of the balance.

accounts of general and local improvements—files or single copies of old newspapers published in the west—statistical information, etc. etc.

In addition Dillon asked his readers for detailed information about county histories and early settlers of each county.[54]

During the next few years the circular prompted a large number of responses. Dillon later claimed that there had been "thousands of replies . . . and a vast store of information was soon accumulated." The Society also accumulated, through Dillon's efforts, several thousand volumes of books and "a large and valuable collection of manuscripts and documentary records. . . ."[55] As early as May, 1860, Calvin Fletcher commented in his diary that Dillon had accumulated "some $2000 or $3000 worth of books and documents" for the Society. The Indianapolis *Sentinel* reported in June, 1859, the Society's collection of "many valuable documents" and noted the recent addition of twenty-one bound volumes of the Cincinnati *Gazette*, a present from J. B. Perrine of Indianapolis.[56]

Though the Society's collections grew steadily in these few years (1859 to 1862), organizationally it was still weak. Exactly what form the Society took is not clear since a new constitution was adopted in February, 1859, and this subsequently was lost, along with a new minute book. Whatever the structure, few people attended meetings. Bethuel Morris, one of the Society's founders and former cashier of the Indianapolis branch of the old State Bank, prepared a lecture for the Society in May, 1859, that was advertised in the Indianapolis papers, but the turnout was so small that the members were discouraged and canceled the meeting.

---

[54] *Proceedings of the Indiana Historical Society, 1830-1886*, pp. 38-40.

[55] Indianapolis *Journal*, October 8, 1873.

[56] Thornbrough, Riker, and Corpuz (eds.), *Diary of Calvin Fletcher*, VI, 57; Indianapolis *Indiana Daily State Sentinel*, June 29, 1859.

That evening Fletcher commented darkly on the Society's prospects in a typical jeremiad:

> There is but little interest in any genuine science or history. Many good men are ashamed of the rulers of the state for the last 20 years. In Mexican wars our governor appointed demagogues to be the officers —2d Regiment ran at 1st fire. Had a corrupt Sup[reme Court] Bench openly charged with taking bribes. Legislature of 1855 by & thro bribes passed the bank bill. Bribes have been common in the several departments of state Governments. [State] library rob[b]ed treasury plundered &c So that many good men & all bad ones do not covet a true history.[57]

In contrast on June 14 an optimistic John Law reported to his old friend Lyman Draper, who was rapidly building an historical collection in Wisconsin, that the Society was "getting along finely" and urged Draper to send books and documents to Dillon, who would pay express charges.[58]

Law and Dillon collaborated in 1859 to publish a lithographed facsimile of an autograph copy of the Patrick Henry secret orders to George Rogers Clark, dated 1778, a document that Law owned. Part of the reason for publishing it was to have something to exchange with other historical societies.[59] Dillon also made some effort to bring speakers to Indianapolis to deliver publishable lectures. The Morris lecture was neither delivered nor published, but Dillon asked his friend Horace Biddle to lecture early in January, 1861, at the Society's new biennial meeting. Biddle backed out at the last minute, and Dillon went to work again, quickly securing the services of Episcopal Bishop George Upfold of Indianapolis. Upfold actually delivered an ad-

---

[57] Indianapolis *Indiana Daily State Sentinel*, May 21, 24, 25, 1859; Thornbrough, Riker, and Corpuz (eds.), *Diary of Calvin Fletcher*, VI, 353.

[58] Law to Draper, June 14, 1859, Draper Collection.

[59] Evansville *Weekly Enquirer*, April 20, 1859.

dress for the Society before an audience of about sixty persons. The lecture was probably published, since Upfold's diary confirms that he prepared this work for publication and delivered the manuscript to Dillon, but the place and date of publication along with the text have not yet been discovered.[60]

After Upfold's presentation, the members at the 1861 meeting agreed to send a committee again to the legislature to request another $500 appropriation. Dillon, as required by law, prepared a report explaining the expenditure of the previous appropriation. Fletcher, a pessimistic member of the committee, gloomily noted in his diary that the prospects were not good. "There is but little interest in the society," Fletcher wrote, discounting the sixty people who attended the meeting. "Our Governor Morton did not attend and but few members of the legislature. I fear Mr. Dillon an honest disinterested man, our secretary, will suffer for want of support." Fletcher's concerns were not allayed after his visits to the legislature with James M. Ray to attempt to secure the money ("Mr. Dillon the secretary cant live without an appropriation," Fletcher fretted again), and his fears about the bill were confirmed when the appropriation failed to pass the house.[61]

The Indiana General Assembly, of course, had much more urgent issues to consider in the "secession winter" of 1860-1861 than the fate of an historical society few people cared anything

---

[60] Horace P. Biddle to John B. Dillon, January 23, 1861, John B. Dillon Papers, Indiana Division, Indiana State Library; Thornbrough, Riker, and Corpuz (eds.), *Diary of Calvin Fletcher*, VII, 38; Indianapolis *Daily Journal*, February 8, 1861; George Upfold diary, loaned for filming by Mrs. Edmund Bingham, Lafayette, Indiana, microfilm copy in Indiana Historical Society Library. See entries for March 5, 6, 7, 1861.

[61] Indianapolis *Daily Journal*, February 8, 1861. The report Dillon prepared was lost by the secretary of state's office by 1873. Indianapolis *Journal*, October 8, 1873; Thornbrough, Riker, and Corpuz (eds.), *Diary of Calvin Fletcher*, VII, 38, 49; Indiana *House Journal*, 1887, pp. 398-401.

about. It is tempting, however, to speculate how different the Society's history might have been had the 1861 legislature renewed the appropriation. If the Society had been able to establish itself as a regular object of public support in the middle of the nineteenth century, it could have created an important research library under Dillon's guidance. As the Society's officers were keenly aware, two other midwestern states had already begun to support historical societies. The Minnesota Historical Society, incorporated in 1849, had acquired an annual state appropriation of $500 by 1856. And the Wisconsin society, also organized in 1849, had an annual appropriation of $1,000 and a library of 14,500 volumes by 1860. On the other hand Kentucky, Illinois, and Michigan, like Indiana, seemed unable to sustain a society on a regular basis; but, unlike the Indiana society, the societies of the former three states admitted their failing and disbanded.[62]

The library Dillon accumulated for the Society between 1859 and 1861 with the support of the General Assembly comprised his greatest service to the Society. It was, by all reports, a valuable collection of material on Indiana history. Unfortunately Dillon's contribution was squandered by the Society. Unable to make a living in Indianapolis, Dillon left for Washington, D.C., in July, 1862, hoping for a federal job from the Republican administration.[63] He was appointed clerk and ex officio superintendent of documents for the Interior Department in 1863 and remained in the position, by the efforts of his friends, until March, 1871. With John Coburn's intercession—by this time

---

[62] Dunlap, *American Historical Societies*, pp. 150, 157, 174; Whitehill, *Independent Historical Societies*, pp. 223, 249, 282, 289; Russell W. Fridley, "Critical Choices for the Minnesota Historical Society," in *Minnesota History*, XLVI (1978), 132.

[63] John B. Dillon to John Coburn, April 3, 1873, William H. English Papers, Joseph Regenstein Library, University of Chicago.

Henry P. Coburn's son was General Coburn, a war hero, and a Republican congressman from Indiana—Dillon was appointed clerk of the House Military Affairs Committee, where he served until Coburn left Congress in 1875.[64] From the summer of 1862 until Dillon returned to Indianapolis in 1875 the Society library was left unattended. Calvin Fletcher, at least, was disturbed about this turn of events: in 1865, the year before his death, Fletcher was still trying to find a way to bring Dillon back to Indianapolis. Fletcher wanted the legislature to hire Dillon to write the history of Indiana in the Civil War, and he urged Dillon to discuss this with the influential James M. Ray, who was in Washington on business. "The deserted collection of historical matter obtained thro' your industry, & the lone apartment, where they are stored," Fletcher wrote to Dillon, "often appear before me in my 'night thoughts.'"[65]

Perhaps if Fletcher had lived through the decade of the 1860s he would have protected the library during the critical time after the building in which it was housed was sold. As it was, at least a large part of the library was apparently lost. How this happened is unclear. The most detailed explanation is in a letter the Society's treasurer James M. Ray wrote to John Coburn some years later:

---

[64] For John Coburn see *Representative Men of Indiana*, 7th District, pp. 249-51. Coburn was chairman of the House Military Affairs Committee, 1871-1875. Indianapolis *News*, January 28, 1879.

[65] Calvin Fletcher to John B. Dillon, January 31, 1865, Dillon Papers. The phrase "night thoughts" is a reference to the poem "Night Thoughts on Life, Death, and Immortality" by E. Young, which was immensely popular throughout the nineteenth century. Fletcher had probably asked Governor Oliver P. Morton in March, 1862, to employ Dillon to write a history of Indiana's Civil War regiments, commenting in his diary that "Poor Dillon" needed the job. Thornbrough, Riker, and Corpuz (eds.), *Diary of Calvin Fletcher*, VII, 368.

Fletcher's concern for Dillon and his work was also expressed in his will. Fletcher left "$500 to my friend John B. Dillon, a worthy man and neglected historian of our State." Quoted in Woollen, *Reminiscences of the Early Marion County Bar*, p. 201.

It is in memory, that, with other friends, an application was made successfully to our Legislature, for permission to have the books of the Society taken charge of and kept by the Librarian of the State, and placed in the State Library. This must have been after Mr. Dillon left for Washington, who, as secretary, had been the custodian of its property, in the western rear room of the State Bank and also by the Bank of the State in continuance to the Historical Society for its uses. It was Secretary Dillon's studio. I remember calling on the State Librarian, after the passage of the legislative permission, as to his taking possession of the Society's books, etc., and that the reply was, that a place for their reception should be prepared, to which they should be removed. For some time after the bank sold its building to the Franklin Life Insurance Company [April, 1868], and after I gave up my official connection with the Company [1870 ?] and used no office room in the building, the same room remained in part occupancy of the large library case and its contents in the same back room. . . .

Ray went on to say that at some later time he discovered that some of the Society's papers were "in the way of being removed to the paper mill," and that he had rescued what he could, placing them in an empty room on the second floor of the building. He then walked away from them, and that is all that is known of the whereabouts of the documents.[66]

No one expressed any interest in either the Society or its erstwhile library until the spring of 1873, when Coburn, home from

---

[66] Letter printed in Indianapolis *Journal,* October 8, 1873. The reference to the Franklin Life Insurance Company confirms the Kentucky and Illinois location. Some of the Society's books were found in the State Library's collections in 1873. Ray's reference to an application for legislative permission to place the Society's books in the State Library is confirmed in Indiana *House Journal,* 1865 Special Session, pp. 736-37.

There is some question about how much was actually lost, since the Society's memorial to the Indiana General Assembly on February 8, 1887, less than a year after the Society's reorganization, claimed that their library included "2,000 books and pamphlets. . . ." Indiana *House Journal,* 1887, pp. 398-401. Either most of the Society's collections had been found again since their loss in 1873, *or* the Society had rapidly, and without mentioning how in the minutes, rebuilt its collections, *or* the Society's memorial inflated the number of its books in order to convince the legislature to give them a room.

Washington, D.C., for a while, wrote to Dillon asking about "the condition of the records, and minutes of the Society" and asking for a list of members. Confidentially Coburn explained that he was thinking of donating the "backpay recently given members of Congress" to the Society, "to put life again into the sleeping organization and restore an activity that would result well." Dillon in turn asked James Ray, then serving in Washington as a Treasury Department official, what had become of the Society's property, prompting the letter quoted above. Dillon confessed that he himself knew nothing certain about the matter and had no records in his own possession.[67]

Coburn was not discouraged and by October had assembled another impressive group of Indiana's first citizens for yet another revival of the Society. The former Senator Henry Smith Lane of Crawfordsville, white haired and erect, Governor Thomas A. Hendricks, and about fifty others attended the meeting, including Dillon from Washington and the state librarian, Mrs. Sarah A. Oren, who discovered 327 volumes belonging to the Society in the State Library collections. The sad tale of the balance of the lost library was related, along with a brief recitation of the rest of the Society's history. Coburn urged more frequent meetings and a regular place of deposit for the Society's books. Professor John L. Campbell of Wabash College, who was a member of the U.S. Centennial Commission, urged the group to raise money to hire a full-time historian and also suggested the need for an historical magazine.[68]

---

[67] John Coburn to John B. Dillon, March 29, 1873, Dillon to Coburn (draft), April 3, 1873, English Papers, University of Chicago.

[68] The *Sentinel* listed in addition to Lane and Hendricks the following persons as present: from Crawfordsville, M. D. Manson, H. B. Carrington, John L. Campbell, Harris Reynolds, and P. S. Kennedy; from Indianapolis, John Coburn, Dillon, "The Revs. Dr. Holliday and Lynch," H. A. Edson, Simon Yandes, Daniel Hough, H. W. Clark, A. L. Roache, D. Wiley, J. B. Julian,

Only about half the group met again in November for a marathon meeting that ran most of the afternoon and all evening. A committee reported some suggested minor changes in the constitution, and a resolution was passed urging the Society to request legislative support. Coburn wanted the group to lobby for a bill to provide for gathering statistics of historical value, and Dillon proposed a resolution calling for a monthly paper on "antiquities and scientific interests." In another move emphasizing the new sense of the unity of science and history Professor Edward T. Cox of New Harmony, a protégé of David Dale Owen and the state geologist since 1869, urged that the Society join forces with the Indianapolis Academy of Science and form a new group, the Indiana Historical and Natural History Society. But the most popular topic of the meeting was a rather macabre proposal for a new memorial. The *Sentinel* had been urging that William Henry Harrison's "remains" be unearthed and brought to Indiana for burial at the Tippecanoe County Battleground, and the meeting declared itself strongly in support of this measure.[69]

After hearing the reminiscences of George W. Carr, a short biography of Calvin Fletcher, and a short speech from Judge Charles Test, the Society adjourned. In January, 1874, the So-

---

James A. Wildman, Henry D. Pierce, L. Abbett, P. D. Hammond, H. F. Keenan, D. H. Oliver, George W. Mears, D. E. Snyder, Samuel Morrison, Charles N. Todd, Thad. M. Stevens, Barton D. Jones, Alfred M. Clark, George Brown, Sarah Oren, "and a few other ladies." Indianapolis *Daily Sentinel*, October 8, 1873; Indianapolis *Journal*, October 8, 1873; *Proceedings of the Indiana Historical Society, 1830-1886*, pp. 42-43; *Indiana State Library Report, 1873-1874*, p. 23.

[69] *Proceedings of the Indiana Historical Society, 1830-1886*, pp. 43-60. For the *Sentinel's* campaign to rebury Harrison at Tippecanoe Battleground, see November 13, 20, 23, 26, December 8, 9, 1873. Apparently the Harrison family decided against the proposal and it was dropped. For Cox see John H. B. Nowland, *Sketches of Prominent Citizens of 1876* (Indianapolis: Tilford and Carlon, 1877), pp. 491-94.

ciety met again briefly to hear the committee on merging with the Indianapolis Academy of Science report that they had decided against it, and then lapsed again into inactivity.[70]

Coburn called another meeting four years later, in January, 1877. This time a new Marion County Courthouse was under construction, and Coburn reasoned that the Society should apply for a room in it. Perhaps if the Society once again could acquire a room of its own, its few remaining collections could be gathered together to form the nucleus of a new library. W. H. H. Terrell, Indiana Civil War Adjutant General and war historian, a new member, offered the Society the use of a room in the post office building until the courthouse would be ready. Terrell also chaired a committee to make new plans for the Society. There were four meetings in February, 1877, and geologist Cox delivered a public address on archaeology at one of them, but Terrell was distracted from the Society's business by the death of a relative, and there seemed to be no other energy available to keep things going. The Society removed its books from the State Library to "the Historical room in the fifth story" of the new courthouse in August, but the new room, apparently inaccessible, failed to bring the anticipated benefits.[71]

Coburn's father-in-law Judge Test and Dillon, perhaps discouraged by the Society's inability to attract public support, founded a new organization in the summer of 1878 devoted to preserving and publishing Indiana history, this one named the Indiana Pioneer Society. Dillon, however, did not live to see this

[70] Indianapolis *Daily Sentinel*, December 18, 1873, January 11, 1874. There was an independent Indiana group appointed to mount an exhibition at the 1876 United States Centennial celebration in Philadelphia. Though John L. Campbell hoped the Society would aid this group, there is no evidence that it did so.

[71] *Proceedings of the Indiana Historical Society, 1830-1886*, pp. 61-64; receipt for hauling books, August 25, 1877, Indiana Historical Society Papers, miscellaneous. Hereafter these papers will be cited as IHS Papers.

group flourish either. He died in his room in Johnson's Building on Washington Street in Indianapolis on January 27, 1879, aged seventy-one, poor in funds as usual, but surrounded by friends.[72]

John B. Dillon was a fine historian, a good man, and appealing human being. He was not, however, either disposed or equipped to lead the Indiana Historical Society during a period when it sorely lacked a leader and when Dillon, by virtue of his role as Indiana historian, must have seemed the logical person to lead such a society. Dillon's services to the Society were those of a scholar rather than a leader: Dillon attended to the library, collecting books and documents. However, without an organization to take charge of and protect his work, Dillon's efforts were largely wasted.

Such sporadic leadership as the Society was able to attract in this period came not from the shy, eccentric Dillon but from a few concerned New Englanders who never quite allowed the idea of a state historical organization to be entirely forgotten. It was Henry P. Coburn, John Law, and then John Coburn from the next generation who were most often involved in efforts to revive the sluggish Society in the half century before 1886. They were aided by a larger group of men who were somewhat more erratic in their support—men like Calvin Fletcher, James M. Ray, Jimmy Blake, Charles Test, James Whitcomb, Aaron B. Line, and Bishop George Upfold. All that this leaderless association was willing to do during these years was to call a meeting every four or five years in hopes that some vague benefit they called "public support" would materialize. What they needed was someone willing to make the Society his special

---

[72] State Board of Agriculture, *Annual Report, 1878*, pp. 392-99, 422-23; Indianapolis *News*, January 28, 1879. The Indiana Pioneer Society met only in 1878 and 1879.

labor—they needed a replacement for John Hay Farnham.

The Society survived for over fifty years without an effective leader. As one reviews the long, rather depressing series of revivals, reorganizations, and new beginnings, the question continually arises, why did they not simply give up?

It seems likely that at least part of the explanation is that a significant number of prominent men never forgot the Society's initial successes and were inspired by them to hope that the early promise could somehow still be realized. The large early meetings attended by all "the best men"; the impressive donations to the Society's collections that Farnham evoked; the concrete presence of the bookcase containing valuable books—all these factors must have haunted the "night thoughts" of other conscientious men as they did Calvin Fletcher's.[73] But it was surely not only the fading memory of Farnham's exciting beginning that preserved the Indiana Historical Society through this period. There was also a continuing and perceived need for such an organization. Historical materials were being lost and destroyed. The story was not being told. In a single generation the state had been transformed from a forest dotted with farms and villages to a rich agricultural heartland with small towns and cities linked by railroads to one another and to the outside world. But the same general story was also true of Indiana's neighbors; without its own recorded history the state was anonymous, undistinguishably midwestern. Especially for the men who had taken on statewide responsibilities—the men who built the roads and railroads and ran the state banks and served in state offices—this historical silence about their work must have been painful to observe. In any event it was just these men who

[73] The achievements of the early Society tended to be enlarged at each reorganization, presumably to inspire the gatherings to equal the accomplishments of their forerunners. See editorial in Indianapolis *Indiana Journal*, March 7, 1843; Dillon's comments, Indianapolis *Journal*, October 8, 1873.

stubbornly revived the notion of an historical society every five years or so until Dillon died in 1879.

Dillon's demise provoked one last meeting of the Society in this first, spasmodic phase of its history. Dillon's old friend Charles Test, who was apparently president of the Society throughout the 1870s, called the meeting in July, 1879, to eulogize Dillon and elect a new secretary. Terrell was chosen, and the Society as usual lapsed into inactivity. It had done little in its first half century except testify to the energy of its founder, Farnham, and to the nagging but ineffectual historical conscience of a group of the state's "best men."

III

A Publishing
Society

1886-1914

Society Library

Indiana State Library

William H. English   Daniel Wait Howe

Jacob Piatt Dunn, Jr.

III

"We profited by their experience and decided to put things into print as far as possible."

J. P. Dunn, Jr.
December 10, 1919

In April, 1886, the Indiana Historical Society was reorganized for the last time; since 1886 the Society has met at least annually. The Society's emergence as a viable organization coincided with and was part of a wider flowering of midwestern letters in which Hoosier literati and Indianapolis played a prominent part. This flowering, sometimes described hyperbolically as "the golden age" of Indiana literature, was prompted to some extent by the common perception that the rural way of life of earlier generations was changing; something valuable and definitively Hoosier was disappearing in the wake of the dramatic new prosperity fostered by the natural gas boom and the concomitant forces of urbanization and industrialization. Even for those who remained on the farms, mechanization was ending a seemingly timeless, traditional way of life only a few generations after its introduction into the forests of Indiana. James Whitcomb Riley, Meredith Nicholson, and Booth Tarkington responded to these changes in imaginative literature; Jacob Piatt Dunn, Jr., Daniel Wait Howe, and William Hayden English responded by writing Indiana history.[1]

---

[1] Clifton J. Phillips, *Indiana in Transition, 1880-1920* (Indianapolis: Indiana Historical Bureau and Indiana Historical Society, 1968), chapter XIII. For Indi-

For all these historians the rebirth of the Indiana Historical
Society was a minor side effect of their research in Indiana
history. In contrast to all the previous, rather grand beginnings,
marked by large public meetings and ambitious plans, the
last reorganizational meeting was an unpretentious private
event, apparently attended by no more than a few dozen men.
The leading figures were English, Howe, and Dunn, none of
whom had been a member of the old Society. Dunn in fact wrote
in 1897 that it was only the reminder by one of the other men
who had been invited to join the new group that there was already an Indiana Historical Society that prompted its reorganization. When the new group asked the members of the old Society to call a meeting and "elect" them to membership, John
Coburn, Addison L. Roache, and William Wesley Woollen were
delighted. Some of the old members were elected officers of the
new Society, but the effective leadership was in the hands of
English, Howe, and Dunn. What prompted these men to form
an historical society in 1886 was their common need for access
to historical materials.[2]

William Hayden English (1822-1896) was the most prominent member of the new Society, and he may have taken the
initiative in its formation. He was a novice historian in 1886 and
a somewhat unlikely one, since one would have supposed that
he was more appropriate as the subject than the author of a his-

---

anapolis in this period see Frederick D. Kershner, "A Social and Cultural
History of Indianapolis, 1860-1914" (Ph.D. dissertation, University of Wisconsin, 1952).

[2] *Proceedings of the Indiana Historical Society, 1830-1886*, p. 7. Dunn identified Jonathan W. Gordon, a Society member since 1859, as the person who
suggested the reorganization. Gordon, a prominent criminal lawyer known for
his work as defense attorney in the Indianapolis treason trials during the Civil
War, was also a political maverick with literary tastes and talents. *Ibid.; Representative Men of Indiana*, 7th District, pp. 48-63; Dunn, *Indiana and Indianans*, III, 1404-1405.

tory. Before the Civil War English, the scion of a family prominent both in politics and war, had been one of the northern leaders of the Democratic party. Elected to four consecutive terms in
Congress before he was forty years old, he had looked forward to
a long and successful political future; instead his entanglement
with pro-slavery forces in Congress in the dispute over the admission of Kansas and Nebraska to the Union left his career in
ruins. Refusing Oliver P. Morton's offer of a regimental com-
mand early in the Civil War, English instead went into the banking business after the passage of the National Bank Act of 1863.
He made a fortune in banking, the streetcar business, and real
estate investments, and built the lavish English's Opera House
in 1880 as a sort of family monument. Nominated by the Democrats for Vice-President in 1880 on the ticket headed by Win-
field Scott Hancock, English was "mercilessly cartooned" by
Nast as a heartless forecloser of mortgages and suffered the
humiliation of failing to carry his home state.[3] A proud and disappointed man, with a commanding figure and a fierce stare,
English was uncomfortable with his unpopularity, and in an attempt to recover former glories he organized in 1885 a reunion
of the surviving members of the constitutional convention of
1850-1851, of which he had been secretary. It was a sentimental
and self-congratulatory occasion. In the course of it, English prepared a collective biography of the members of the convention.
After this taste of historical research he hit upon the notion of
collecting materials for and writing the early history of the state.
The project seized his imagination, and he devoted the last decade of his life to accumulating an astonishingly large collection
of information about early Indiana history. This effort culmi-

---

[3] For English see F. Gerald Handfield, Jr., "William H. English and the Election of 1880," in Ralph D. Gray (ed.), *Gentlemen from Indiana* (*Indiana Historical Collections*, L, Indianapolis: Indiana Historical Bureau, 1977), pp. 83-
116. Quotation in Indianapolis *News*, January 8, 1909.

nated in English's publication in 1896, the year of his death, of
a two-volume history of George Rogers Clark's military ex-
ploits in the Northwest Territory during the Revolutionary War,
planned as the first segment of a series of volumes revealing the
fruits of his work.[4]

As English undertook his researches in 1885, he discovered
the sad state of historical materials in Indiana. The State Library, temporarily housed in rooms at the corner of Market and
Tennessee streets awaiting the construction of the new capitol,
contained a valuable but somewhat haphazard collection of
books and documents. There was no complete set of Indiana
state and territorial laws, no card catalogue, and no order to federal publications. A large number of the books, which sup-
posedly numbered 23,000 volumes, were falling apart, and a
significant percentage was composed of duplicates. The large
pamphlet collection was unusable because the pamphlets were
unbound and uncatalogued. The collection of state publications
was fragmentary; of state manuscript documents, nil. No state
archives existed except the files of the secretary of state, which
were inaccessible and incomplete. There were no printed collections of Indiana historical documents. The best sources for information on early Indiana history were the collections of the
Wisconsin State Historical Society, the Chicago Historical
Society, and the Library of Congress.[5]

Fortunately, English was not alone in his concern about improving access to Indiana's historical material. He was joined in
this interest by Howe and Dunn, each of whom had indepen-

---

[4] Indianapolis *Sentinel,* October 6, 1885; proof clipping, n.d., *City of Indianapolis,* in William H. English file, William H. English Papers, Indiana Historical
Society Library; William H. English, *Conquest of the Country Northwest of
the River Ohio, 1778-1783* (2 volumes. Indianapolis: The Bowen-Merrill Company, 1896).

[5] *Indiana State Library Report, 1885-1886,* p. 8; ibid., *1887-1888,* p. 7.

dently discovered the same problems as English in the course of their own researches.

Daniel Wait Howe (1839-1921), a Marion County superior court judge, a Republican, and a Civil War veteran, began to take an interest in legal history in the 1880s, perhaps prompted by the publication of books like Berry Sulgrove's *History of Indianapolis* (1884) and William Wesley Woollen's *Biographical and Memorial Sketches* (1883), reminiscences of men and events in many cases known well to Howe. Perhaps even more likely, he was prompted by his searches in Indiana legal history for precedents to guide his opinions on the bench.

Born in Patriot, Indiana, Howe was educated at Franklin College and, after the Civil War, at Albany Law School in New York. He moved to Indianapolis in 1873 and was elected Marion County superior court judge in 1876, an office he held until 1890. He was active in Republican politics at the city and state levels, and he was a devoted Mason. A polished writer, modest and judicious in manner, Judge Howe was also, like English, proud of his family heritage—though while English boasted of being descended from one of George Rogers Clark's lieutenants, Howe was a member of the New England Historic Genealogical Society, and wrote a paean to the Plymouth Colony, *The Puritan Republic* (1899).[6]

By 1886 Howe had done considerable research and personal collecting in compiling a bibliography of Indiana territorial and state laws, which was published as an appendix to the state librarian's biennial report for 1885-1886. He had also prepared a work on "Laws and Courts of Northwest and Indiana Territories," which he volunteered as the first paper to be published by

---

[6] For Howe see Dunn, *Greater Indianapolis*, II, 753-55; James Woodburn, "Judge Daniel Wait Howe and the 'Political History of Secession'," in *Indiana Magazine of History*, XI (1915), 70-76; Indianapolis *News*, October 29, 1921.

the new Society in the spring of 1886.[7] He also contributed essays for the Society's *Publications* in 1899, 1902, 1908, 1912, and 1914, in addition to his book-length works, *The Puritan Republic, Political History of Secession* (1914), and *Civil War Times* (1902).

Joining the sixty-four-year-old English and the forty-seven-year-old Howe in their determination to improve the historical collections of the state was a young man who proved to be even more prolific than Howe and who became more closely identified with the Indiana Historical Society than any other officer. Jacob Piatt Dunn, Jr. (1855-1924), or "Jake" as he was affectionately dubbed, was born in Lawrenceburg to a pioneer Indiana family. His parents moved to Indianapolis when he was a child, and he lived in the capital most of his adult life, but he was far from parochial. He was graduated from Earlham College in 1874 and took a law degree at the University of Michigan in 1876. In 1879 he went to Colorado to look after his father's mining interests. In his approximately five-year stay he also prospected for silver and worked for a Denver newspaper as a reporter. Dunn, fascinated by the Indian wars of the Far West (Custer had died in battle only a few years before, and Helen Hunt Jackson's *A Century of Dishonor* was published in 1881), explored the subject in his first book, *Massacres of the Mountains*, which he published in 1886 after returning to Indiana. Colorful and even-handed, the work confirmed a taste and talent for historical writing that lasted throughout his life. Dunn returned to Indianapolis in 1884, turned his attention to Indiana history, and almost immediately became the leader in the movement to improve the State Library.

---

[7] Daniel Wait Howe, "Catalogue of Laws of Indiana Territory and State of Indiana," in *Indiana State Library Report, 1885-1886*, pp. 47-51; *Minutes of the Society, 1886-1918* (Indiana Historical Society *Publications*, VI, No. 4, Indianapolis, 1919), p. 464.

A handsome, engaging, easygoing man with a droll sense of humor, Dunn enjoyed a long and successful career as a political man of letters. As a reform Democrat, he was an important factor in the campaigns for the Australian ballot (1889) and the Indianapolis city charter (1891). In addition to his numerous historical monographs, Dunn worked as an editorialist on a variety of Indianapolis newspapers from 1886 to 1921; he was also president of the Public Library Commission (1899 to 1914), state librarian (1889 to 1892), Indianapolis city controller (1904 to 1906, 1914 to 1916), and private secretary to Senator Samuel Ralston (1923 to 1924). But in all of this varied public career Dunn never lost his interest in Indians and his taste for adventure. He became an expert in Indian languages and crusaded in later years for funds to enable the Bureau of American Ethnology to preserve accounts of many fast-disappearing dialects. And in 1922, at the age of sixty-seven, Dunn the vigorous adventurer went looking for manganese in Santo Domingo and Haiti (at the same time seeking Christopher Columbus's lost mine).[8]

Like his contemporaries Theodore Roosevelt, Woodrow Wilson, Henry Cabot Lodge, and, nearer to home, Albert Beveridge and Claude Bowers, Dunn perceived no conflict in his roles as historian and politician. For the Progressive generation history, properly understood, was the key to the future. As Dunn put it in 1910, "a state cannot possibly profit fully by its experience unless it provides for handing it down from one generation to another by the preservation of its history."[9] This view of history

---

[8] Caroline Dunn, *Jacob Piatt Dunn: His Miami Language Studies and Indian Manuscript Collection* (Indiana Historical Society *Prehistory Research Series*, I, No. 2, Indianapolis, 1937), pp. 31-43; Indianapolis *Star*, June 7, 1924; Indianapolis *News*, June 7, 1924.

[9] Jacob Piatt Dunn, Jr., "The Duty of the State," in *Indiana Magazine of History*, VI (1910), 137-38.

as the handmaiden of politics was later challenged by the new seminar-trained historians from Johns Hopkins University and elsewhere, who increasingly dismissed the informally researched narratives of lawyer-historians like Dunn, Howe, and English as amateurish and unscientific. (Unfortunately professional historians succeeded too well in convincing their students and the general public that history was a rarified science; they surrendered to popularizers and journalists the historian's role as an educator of the public.) But in 1886, with formal graduate training in history underway in only a handful of eastern universities, there were no doctors of philosophy present to challenge the credentials of Indiana's lawyer-historians. They wrote well and were practiced in using and evaluating evidence; that they were also more trained to argue a case than to search objectively for the truth was undeniable, though it is also clear that legal training is no prerequisite for producing bias in historical writing and that graduate training in history is no guarantee of objectivity. They were modest, scrupulous historians, and the state was fortunate that they undertook to begin to prepare its history.

Drawn together by their need for access to historical materials, English, Howe, and Dunn and a handful of supporters formed a new historical society in 1886 based on the old Indiana Historical Society. There was little left of the old organization: there were no available copies of any of the pre-1886 publications; the original minute book revealed only a fragmentary record of the old Society's activities; many of the 327 books that Dillon had hired men to haul over to the Society's room in the Marion County Courthouse in 1877 had been subsequently lost or stolen; and few of the old members were still alive. In an attempt to rescue the work of the old Society the new secretary, Jacob Piatt Dunn, Jr., undertook the task of tracking down all the Society's old publications so that the new Society could publish them together in one volume. It took him ten years to find them, and he may have missed one, the 1861 lecture by Bishop George Upfold. Still the Society triumphantly published "Volume I" of the *Publications* in 1897, eleven years *after* the appearance of Volume II, which reflected the earliest of the new Society's work.[10]

In one important way the new members reshaped the old Society: while the old constitution had specified an open membership, achieved simply by signing the documents and paying the dues, in the new Society members were to be elected by secret ballot, with a three-fourths majority required. Hence the Society was transformed into an exclusive club, emulating the other prestigious gentlemen's clubs in Indianapolis, like the Indianapolis Literary Club and the Contemporary Club, of which several of the younger new organizers were faithful members. Although the secret ballot lessened the pressure to accept a candidate proposed by an influential member and permitted members to exercise their prejudices, in fact the minutes do not indicate that any applicant ever failed to be elected. Nevertheless, with or without the blackball, the members selected in the early years of the reorganized Society were all prosperous, "prominent" men. The first election is representative: in addition to Howe, English, and Dunn, William De M. Hooper, John R. Wilson, Addison C. Harris, John H. Holliday, John C. Shoemaker, William R. Holloway, Elijah Halford, John A. Finch, George C. Hitt, and Byron K. Elliott were elected.[11]

The new Society insured that their approach would prevail by resolving in the April 17, 1886, meeting to expel all old members

---

[10] *Proceedings of the Indiana Historical Society, 1830-1886*, pp. 5-8.

[11] *Minutes of the Society, 1886-1918*, pp. 463, 464-68. Half of these men (Holliday, Shoemaker, Holloway, Halford, and Hitt) were newspaper executives, the others were successful lawyers.

who failed to pay their dues within thirty days. Since there appear to have been no public notices of the new group's meetings and since there were few surviving members of the old group anyway, the takeover was complete.

To an egalitarian generation the vices of the restricted membership policy are evident: for instance, the Society not only promoted snobbism, but also skewed its presentation of the state's past somewhat by a tendency toward filiopietistic emphasis on Great White Men and "good" families. But the virtues of the elitist society must also be noted. There were, in fact, only a very small number of persons interested in supporting, writing, and preserving the state's history in 1886; they were already a self-selected elite, and, in view of the dismal failure of the Society in its early "popular" phases, one cannot but sense that the elaborate membership rules were a sort of morale booster: in short it enabled them to see themselves as a successful elite rather than an unsuccessful attempt at a popular movement.

Certainly the contrast between the new society and the old is marked. The new group boasted durable leaders and a handful of diligent members willing to serve as officers for years on end, to attend meetings regularly, to pay their dues, to serve on committees, to prepare monographs on Indiana history, and to bring new members, similarly dedicated, into the Society. The old society had demonstrated few of these strengths.

It is difficult to evaluate the new Society's success in attracting members for most of the first thirty years of its life, since there were no systematic records kept. The first membership roster was published in 1906, twenty years after reorganization, and it revealed only eighty-seven regular members and ten honorary ones. Certainly the Society was not aiming for large numbers: only 112 men were elected to membership in the first decade, and it is likely that a significant number of these refused the honor. In the first year, 1886, forty-seven men were elected, but only twenty-eight had paid their dues by the end of the year. Most years only a handful of new members were elected, but in 1891 and 1914, both years in which great progressive issues were stirring, members were elected in greater numbers: 34 in 1891, 50 in 1914. By 1914 the Society reported 102 regular members, of whom approximately one half were newly elected. Certainly it was a small society throughout this period.[12] The members were mostly professional men: prominent lawyers, jurists, doctors, journalists, and a scattering of college and university teachers.

Although the progressive young Secretary Dunn proposed in 1888 that women be eligible for membership, it was not until 1906 that the Society ceased to be strictly a gentlemen's club. Eliza Gordon Browning (1856-1927), the first woman member, had been head of the Indianapolis Public Library since 1892. "Lide" Browning became a Society stalwart, one of the handful of members who actually attended annual meetings. She edited a publication for the Society in 1909, and in 1910 she began an eleven-year period of service on the executive committee. Her election did not immediately signal the beginning of significant female participation, however, since the Society waited four more years to elect another woman to membership.[13]

Generally the Society reflected the male Protestant establishment. A refreshing departure from this pattern was the instance of the Rev. Denis O'Donaghue, Roman Catholic Auxiliary Bishop of Indianapolis, a Washington, Indiana, native who was

---

[12] *Ibid.*, pp. 463-90, 510-11, 551-56; Indiana Historical Society, *Charter, Constitution, Officers and Members and List of Publications* ([Irvington]: Cottman, 1906).

[13] *Minutes of the Society, 1886-1918*, pp. 477, 512, 530, 534; Eliza G. Browning (ed.), *Lockerbie's Assessment List of Indianapolis, 1835* (Indiana Historical Society *Publications*, IV, No. 7, Indianapolis, 1909).

Society Library

above, Indiana State Capitol, 1902;
left, William Wesley Woollen,
historian, pre-1861 member of the
Society, president, 1896-1900

Indiana State Library

Society Library

above, Charles Coffin, Society
treasurer, 1894-1931; Eliza G.
Browning, first woman member of the
Society; *right,* Will E. English, a
Society vice-president, 1896-1926

Indiana State Library

above, George S. Cottman, founder and editor of the *Indiana Quarterly Magazine of History*; *left*, The *Magazine* appeared with this cover design until 1913.

Butler University *Drift*

Vol. IX   December, 1913   No. 4

Indiana Magazine
of History

Published Quarterly by
The Department of History of Indiana University
with the cooperation of the Indiana Historical
Society and The Indiana State Library

CONTENTS

Subscription Price, $1.00 per year   Single Copy, 25 Cents

Entered as second-class matter September 16, 1913, at the postoffice at Bloomington, Indiana, under
the Act of March 3, 1879.

above, Christopher B.
Coleman, 1904; *right,* the
new *Indiana Magazine of
History,* 1913

Indiana University Alumni Magazine

right, James A. Woodburn in the
1890s; *below*, Demarchus Brown,
state librarian, 1906-1926; Dr. Frank
Wynn, a leader in the movement to
celebrate the state centennial in 1916

Indiana State Library

Indiana State Library

elected to membership in 1894 and to a vice-presidency in 1900, serving until he was transferred to Louisville in 1911.[14]

The overwhelming majority of members were Indianapolis residents. In 1911, for instance, forty-nine of the sixty-four members lived in the capital. Not only was the Society essentially a gentlemen's club before it linked up with the state in 1915, it was an Indianapolis gentlemen's club.[15]

The first goal of this small, elite group was to preserve historical materials. This was accomplished by publishing historical work and by improving the state's historical collections.

The new Society's first order of business was to publish the work of its own members. This policy was the Society's main priority throughout its first thirty years as an active organization and has continued ever since to hold a place in the Society's program. By publishing, the Society preserved historical materials. Moreover, preparing articles for publication did not depend upon legislative grants, permanent quarters, or wide public support; it depended only upon the work of individual historians. The new Society felt confident that its members could supply historical writings and to an impressive extent this was so. In the first twenty-eight years of its new life the Society issued forty publications, all but a few of which were prepared by its own members.

The Society's publishing program was subsidized by the Bowen-Merrill Company of Indianapolis, later Bobbs-Merrill. Initially, the publishers printed the material at their own expense, furnished the Society with 100 free copies, and agreed to pay a 10 percent royalty on sales above 200 copies. Sales, of course, rarely achieved 200 copies. Even after Bowen-Merrill

---

[14] For O'Donaghue see Indianapolis *News*, November 7, 1925.

[15] Indiana Historical Society, *Charter, Constitution, Officers and Members and List of Publications* (Indianapolis: Edward J. Hecker, 1911).

suffered a devastating fire in 1890, they continued this charitable arrangement.[16] After the Society secured an appropriation from the legislature in 1899 authorizing $600 a year to the Society for publications in 1900 and 1901, the arrangement changed. The Society was asked to purchase Bowen-Merrill's stock of Society publications for $810, and the publisher agreed to act as the Society's agent for sales but no longer would print the material free of charge. Bobbs-Merrill continued to act as the Society's agent for booksales until the 1950s. All of the company's dealings with the Society were offered as a public-spirited gesture; Bobbs-Merrill never even recovered expenses from the commissions earned.[17]

The Society applied to the legislature for modest amounts of aid during this period. Within the first year of the Society's reorganization a committee composed of English, Coburn, Superior Court Judge John A. Holman, and U.S. District Attorney Charles Holstein asked the Indiana House of Representatives for a room in the new State Capitol, one adjoining the State Library rooms, so that the state librarian could oversee the Society's collections (described as "a library of some 2,000 books and pamphlets") and make them accessible to the public. The Society also wanted a state appropriation to publish the executive journal of the Indiana Territory, pointing out that most states had already begun to publish their older state documents and that Indiana ought to do her part. Without the publication of the executive journal, the Society's committee argued, Michigan, Illinois, Wisconsin, Arkansas, and Missouri were "left with incomplete records," since the journal covered all the old Indian Territory for a period. But the strongest section of the committee's 1887 memorial to the legislature was a request for improving

---

[16] *Minutes of the Society, 1886-1918*, pp. 464, 468, 471, 479, 481.

[17] *Ibid.*, pp. 495, 514-15, 534-35. See also Bobbs-Merrill file, IHS Papers.

the collections of the State Library. The library's growth had
been severely hampered by inadequate funding. Since 1852 its
annual budget for purchasing new materials and maintaining
the old ones had been $400. The Society outlined the State Li-
brary's "pressing wants":

> its broken sets of books should be completed, its damaged volumes re-
> bound, a complete card catalogue made, its deficiencies filled, and in
> the future it be kept abreast of the constant increase of knowledge by
> the purchase of books of intrinsic worth.

To accomplish all this the Society recommended allocations of
$5,000 the first year and $2,000 annually afterwards. The committee also recommended the appointment of a purchasing board
to help the librarian spend the larger sums of money and asked
that the Society be allowed one representative on the board.[18]

Although the bill failed to pass in the 1886-1887 legislative
session, which was among the most "chaotic and unproductive"
in the state's history, by December, 1887, the Society was assigned Room 87 on the second floor of the new capitol, next to
the rooms assigned for the State Library. The recommended improvements in the State Library passed the next session of the
General Assembly after a strenuous lobbying effort led by Dunn,
who got the support of a broad variety of organizations, ranging
from the Knights of Labor to "the State Board of Agriculture,
Horticultural Society, Horse Breeders, Sheep Breeders, Short
Horn Breeders, Hog Breeders, Bee Keepers, etc. . . . on condition
that the literature of their various lines be put in the library. . . ."
Only the Society's request for a legislative appropriation to support the publication of the executive journal failed to be passed
in the first decade. The Society's plan in 1888 to ask the legislature to appropriate $1500 a year for its work was laid aside in

-----

[18] Indiana *House Journal*, 1886-1887, pp. 398-401.

order to concentrate all efforts on getting the new State Library appropriations passed.[19]

For several reasons the Society's officers decided in this period not to attempt to build its own collections. There was no adequate place to keep a significant independent library in the state capitol. The legislature then, as later, was annoyed and confused by requests for support from more than one historical institution. And the State Library had priority in this regard. Moreover, until 1896 the other members probably hoped that English would simply provide a library for the Society. He was extremely rich; he had a tremendous private historical collection; and he seems to have dropped hints about this from time to time.[20]

Meanwhile the members worked hard collectively and individually to improve the State Library. Howe, Dunn, English, and Judge Addison L. Roache were all thanked specifically for their work and their donations by State Librarian Lizzie Callis-Scott in November, 1888. Dunn was rewarded for his leadership in the campaign for the new bill by being elected state librarian in 1888. During his two terms (1889-1892) Dunn and the purchasing board improved the library considerably, achieving such impressive results that the legislature concluded that all had been done that needed to be done and promptly cut the $2,000 annual appropriation by half. This lapse was somewhat compensated for by the removal of the office of the state librarian from politics in 1895, when the management of the library was placed under the State Board of Education. Certainly by the end of the Society's first decade it had achieved a real transformation in the State Library.[21]

---

[19] Phillips, *Indiana in Transition*, p. 24; *Minutes of the Society, 1886-1918*, pp. 475, 477, 478; Dunn, *Greater Indianapolis*, I, 510.

[20] Dunn, *Greater Indianapolis*, I, 509-10; Indianapolis *News*, February 8, 1896.

[21] *Indiana State Library Report, 1887-1888*, p. 8; ibid., *1889-1890*; ibid., *1891-1892*; ibid., *1893-1894*, p. 16; ibid., *1895-1896*, p. 16.

The Society's hope that English would give the organization his historical collections and funds to provide a permanent head-quarters proved evanescent. English died in 1896 and left the group a $2,500 bequest instead, the interest on which was to be used to support the publications program. By 1896 English's son, Will E. English (1850-1926), was an active member of the Society and had even contributed a monograph on the Indianapolis Masonic Order to the *Publications* series in 1895. He inherited his father's large collection of books, documents, and extensive notes on Indiana political figures and still hoped to prepare a manuscript to complete his father's grand design for a history of Indiana. Some members perhaps transferred their hopes for a Society library provided by the English family to Will E., but certainly nothing was done directly throughout this period to attempt to build the Society's own fragmentary collections into an historical library.[22]

The Society continued to seek legislative support for its publications program and was sometimes successful. A bold request in 1897 for $2,000 one year and $500 a year thereafter, supported in principle by lame-duck Governor Claude Matthews, a Society member since 1891, was rewarded in 1899 by a two-year appropriation of $600 a year. There was some confusion about the appropriation, since the bill directed the Bureau of Printing "to cause to be printed the annual report of the Indiana Historical Society, not to cost to exceed [sic], $600 for each year." A Society committee had to inquire of the State Printing Board what the money was to be used for; but it turned out that there were no unreasonable limitations. The Society was issued warrants on the state treasury through the printing board. Approximately one fourth of the $1,200 was used to pay the state

---

[22] *Minutes of the Society, 1886-1918*, pp. 487-89; for William H. English's will see Indianapolis *Journal*, February 11, 1896. Will E. English was a vice-president of the Society from 1896 to 1926. For the Society's acquisition of a part of the English collection see below, pp. 242-43.

printer to print the annotated executive journal of the Indiana Territory, which included 157 pages of text, a 16-page subject index, and a 42-page name index. It was the most ambitious work the Society had yet produced. After a four-year lapse in appropriations the Society went again to the General Assembly to request support of $300 a year. This was granted in 1907 and was continued by successive legislatures through 1917, enabling the Society to increase its pace of publication somewhat.[23]

As the reorganized Indiana Historical Society prepared to celebrate its twentieth anniversary in 1906, there were signs of renewed vitality and expanded plans. Suddenly in December, 1905, there was an unusually large number of members at the annual meeting, and fifteen new members were elected. The Society agreed to participate in the meetings of the History Section of the State Teachers' Association. Early in 1906 there was an unprecedented meeting and stocktaking, with a full report on all members who had either resigned or died followed by an order to print the first full roster of active members. The Society called for a report from Bobbs-Merrill on its stock of Society publications. Plans were approved to host the joint professional meetings of the American Historical Association, the American Economic Association, and the American Political Science Association in 1910, and the constitution was altered to make election to membership a little easier. The Society decided to ask again for a legislative appropriation.[24]

At least a good measure of the inspiration behind this unusual activity came from an Irvington printer with literary tastes and

---

[23] *Minutes of the Society, 1886-1918,* pp. 491, 492, 493-94, 495; *Laws of Indiana,* 1899, pp. 529-30, 1907, p. 682, 1909, p. 491, 1911, p. 283, 1913, p. 588, 1915, p. 353, 1917, p. 207.

[24] *Minutes of the Society, 1886-1918,* pp. 505-14.

connections and an enthusiasm for history. George S. Cottman (1857-1941) began writing brief historical sketches and nature articles for Indianapolis newspapers before the turn of the century. He was elected a member of the Indiana Historical Society in 1900 and was totally unimpressed by the organization. He was later to remember it in the following terms:

> the State Historical Society, though it had a tenacity of life equal to that of the Democratic party, was virtually a homeless nomad unprepared to do more than hold occasional meetings and publish monographs when there chanced to be a little money in the treasury.

It was not a generous assessment, but Cottman set out to change things.[25]

In 1905 Cottman independently launched a new historical magazine, *The Indiana Quarterly Magazine of History*. Though not the first magazine to specialize in Indiana state and local history—the *Indianian*, a monthly published by B. F. Blair from 1897 to 1901, was edited by the historian W. H. Smith after July, 1899—the *Magazine*, predecessor of today's *Indiana Magazine of History*, was the first to succeed. It was launched with the assistance of state librarian and fellow Society member William E. Henry, who provided a list of subscribers. Cottman editorialized in every issue for improvements in the preservation and dissemination of state and local history, and at the same time he urged the Society to begin to co-operate with other historical organizations, like the State Teachers' Association history section, the patriotic societies, and local historical societies. Far from being an arm of the Indiana Historical Society, Cottman in some ways made the Society an arm of the magazine.[26]

---

[25] George S. Cottman, "The Indiana Magazine of History: A Retrospect," in *Indiana Magazine of History*, XXV (1929), 280-87; *Minutes of the Society, 1886-1918*, pp. 506, 509, 513.

[26] *Minutes of the Society, 1886-1918*, pp. 506, 509, 513; Dunn, *Greater Indianapolis*, I, 399.

For three years Cottman ran the magazine entirely on his own: he was editor, printer, and publisher, and he never made any money on the enterprise. Still, the publication was well received; its rather small readership believed it filled an important need. When Cottman announced to the Society at the end of 1907 that he was moving to Oregon, the organization faced the prospect of the extinction of a journal that had made itself useful not only to the Society but also to a number of other organizations. In an unusually venturesome move, the Society resolved to keep the magazine going. The members voted a shoestring appropriation of $150 and Christopher B. Coleman (1875–1944), Butler University professor of history, agreed to take over the editorship.[27]

Coleman had only joined the Society the previous year. He was one of the handful of members with professional training in history and was, in all respects, an up-and-coming young man. After being graduated from Yale in 1896 Coleman took a divinity degree at the University of Chicago in 1899 and then studied history for a year at the University of Berlin in 1904-1905. Beginning what was to be a long and fortunate association as an officer of the Society, in 1907 Coleman took over both the magazine and Cottman's office as corresponding secretary.

As the Society had been swept up into Cottman's history magazine, it found itself increasingly overwhelmed by other events and projects initiated elsewhere. Dunn and Howe were both deeply involved in writing projects. Dunn especially was engrossed in his truly monumental histories of Indianapolis and of Indiana. Neither man was an administrator or businessman; they were working at writing history, not running a public agency. The Society under their leadership spoke out occasionally for

---

[27] *Minutes of the Society, 1886-1918*, pp. 519, 521; Cottman, "The Indiana Magazine of History: A Retrospect," in *Indiana Magazine of History*, XXV, 281-88.

more funds for institutions like the Indiana State Library and the Bureau of American Ethnology, and it co-operated in a small way with other state groups, such as the Academy of Science, and sent delegates to the national Conference of State and Local Historical Societies.[28] But there was a newly emerging history establishment in Indiana, composed of seminar-trained historians, public school history teachers, and librarians, as well as energetic independents like George Cottman and the founders of numerous local historical societies, and this establishment was beginning to demand a kind of leadership that the Society was not quite prepared to provide.

The histories of the plans for celebrating the state's centennial and the fate of the *Magazine* illustrate the Society's somewhat subordinate role. The initiative for a centennial celebration in 1916 came from the Indiana University History Club in 1907. Indiana Historical Society President Howe responded in December, 1908, by proposing that the Society "co-operate in any movement that may be undertaken to celebrate the Centennial. . . ."[29] Howe did not propose to undertake to lead such a movement, only to co-operate if some other organization were to lead the way.

The Society did prepare a memorial to the state legislature in 1910 requesting "an adequate permanent building, on grounds adjacent to the State Capitol, for the housing of the State Library and State Museum, and other agencies devoted to the preservation of historical material. . . ." Professor James A. Woodburn,

---

[28] *Minutes of the Society, 1886-1918*, pp. 520, 525, 530, 538, 561; Amos W. Butler to J. P. Dunn, December 23, 1908, November 5, 1909, in Butler Papers, Lilly Library, Indiana University, Bloomington.

[29] Woodburn, "The Indiana Historical Society: A Hundred Years," in Coleman (ed.), *Centennial Handbook*, p. 33. Woodburn also says the Society was "a vital factor in the creation of the Indiana Historical Commission," but it is more correct to say that Woodburn was such a factor. *Ibid.*, pp. 38-39; *Minutes of the Society, 1886-1918*, p. 523.

chairman of the history department at Indiana University since 1890 and a Society member since 1895, was a moving force both for the building project and for the centennial celebration; he replaced Bishop O'Donaghue as third vice-president in 1910.[30]

In December, 1911, the Society appointed a committee of three to request a legislative appropriation "for the purchase and preservation of relics and documents relating to the history of Indiana." The committee members were Dr. Frank Wynn, State Librarian Demarchus Brown, and the irrepressible George Cottman, back from Oregon, editing the magazine again and active in the Society. Since Wynn, a prominent Indianapolis physician, was eventually to become the president of the Indiana Historical Commission, and since the appropriation requested here was to be solicited independently of the historical building request, one is tempted to see in the committee the germ of the idea of the Indiana Historical Commission, created by the General Assembly in 1915.[31]

In 1913 the Centennial Commission recommended to the legislature that the state appropriate two million dollars for a centennial memorial building. Considerable support for the idea had been demonstrated previously at a conference organized in May, 1912, by Dr. Wynn, who had gathered together 150 luminaries from around the state to consider an appropriate memorial. Woodburn campaigned for the building before groups like the Indianapolis Literary Club, the Colonial Dames of Indiana, and the history section of the Indiana State Teachers' Association, which had been meeting with the historical society since 1906. There was, unfortunately, some controversy among the Commission members and others about where the building

---

[30] *Minutes of the Society, 1886-1918*, pp. 531, 534; James A. Woodburn, "The Indiana Centennial, 1916," in *Indiana Magazine of History*, VII (1912), 1-14.

[31] *Minutes of the Society, 1886-1918*, p. 537.

should be constructed and what form it would take. Dunn was quoted by the Indianapolis *News* as asserting that the Commission "fooled away 2 years" and failed to make a specific proposal. The General Assembly was unwilling to accept responsibility for the project and referred the memorial building proposal to the voters. A disappointed Jacob Dunn described this as

> a repetition of the picayune politics that caused the State to be discommoded for years by the Old State House, until we had a legislature in which the two houses were of different political majorities, and neither party had to take the responsibility of the expenditure.

The voters, perhaps predictably, rejected the opportunity to spend $2 million on an historical building.[32]

The Centennial Commission then presented "Plan B" to the legislators in 1914. Time was running out. If the assembly would not authorize a $2 million building, would they authorize $25,000 for an Indiana Historical Commission, $20,000 to be spent for celebration, $5,000 for editing and publishing historical documents? Professor Woodburn and Governor Ralston worked together to design the legislation, and it became law in March, 1915.[33]

The underwriting of the Indiana Historical Commission in 1915 marked the first significant state commitment of funds to history in Indiana. The Indiana Historical Society participated in the drive to achieve this commitment, but no one would have said that the Society was a leader in this project. Individual members were very active, but the Society itself played a small role.

---

[32] Woodburn, "The Indiana Historical Society: A Hundred Years," in Coleman (ed.), *Centennial Handbook*, p. 33; Indianapolis *News*, December 18, 1912, November 21, 1914; Dunn, *Indiana and Indianans*, II, 781.

[33] John A. Lapp to James A. Woodburn, December 29, 1914, Woodburn Papers, Lilly Library, Indiana University, Bloomington.

Similarly, others took the lead in beginning to collect historical documents in Indiana. With no historical society library to
offer an obvious place of deposit for the papers of prominent
persons, many private collections were simply lost. In 1906 Demarchus Brown, the new state librarian, oversaw the creation of
a department of Indiana archives, the forerunner of the present
Indiana Division of the State Library. Though there was no
room in the cramped quarters in the capitol to store state records, the new department could and did begin to collect books
and manuscripts.[34]

The history department at Indiana University also stepped
forward to fill the vacuum in leadership in collecting Indiana
history. The Indiana Historical Survey was initiated by the department in 1912 under the direction of Professor James A.
Woodburn, inspired by the plans for the centennial celebration.
The real workhorse of the Survey, however, was Logan Esarey,
a new Indiana University Ph.D. with a strong commitment to
Indiana history. Esarey developed a seminar in Indiana history
with Woodburn's support and began to collect newspapers and
documents.[35]

Meanwhile Cottman continued to edit the *Indiana Quarterly
Magazine of History* with minor financial assistance from the
Society. The magazine never made a profit, and Cottman was
somewhat discouraged about the project. Woodburn pointed out
that the Survey needed a vehicle for its publications and offered
to take over the struggling magazine "for a year or two to see
what we can do with it." Esarey took over the editorship in 1913,

---

[34] Esther U. McNitt, "Short History of the Indiana State Library," in *Library
Occurrent*, X (1931), 26-27.

[35] Woodburn outlined the goals of the Survey in "Indiana History and Its
Celebration," in *Suggestive Plans for a Historical and Educational Celebration
in Indiana in 1916* (Indianapolis, 1912). See also R. Carlyle Buley, "Logan
Esarey, Hoosier," in *Indiana Magazine of History*, XXXVIII (1942), 348-50.

publishing the best results of his seminar on Indiana history in the magazine. The level of scholarship reflected in the journal was, of course, raised considerably, and the Society was duly impressed. The members increased the level of support for the magazine from $100 to $200 in 1913, and in 1914 they also agreed to pay the magazine one dollar for each member's subscription.[36]

After nearly three decades of regular activity the Indiana Historical Society lacked most of the standard trappings of an American state historical society. It did not possess a library, a museum, or even a permanent meeting place. The Society had been shuttled around from one room to another in the capitol since 1888 and was finally expelled from the building altogether in 1914. Dunn, who was serving the second of his two terms as city controller at the time, provided a closet in the City Hall in which the Society's few possessions could be stored.[37] Nor did the Society publish its own historical magazine.

The Society remained in 1914 pretty much what it had been in 1886, a small private club for publishing local history. It is not easy to understand why this was so. Certainly the Society was favored with intelligent and faithful leaders: Daniel Howe was president of the Society for twenty years; Dunn was secretary

---

[36] Cottman, "The Indiana Magazine of History: A Retrospect," in *Indiana Magazine of History*, XXV, 281-88; James A. Woodburn to George S. Cottman, February 22, 1913, Cottman Papers, Indiana Division, Indiana State Library; *Minutes of the Society, 1886-1918*, pp. 547-48, 554. See also William O. Lynch, "A History of the *Indiana Magazine of History*," in *Indiana Magazine of History*, LI (1955), 1-30.

[37] The Society occupied Room 87 from 1888 to 1905. After 1905 the Society was assigned Room 121 for some unspecified period. It was apparently not appropriate as a meeting room, for all the subsequent meetings through November, 1911, were held in President Howe's law offices; from December, 1911, through April, 1916, meetings were either held in Howe's office or the Union Trust Company assembly room. At some point before 1914, the Society was asked to leave Room 121 and occupy an unspecified room in the basement. *Minutes of the Society, 1886-1918*, pp. 476, 505, 553.

for nearly forty years. The members, though few in number, included many of the state's best educated, most progressive public figures. Though the state was a conservative one, so were its neighbors, and yet by 1914, even leaving Wisconsin and Minnesota out of the reckoning on the grounds that those states were unusually generous in expenditures for history, Indiana had fallen behind every other midwestern state in promoting scholarly research, collection, and publication in state history.[38] The oldest continuously existing historical society west of the Alleghenies, Indiana's was also among the least productive. Perhaps the reason was that the Society's leaders were historians, not administrators or promoters or empire builders. Moreover, for them the Society was only one interest among many. The Society still had not attracted a leader who wanted to make an historical agency his or her lifework. Meanwhile, Indiana's new historical establishment had taken over the leadership of Indiana history by 1914. The Society's task for the coming decade was to find a new role for itself.

---

[38] Buley, "Logan Esarey, Hoosier," in *Indiana Magazine of History*, XXXVIII (1942), 348-49. Buley pointed out that Michigan had published forty volumes of *Pioneer and Historical Society Publications* by 1913; Ohio, twenty-two volumes of *Archaeological and Historical Society Publications* and nine volumes of *Historical and Philosophical Society Publications;* Illinois, nine volumes of *Illinois Historical Collections,* five volumes of the *Journal,* and thirteen volumes of *Transactions of the Illinois Historical Society,* and Indiana had produced only four volumes of *Publications* and eight volumes of *Indiana Magazine of History.*

IV

The Society Transformed

1915-1924

Indiana Historical Commission

Charles W. Moores   Harlow Lindley   John Cavanaugh   Lew M. O'Bannon
                          Secretary

James A. Woodburn   Samuel M. Foster

        Frank B. Wynn   Gov. Samuel M. Ralston   Charity Dye
        Vice-President   President

IV

"From the bluffs of the Ohio to the sand dunes of Lake Michigan there has been a general outburst of patriotic interest in Indiana and its history."
The Indiana Centennial 1916
(1919)

The celebration of the centennial of Indiana's admission to the Union provoked an unprecedented interest in the state's history. Under the leadership of the Indiana Historical Commission (IHC) a variety of programs was planned in every county, creating a state network of citizens interested in local history. In order to provide lasting institutions to benefit from these new energies, the IHC urged its agents to form or reactivate local historical societies. In an extension of the same effort the commission also made a determined effort to widen and increase the membership of the Indiana Historical Society.

The Society had roughly 130 members in 1915; a decade later, with the assistance of the commission staff, the membership numbered more than a thousand.[1] The new members, recruited primarily from among the commission's agents, were citizens who had volunteered to take an active interest in organizing the centennial celebration. As organizers of local historical societies,

---

[1] Minutes of IHS, December 29, 1921, December 28, 1922; *The Indiana Centennial 1916* (*Indiana Historical Collections*, V, Indianapolis, Indiana Historical Bureau, 1919), p. 63.

they looked to the capital for aid and encouragement. They wanted to know what other local societies were doing, how to run a museum, how to raise money, where to find experienced and interesting speakers, and how to write local history. In fact, it was the IHC, not the Society, that attempted to meet their needs. The Indiana Historical Society had never concerned itself with these kinds of questions, and it did not begin to do so during the IHC years. Why then did the commission encourage the local societies to support the state society, and why did the local people accede to this encouragement to some degree?

The commissioners realized from the beginning of the IHC's existence in 1915 that an organized public sentiment was essential to maintain a state-supported historical agency. The General Assembly appropriated $25,000 in 1915 "for the use of the commission until January 1, 1917. . . ." The act creating the commission suggested that it might be allowed a longer life than two years, since three of the nine commission members were to be appointed to four-year, rather than two-year, terms, but this provision merely suggested a possibility.[2] In fact, the continued life of the commission after January, 1917, depended upon the General Assembly and the governor. Therefore, it was imperative that the commission organize public support for its continued existence.

In other midwestern states the state historical societies combined the features of large voluntary organizations of citizens interested in history with those of state agencies manned by professional historians. In Indiana there was neither a large citizen organization nor a permanent state agency to collect, publish, and preserve historical material. In order to achieve the permanent state agency, the IHC needed the enlarged citizens group; though the Society was not the kind of organization the commission wanted, the Society simply could not be avoided. An

---

[2] *Laws of Indiana*, 1915, pp. 455-57.

Indiana Historical Society already existed. The commission's strategy, therefore, was to influence the Society as much as possible to become a popular, ready-made lobby for a state historical agency.

Turning an old, dignified, elitist club for amateur historians into a large enthusiastic state lobby for historical interests was a rather large order and did not meet with either rapid or complete success. However, the Society did change under the influence of the IHC; and by 1925 a permanent state agency, though not a state-supported historical society, was established.

The Society's history in this decade is for the most part significantly influenced by the activities of the Indiana Historical Commission. Of the nine-member commission, five persons were apparently quite active: the president, Governor Samuel Ralston, a very capable administrator and strong supporter of the commission; the secretary, Harlow Lindley of the State Library's Indiana Department; James Woodburn, chairman of the commission's publication committee; Dr. Frank Wynn, chairman of the centennial celebration committee; and Charity Dye, an Indianapolis schoolteacher and Federation of Women's Clubs leader. The IHC appointed a director, Walter C. Woodward of Earlham College, and an assistant director, Lucy M. Elliott of Tipton. The commission was largely composed of Society members, but its leadership was not identical with the Society's leadership, and the commission initiated programs unlike anything the Society had ever attempted. The Indiana Historical Society's response to IHC initiatives was, so far as the records indicate, cordial and supportive, though at times one senses a certain bewilderment at all the unusual activity and a certain loss of control.[3]

---

[3] For the commission see Kate Milner Rabb's brief history in *Indiana History Bulletin*, II (1925), 163-69. For the Society's mixed response see for instance Woodburn, "The Indiana Historical Society: A Hundred Years," in Coleman (ed.), *Centennial Handbook*, pp. 35-37, in which he seems nostalgic for the small, old Society.

The commission had $20,000 with which to prepare a centennial celebration, and in the course of 1915-1916 it surely created $20,000 worth of interest in history. In a barrage of bulletins, Walter C. Woodward and his assistant Lucy Elliott sent out scores of suggestions, instructions, and exhortations to local historical society leaders, but the schools and colleges were the main targets. And no one was left out:

> The Commission urges that there be brought into cooperation all cultural and business influences; clubs; historical and patriotic organizations; athletic, musical and art associations; religious bodies, and fraternal orders; civic and commercial bodies, industrial and agricultural interests; town, county, and state boards.[4]

With the assistance of this powerful troupe of celebrants, the commission undertook an extensive program. In 1915 Charity Dye edited a column called "The Centennial Story Hour" for school children; it appeared in the Sunday edition of the Indianapolis *Star*. She was also an indefatigable public speaker and led the State Federation of Women's Clubs into the work. The commission produced not only a slide show on Indiana history, but also and even more ambitiously a motion picture called "Indiana." Produced by an Indiana company, the film featured a benign James Whitcomb Riley and a lapdog, both surrounded by children. Indiana-born artist Janet Scudder designed a commemorative medal based on the state seal, but for pageants the planners decided to look outside the state for experts. A pageant master from New York was brought in to write and direct shows at Bloomington, Corydon, and Indianapolis; however, most communities had to get along with mere local talent, guided by the commission's instructional bulletins.[5]

---

[4] Indiana Historical Commission, *Bulletin No. 3* [1915], p. 4.
[5] *The Indiana Centennial 1916*, pp. 26, 27, 31, 35, 39.

The commission estimated that a quarter of a million Hoosiers watched historical pageants in 1916, and thirty to forty thousand were actors in the pageants. It is difficult to imagine what most of these productions were like from the brief published descriptions, but the Bloomington pageant, reflecting the participation of the university community and the talents of the New York pageant master, seems to have been unique. The first part featured masses of young women dressed in blue to embody spirits of Hope and men in purple personifying spirits of Determination. As described by the author the two kinds of spirits "meet and join in a whirling dance of exquisite joyousness. . . ." The Indians were simple "heavies" in this pageant, and they were quickly driven off by Hope, Determination, and the Pioneers. In Part II Light and Truth arrived, personified by a procession of figures from Moses to someone representing Harvard and Yale; then the State of Indiana called for her own university and dressed a child in academic robes. Most pageants were less symbolic and represented more concrete historic events, with pleasing opportunities for local citizens to dress up in historic costumes.[6]

At Indianapolis the centennial celebration lasted two weeks, from October 2 to 15. There were parades, daily pageants at Riverside Park, and "Indiana Authors' Night" at the Masonic Temple. Even President Wilson came to town for Historical Highway Day to campaign for good roads as the key to "the nationalization of America." As a final 'hurrah' Admission Day, December 11, 1916, was celebrated throughout the state with school programs and public speeches.[7]

In the midst of the excited plans for the celebration journalist Juliet Strauss suggested in April, 1915, that a state park system

---

[6] *Ibid.*, pp. 40, 212-16.

[7] *Ibid.*, pp. 280-82, 302, 305.

would make a splendid permanent memorial of the centennial, pointing out at the same time that a beautiful wilderness area in Parke County called Turkey Run had come onto the market. Through the combined efforts of Governor Ralston, the conservationist Richard Lieber of Indianapolis, Dr. Wynn, and fund-raisers Sol S. Kiser and Leo M. Rappaport, the tract was finally purchased from a lumber company for $40,000 in November, 1916. The IHC state park committee, meanwhile, had purchased McCormick's Creek Canyon in 1916, with the aid of an Owen County citizens' group, so that by the end of 1916 the State of Indiana owned two excellent sites for state parks. Their contribution to the preservation of the natural history of the state was an important one.[8]

These were the commission's primary accomplishments in 1915-1916. But there was, as the IHC pointed out, a great deal yet to be done. Only three of the many planned publications had yet come forth; local historical societies wanted co-ordination and guidance; the schools needed help in preparing courses on Indiana history; and historical relics from all over the state needed protection. The commission and its supporters hoped that the statewide enthusiasm generated by the centennial would persuade the legislature to extend the life of the agency.[9]

Buoyed by their successes and their enthusiastic supporters around the state, the IHC staff also made plans to consolidate the historical programs of the state under the commission's leadership. The young assistant director of the commission, John W. Oliver (1886–1972), a recent University of Wisconsin Ph.D., was especially appalled by the multiplicity of historical agencies

---

[8] Suellen M. Hoy, "Governor Samuel R. Ralston and Indiana's Centennial Celebration," in *Indiana Magazine of History*, LXXI (1975), 253-59; *The Indiana Centennial 1916*, p. 49.

[9] *The Indiana Centennial 1916*, p. 64.

in Indiana. His model was the State Historical Society of Wisconsin, which incorporated an historical library, an archives, a museum, a publications program, and a co-ordinator of all the other historical groups in the state into one program, led by one director. In Indiana no two of these functions were performed exclusively by the same agency. In an effort to simplify the confusion of functions, the IHC staff proposed a new organization for the commission in 1917. The result was a bill proposing a new Indiana Historical Commission,

> reducing its unwieldy membership of nine down to a working body of three, and provided especially for uniting the work of the Indiana Historical Society with the Indiana Historical Commission. . . .

The new agency asked for $5,000 per year, "barely enough," as Oliver observed, "to provide for a permanent secretary to look after their work."[10]

The bill foreshadowed the relationship between the Society and the state historical agency that would emerge in 1924, when the Society appointed IHC Director Christopher B. Coleman to be the IHS's secretary, achieving effectively, though not formally, a merger of institutions. The Society's leadership did not resist the plans for this merger either in 1917 or in 1925.[11] The officers were apparently at all times attracted by the energetic program of the commission and eager to profit from the presence in Indianapolis of a full-time historical officer employed by the state. Partly too the leadership's submissive willingness to be

---

[10] John W. Oliver, "Co-operation among State Historical Agencies," in *Proceedings of the Indiana State History Conference, 1919*, p. 33. For Oliver see *Western Pennsylvania Historical Magazine*, LV (1972), 291-92.

[11] Charles W. Moores to W. E. English, January 13, 1923, "Historical Commission Correspondence" folder, Box 3, Records of the Indiana Historical Commission (IHC), Archives Division, Commission on Public Records, Indiana State Library and Historical Building.

appropriated by the new state agency reflected the end of an era. By 1917 the Society's principal officers were old men, ready to relinquish leadership to a new generation.

Despite the Society's support and considerable statewide enthusiasm, the movement to consolidate the commission and the Society in 1917 failed. Although the IHC bill passed both houses of the General Assembly, it did not become law because Governor James P. Goodrich refused to sign it on grounds of economy.[12] With the failure of the bill, the commission simply ceased to be in 1917. It looked as though Indiana's commitment to a publicly-supported history program was going to expire after a single appropriation, just as it had done in 1861. However, while one might speculate that the Civil War killed the Society's appropriation in 1861, certainly the World War saved the commission in 1919. After the United States entered the war and Indiana began to mobilize its resources in unprecedented ways, the need for a state agency to chronicle the state's war record became clear. Governor Goodrich summoned the former IHC members in December, 1918, and set them to work organizing a complete county-by-county war history. Goodrich dipped into his contingency fund to finance the work until the legislature acted in 1919.[13]

The Indiana Historical Commission was allocated $10,887.28 in 1919, $9,717.54 in 1920, $8,862.93 in 1921, and $15,000 in 1922. There was apparently a move to abolish the agency in 1923, but with the help of a Society-sponsored letter-writing campaign the IHC survived the challenge. Since 1919 the State of Indiana has regularly funded an historical agency.[14]

The Indiana Historical Society discovered that it lost its own

---

[12] Oliver, "Co-operation among State Historical Agencies," p. 33.

[13] *Ibid.*

[14] Minutes of IHS, December 28, 1922.

appropriation when the IHC was funded again in 1919. Since 1919 the Society has not received a regular appropriation from the state. The Society had scarcely been a grateful recipient of its yearly $300 in any event. Howe complained in the Society's report to the state for 1918 that "the assistance heretofore rendered by the State to the society is insignificant when compared to the generous allowance made by other States to similar societies," and again in 1919 Howe remonstrated that it was not economy "in order to save a few dollars, to permit to go to waste historical documents and data essential to the preservation of a full and accurate history of the state. . . ." The Society continued for several years to receive $300 a year for its publications indirectly from the state through the generosity of the Indiana Historical Commission.[15]

The next important move to co-ordinate the state's historical work came in 1919, not from the revived commission, but from the Society of Indiana Pioneers, another of the state's historical institutions, on the suggestion of Amos Butler. The Pioneers had been organized in 1916 by John H. Holliday, and membership in the group was limited to the descendants of Indiana pioneers. Butler, also a Society member, was widely known for his work as administrator of the Conference on Charities and Corrections and as director of the Indiana Academy of Science. Joining the Pioneers were the Society, the IHC, and the state library association, all of which issued an open invitation to individuals and agencies interested in Indiana history to attend a state conference in Indianapolis. The Indiana History Conference was an immediate success. It played an important role in promoting state and local history by providing a forum in which many his-

---

[15] *Indiana Year Book, 1918*, p. 578; *Indiana Year Book, 1919*, p. 644; Jacob P. Dunn, "The Indiana Historical Society," in *Proceedings of the Indiana State History Conference, 1919*, p. 20. Dr. Frank B. Wynn, who was IHC president from 1920 to 1925, was also corresponding secretary of the Society after 1919.

above, James Whitcomb Riley in a scene from the Centennial motion picture *Indiana; left,* Charity Dye, active member of the Indiana Historical Commission

opposite, above, The spirits of Hope and Determination are personified in the Centennial pageant at Bloomington; *below,* A young girl sings her thanks for a new shawl as Governor William Henry Harrison and townspeople listen at the Corydon Centennial pageant, 1916.

Indianapolis *Star*, 1932

Society Library

Society Library

Society Library

The Rutherford B. Hayes Library

opposite, above, Lucy M. Elliott, Society assistant secretary and treasurer, 1921-1923; Charles W. Moores, Society president, 1920-1923; *below,* William Henry Smith, founder of the Associated Press, historian, and journalist; Delavan Smith, Indianapolis newspaper publisher, who left the Society his father's library and $150,000 in 1922

above, Lucy Webb Hayes, President Rutherford B. Hayes, and William Henry Smith on the porch of Spiegel Grove, Fremont, Ohio, in December, 1887; *right,* Jacob Piatt Dunn

torical institutions could exchange ideas. The conference was also credited with having provided the persuasive impact on the members of the Board of Education that led to the board's decision in 1921 to include a chapter on Indiana history in the history textbook adopted for use by the state.[16]

The first conference was held on December 10 and 11, 1919, a Wednesday and Thursday, in order to celebrate Admission Day. In later years the conference was always held on Friday and Saturday for the greater convenience of the participants. The first evening's speakers included Governor James P. Goodrich, who was in bad odor with many of the participants for having vetoed the IHC bill in 1917, Professor Thomas F. Moran of Purdue, Dunn, Lindley, Woodburn, Cottman, and John Oliver. The next day the speakers ranged from the director of the Terre Haute vocational schools Herbert Briggs, who argued for teaching Indiana history in the public schools, to the DAR state regent Mrs. Frank Felter, who was anxious to preserve the historical documents collected by her organization.[17]

All of the early conferences combined reports of local historical activities with reports from various state agencies and institutions, and from an early date speakers were sought from outside the state to bring a wider perspective to the audience and to suggest new goals for Indiana. For instance, Benjamin Shambaugh of the Iowa Historical Society addressed the second conference in 1920 and the fourth in 1922. Hamlin Garland came from New York to speak in 1922, and in 1923 the conference heard three outsiders: William C. Mills, director of the Ohio State Archaeological and Historical Society; Charles E. Brown, chief of the Wisconsin State Historical Museum; and Dr. Har-

---

[16] *Proceedings of the Indiana State History Conference, 1919*, pp. [3, 5,] 39, 84; *Indiana Year Book, 1921*, p. 374.

[17] *Proceedings of the Indiana State History Conference, 1919*, pp. 9-35, 36-39, 42-44.

vey W. Wiley, the pure food reformer and chief chemist of the U.S. Department of Agriculture, 1883–1912, who was born in Jefferson County.[18]

In 1920 Daniel Wait Howe resigned from the office of president of the Indiana Historical Society. He was eighty years old and in ill health, and he had served for twenty years. Modest and graceful, Howe exemplified the best features of the Society in the period 1886-1920. He was a gentleman, a responsible citizen, and a scholar. Upon accepting his resignation, the Society voted him honorary president for life. When he died a year later, the Society learned that Howe had provided generously for the future of the institution. He left a one-third residuary interest in his estate to the Society, to be delivered on the deaths of his wife and daughter. In 1957 the Society received more than $19,000 from the Howe estate.[19]

As Howe left the presidency other changes followed. For the first time in 1920 the Society planned a concerted effort to increase its membership significantly. Throughout 1921 Lucy M. Elliott, the assistant director of the commission and a new Indiana Historical Society member, mailed applications to members of the Society of Indiana Pioneers. Elliott and board member Mabel Cobb Morrison (1869-1925) also worked as a Society committee to plan co-operation with other groups interested in history, a chore which probably suggested further opportunities to acquire members. The results were impressive. The Society's membership rose from 130 in 1920 to 700 in 1921; by 1922 there were more than a thousand members.[20] After nearly a century the little club became a large organization in just a year or two.

---

[18] *Ibid., 1920*, pp. 18-21; *ibid., 1922*, pp. 27-31, 69-76; *ibid., 1923*, pp. 15-21, 63-70, 75-86.

[19] Minutes of IHS, December 30, 1920. E. C. McKinney to Indiana Historical Society, January 15, 1957, "Finance, Fletcher Trust Co." folder, IHS Papers.

[20] Minutes of IHS, December 30, 1920, December 29, 1921, December 28, 1922.

Charles W. Moores (1861-1923), Howe's successor, presided over these brief years of expansion, especially urging the erection of a permanent building for historical records and relics. Moores, a descendant of Samuel Merrill, was a prominent lawyer and responsible citizen, having served on the boards of Butler College, the Indianapolis School Commissioners, and the Indianapolis Art Association. In the last month of his life Moores was chosen special prosecutor to investigate Governor Warren T. McCray, an investigation that resulted in McCray's indictment and conviction for mail fraud. But Moores died after only three years of service as Society president on December 7, 1923, the day of the Society's annual meeting. It was the second time a president had died on the day of a meeting; the first was John Law, who died in 1873.[21]

Another sign of change was the absence of J. P. Dunn at the annual meeting of 1921. After thirty-five years of continuous service, Dunn missed an annual meeting; he was searching for manganese in Haiti. The Society elected Lee Burns recording secretary to replace Dunn, but Burns refused the office. Lucy Elliott "carried on the work of the Society without authority and without compensation" until April 13, when the executive committee appointed her assistant secretary and treasurer at an annual salary of $500. Dunn continued to be identified as the Society secretary until his death in June, 1924. He wrote the minutes of the annual meeting in 1922, but he went to Washington in 1923 as secretary to Senator Samuel Ralston. It seems clear that Dunn was not acting as secretary after Elliott moved into the position of ad hoc membership secretary in December, 1920.[22]

---

[21] *Ibid.*, December 7, 1923.

[22] *Ibid.*, December 29, 1921, April 13, 1922, December 28, 1922; Lucy M. Elliott to James Woodburn, January 11, 1924, Woodburn Papers.

Lucy Elliott (1869-1953) was the first paid officer of the Indiana Historical Society. The Society was uncomfortable with the notion of paying its members—though Dunn had been appropriated small sums in return for preparing indexes—and presumably was more uncomfortable with the notion that a non-officer could be empowered to act for the Society. Hence Elliott received an unusual appointment to an office not mentioned by the Society's constitution, assistant secretary and treasurer.[23]

Elliott, a stenographer from Tipton, Indiana, played a useful role in the Society from 1921 to 1924. As assistant director of the Indiana Historical Commission from 1915 to 1924, she was active in organizing the statewide centennial celebration and in fostering the interest provoked by it. She encouraged local enthusiasts to organize historical societies with personal visits, friendly letters, and, after 1922, with a weekly newsletter reporting statewide news of local groups. The newsletter was extremely successful and led to the publication of the *Indiana History Bulletin*, begun in November, 1923, and still published monthly by the Indiana Historical Bureau.[24]

Elliott was part of the commission effort to bring the Society under the IHC's leadership in 1917, and she believed that the Society should play a greatly expanded role in the state. With her contacts and her driving energy, Elliott succeeded in increasing the Society's membership. She was also, however, impatiently critical of the Society's leaders. In an irate letter to the new president, James Woodburn, in January, 1924, responding to his request for a statement of what amount of money the Society owed her for her services, Elliott complained that the offi-

---

[23] *Minutes of the Society, 1886-1918*, p. 491; Minutes of IHS, December 29, 1921.

[24] *The Indiana Centennial 1916*, pp. 24, 27, 200, 235. Dorothy L. Riker called Elliott's work with the mimeographed newsletter to my attention. See files of the "Centennial news letters" in Indiana Division, Indiana State Library.

cers left all the work to her. She made her further service to the Society conditional upon their acceptance of her "ideals as to the future of the Society" and upon their assurance of "interest in the success of the Society fifty-two weeks in the year rather than at the rare intervals of eighteen months, more or less." It was a rash letter, and Woodburn responded by terminating her appointment.[25]

The problem of just how this expanded new Society was to be administered, however, was not solved so easily. Elliott had done all the Society's work in addition to performing her duties for the IHC. She had enlarged the membership to more than a thousand; she collected the dues, corresponded with Logan Esarey about the members' subscriptions to the *Indiana Magazine,* and sent out renewal notices and membership applications. She demonstrated unarguably that the Society needed someone to do all these things.[26] Moreover, the Society needed a head-quarters. Just as the commission had provided the staff to handle the Society's growing administrative work, it had provided space for the Society's records. Though Woodburn and his fellow of-ficers were not about to accept either Elliott's rebukes or her vi-sion of an historical society on the Wisconsin model, they were for the time being dependent upon the IHC for staff and office space.

Their sense of dependence had been greatly mitigated, how-ever, by an event in the summer of 1922 that more than any-

---

[25] Elliott to Woodburn, January 11, 1924, Woodburn to Elliott, January 16, 1924, Woodburn Papers. See also the alarmed responses of the other officers: Charles E. Coffin to Woodburn, January 22, 1924, Lee Burns to Woodburn, January 23, 1924, *ibid.* See also Elliott's address to the Indiana History Confer-ence in 1921, *Proceedings of the Indiana History Conference, 1921,* pp. 9-16.

[26] In fact Elliott continued to perform all those chores, stripped of her official title, until Coleman took over the leadership of the commission in 1924 and abolished her position. The assistant director was then replaced by an as-sistant editor and a secretary. *Indiana History Bulletin,* I (1924), 130.

thing else in the Society's history changed its character and gave it a permanent identity.

The Delavan Smith Bequest

Delavan Smith (1861-1922) surprised a lot of people when his will was published. A reserved, unpretentious person with a consuming interest in his fellow man, he was given to private generosities. No one was surprised that he had left money to charity, but the objects of his philanthropy were apparently unaware of his intentions before he died. The two largest bequests were a million dollars to the Indianapolis Foundation and $150,000 plus a rare book library worth a quarter of a million dollars to the "Indiana Historical Association."[27]

Smith, the publisher of the Indianapolis *News* for nearly thirty years, was the son of William Henry Smith (1833-1896),

---

[27] Item 18 of the will of Delavan Smith reads:

> I give and bequeath to the Indiana Historical Association one hundred and fifty thousand dollars ($150,000.00) for the erection of an assembly room, library stack room, museum, reading room, etc. for the use of the Association, the bequest being for the purpose of endowment for building, operation and purchase of books. I also give and bequeath to said Association my library at my home in Lake Forest, largely of Americana, to be the nucleus of a permanent library for the Association. The whole to be a memorial to my father, William Henry Smith. The books not suitable for the purposes of the Association may be disposed of and the proceeds invested in books to replace those sold. Acceptance in writing of the conditions above stated shall be delivered to the Executor of this will before payment or delivery of any part of these bequests, and failing such acceptance, I give and bequeath the said sum of money and library for similar purposes to the town of Lake Forest, Illinois, or to the Hayes Memorial at Fremont, Ohio, but in either case conditioned upon the memorial being established. My cousins, Warren C. Fairbanks, Frederick C. Fairbanks, and Richard Fairbanks, or any two of them, shall determine whether said bequests shall go to said town of Lake Forest or to said Hayes Memorial.

Proceedings of the Indiana History Conference, 1924, p. 23.

founder of the Associated Press, historian, and journalist. The money and books left to the Society were to be used to establish a memorial library to honor William Henry Smith.

The library Delavan Smith gave to the Society was collected for the most part by William Henry Smith as a tool for his own historical research. An important political figure in Ohio during and after the Civil War, the elder Smith served as secretary of state under Governor John Brough and as the most zealous and effective promoter of Rutherford B. Hayes. As general manager of the Western Press Association after 1870, Smith was in a position to influence national politics strongly, and he used his power to help Hayes secure the presidency in 1876. To a great extent Smith's historical work resulted from his political career. As secretary of state in Ohio he discovered that the Arthur St. Clair Papers were in private hands and in disrepair. Through his efforts and those of his friends, the State of Ohio purchased the St. Clair Papers, and Smith secured the task of editing them. His two-volume life and letters of St. Clair appeared in 1882. Similarly Smith's later works on western antislavery—*The First Fugitive Slave Case of Record in Ohio* (1894), *A Sketch of Governor Jeremiah Morrow* (1888), *A Political History of Slavery* (posthumously published, 1903), and his work on the life and times of Hayes—essentially grew out of his relationship with Rutherford B. Hayes, whose career Smith saw as an embodiment of the best ideals of the western antislavery movement.[28]

As an historian William Henry Smith was a good Republican; he was undeniably biased in his interpretations. He was also, however, shrewd, knowledgeable, and keenly aware of the importance of preserving documents and publishing them accurately. His library included a rich collection of documents

---

[28] For William Henry Smith see Indianapolis *News,* July 27, 29, 1896. This William Henry Smith is not to be confused with the William Henry Smith (1839-1935) who edited *The Indianian* and wrote a history of Indiana. For the latter Smith see Indianapolis *Star,* February 13, 1935.

relating to the Northwest Territory, most of them copied either from the Ohio archives or from material in the British Museum. In addition, he collected rare editions of early American travel literature, biography, memoirs, periodical publications, and American literature. His son Delavan took a serious interest in the library and added to the collection after his father's death in 1896.[29]

Like his father, Delavan Smith saw himself as a midwestern man. Born in Ohio, he was educated in Illinois and Massachusetts and spent most of his professional career in Chicago and Indianapolis. Many of his childhood vacations were spent in Wayne County, Ohio, in the home of his aunt and uncle, the parents of his first cousin Charles Warren Fairbanks, who was later Senator from Indiana from 1897 to 1905 and Vice President of the United States, 1905 to 1909. When Fairbanks needed newspaper support in Indianapolis, the family rallied; his uncle William Henry Smith bought the Indianapolis *News* in 1892 from John H. Holliday and gave it to his son and son-in-law to run.

For thirty years Delavan Smith was associated with the Indianapolis *News*. It was by all accounts a well-produced newspaper, and it featured outstanding columnists, including Jacob Piatt Dunn from time to time. Smith himself lived most of the time in Lake Forest, Illinois, but he was also a responsible citizen of Indianapolis. He joined the Indiana Historical Society in 1905. He never married.[30]

The Delavan Smith bequest transformed the Society from a

---

[29] *Proceedings of the Indiana History Conference, 1922*, p. 42. It was, however, to Charles R. Williams, Delavan Smith's co-publisher of the *News* and his sister's husband, that William Henry Smith entrusted the task of finishing the Hayes biography, a task imposed as a deathbed request from Smith. Charles R. Williams, *The Life of Rutherford Birchard Hayes* (Boston: Houghton Mifflin Co., 1914).

[30] For Delavan Smith see Indianapolis *News*, August 26, 30, September 1, 2, 5, 1922.

homeless, unsubsidized publishing enterprise to a significantly endowed institution with a fine library of rare books. The Society was now in a position to begin at least the process of building a research institution to fulfill its initial object, that of "collection of all materials calculated to shed light on the natural, civil, and political history of Indiana. . . ." As Calvin Fletcher's granddaughter Laura Fletcher Hodges said in appreciation of the gift at the history conference in December, 1922: "The society is now face to face with the realization of long deferred hopes and ambitions."[31]

The Delavan Smith will was challenged by his relatives, and the estate was not settled for fifteen months. The Society was not actually able to claim its bequest until early in 1925. Meanwhile, the Society's officers sought likely quarters. The proposed war memorial building seemed to be a logical home, and the legal consensus was that the terms of the bequest would allow such a location.[32] In fact, however, it was to be ten years before the William Henry Smith Memorial Library would find a home.

In July, 1924, Jacob Piatt Dunn, Jr., died in Indianapolis after a brief illness. He was sixty-nine years old, the last of the original members of the Society as reorganized in 1886. Daniel Wait Howe had written to the Society in January, 1921, that "Too much credit cannot be given to your Secretary, Mr. Jacob P. Dunn, for his untiring efforts," and Woodburn observed in his eulogy that Dunn "was the chief editor of its publications and at times he was almost the Society itself."[33] His greatest legacy to the Society was seven volumes of Indiana Historical Society

---

[31] *Proceedings of the Indiana History Conference, 1922*, p. 39.

[32] *Ibid.*, *1924*, pp. 23, 25; Indianapolis *Star*, October 16, 1923.

[33] Daniel Wait Howe to Indiana Historical Society, January 8, 1921, in Minutes of IHS; James A. Woodburn, "Charles W. Moores and Jacob P. Dunn: In Memoriam," in *Proceedings of the Indiana History Conference, 1924*, pp. 7-11.

Publications, five numbers of which he also authored. To Indiana history he gave monumental works that are amazing in their breadth and accuracy and always entertaining to read: *Indiana and Indianans* in five volumes and *The History of Greater Indianapolis*, in addition to the shorter works he prepared for the Society. To national history he contributed expertise on Indian history— *Massacres of the Mountains* (1886), *True Indian Stories* (1908)—and Indian languages as well as his good lobbying work for the Bureau of American Ethnology.

The editor of the *News* described Dunn as "individual and distinctive, admired for his intellectual qualities and loved for his genial companionship," adding that he was "a dreaded foe of sham." Ralston praised his longtime friend as "not only loyal to truth at whatever cost, but he was loyal to a friend. And trustworthy—absolutely so. I shall miss him."[34]

Dunn's death marked the end of an era in the history of the Society. The elite publishing society founded in 1886 had already expanded to embrace new members and new ambitions, and in 1924 stood on the threshhold of new opportunities. As Dunn passed from the scene some observers may have wondered whether the elite publishing society he co-founded would simply disappear, transformed beyond recognition into a large modern society. That this did not happen is attributable to Dunn's many-faceted successor, Christopher B. Coleman.

------

[34] Indianapolis *News*, June 7, 1924.

V

The
Christopher B.
Coleman
Years

1924-1944

Christopher B. Coleman

V

"The historical society is an organization of adults who . . .
band together for the application of their trained intellects to the
problems for which historical work may afford a solution."
Christopher Bush Coleman, 1933

Christopher Bush Coleman was elected secretary of the Indiana Historical Society in September, 1924; at the same time, he was appointed director of the Indiana Historical Commission, succeeding Harlow Lindley, who resigned in April. It is not clear to whom should go the credit for placing Coleman in the position of Indiana's chief historical officer in 1924, but there is no doubt that it was a clever stroke. He was singularly well equipped to gather together the scattered reins of Indiana's various historical agencies. Coleman was a propertied gentleman, comfortable with the Indianapolis elite from the small, pre-IHC Society; he was a professionally trained historian, replete with Ph.D. from Columbia and solid connections with both the state and national historical establishments; he was a skilled administrator, having served for seven years as Butler University's vice-president and for four years as chairman of his department at Allegheny College; he was interested in the historical society movement and viewed his work in it as a satisfying lifework; he was a Democrat at a time in the state's history when it was essential for the welfare of the State Library that he be a Democrat; and he was, by nearly all accounts, an extremely appealing human being. Even his vices—he chainsmoked cigars and made terrible puns—were regarded with affection by his friends and co-workers. A dignified man (he was always "Dr. Coleman" to his staff and all but intimates), he was not at all stuffy. Caroline Dunn, Society librarian from 1939 to 1973, remembered that "everybody was crazy about him." He normally had lunch with members of his staff, encouraging a running exchange of ideas. He was able to garner goodwill for the historical agencies he represented and to run "a happy ship," tactfully directing an able and generally underpaid staff.

All of these characteristics were already evident in 1924. Coleman was forty-nine years old, a familiar figure in Indianapolis since his arrival in 1900 as a new member of the history faculty at Butler. He was born in Springfield, Illinois, the grandson of one of Abraham Lincoln's former law partners. He was educated at Yale (B.A., 1896) and took a divinity degree at the University of Chicago (1899), specializing in church history. He took a year off from his teaching duties at Butler in 1904-1905 to pursue graduate studies in history at the University of Berlin and went on to complete a doctorate at Columbia University in 1914.[1]

During the first segment of his years in Indianapolis (1900-1919) Coleman acquired a circle of friends who would prove to be lifelong, men like Indianapolis architects Lee Burns and Anton Scherrer, both of whom shared his devotion to local history. Burns (1872-1957), the son of Indiana's legal code writer Harrison Burns (of *Burns' Statutes*), worked with Coleman as a member of the Butler University board of trustees and was, like Coleman, a devoted member of the Contemporary Club and the Indianapolis Literary Club. Burns and Coleman played bridge

---

[1] For Christopher B. Coleman see memorial issue of *Indiana History Bulletin*, XXI (1944), 355-78. Interviews with Dorothy L. Riker, Gayle Thornbrough, Caroline Dunn, and Hubert Hawkins, fall and winter, 1979.

together every week for forty years with several other prominent Indianapolis businessmen, and Burns became chairman of the Society's executive committee in January, 1924, nine months before Coleman was elected secretary.[2] Scherrer (1878-1960), though not an officer of the Society until 1945, was a member from 1932 and wrote a popular newspaper column on Indianapolis history for the *Times* from 1936 to 1949. Scherrer also shared Coleman's interest in art.[3]

These were some of the resources Coleman brought to the Society and to the IHC in 1924. His situation was an unusual and challenging one. The question of how the Society and the commission should work together had been explicitly raised in 1924, after the Society's President James Woodburn had told IHC Assistant Director Lucy Elliott that her services as assistant secretary and treasurer of the Society were no longer needed. A three-member "Committee on Mutual Relations to the Indiana Historical Commission" was appointed, consisting of Evans Woollen, an Indianapolis banker and the Society's first vice-president; Kate Milner Rabb, IHC member and the author of the Indianapolis *Star* column "A Hoosier Listening Post"; and Harlow Lindley, IHC director. This group reported its recommendations to the IHC in April, 1924. Only a truncated version of the report survives, but there is enough to indicate that the committee was not at all sure how the relationship between the two agencies should work. The committee pointed out that while the state "needed a central organization" to provide "an efficient historical program," in fact the Society "cannot be brought under state control because it operates under a private charter. . . ." The committee therefore recommended further study by a joint

---

[2] Indianapolis *Times*, October 12, 1940; Indianapolis *News*, January 8, 1957.

[3] Indianapolis *Star*, January 9, 1960; Indianapolis *News*, January 9, 1960; Indianapolis *Times*, September 21, 1953.

IHS-IHC group, but meanwhile, in answer to the urgent question of who was going to do the Society's clerical work, the committee proposed that it "be cared for by the office staff of the Indiana Historical Commission."[4]

Coleman, then, had few guidelines as he commenced his unusual new administrative position. He was to consolidate and co-ordinate the historical work of the state while preserving the separate identities of the state agency and the private society. Financially, the Society was dependent upon the IHC. The small income from dues and from the English fund was barely enough to provide members with the *Indiana Magazine of History*, to provide the magazine with a small subsidy, and to support the Indiana History Conference. The commission, by contrast, had a budget of $15,000 for 1923 and 1924, i.e., a modest $7,500 per year, with which to support two staff members and a publications program. This allocation was doubled in the next session of the legislature, and it remained at approximately $15,000 per year for the next twenty years. Certainly this was little enough to support a director, two editors, a secretary, and a publications program, but it was a great deal by Society standards. The Smith bequest of $150,000 generated a modest income, but the provision of the bequest restricted its expenditure to meeting library expenses.[5] Clearly what both institutions needed was a larger financial base, and by pooling their resources they achieved this.

---

[4] Lee Burns, "The Indiana Historical Society, The Indiana Historical Commission, The Indiana Library and Historical Department, The State Library Building Commission: A memorandum showing the close relationship between these organizations," mimeographed pamphlet, August, 1944, in Indiana Division, Indiana State Library, pp. 3-4; Minutes of IHS, January 4, 1924.

[5] The Commission/Bureau appropriations are summarized in a memorandum in a folder marked "Historical Bureau 1931," Records of the Indiana Historical Bureau (IHB), Box 4, Archives Division, Commission on Public Records, Indiana State Library and Historical Building. The Smith fund earned approximately $7,000 to $8,000 per year during the period from 1925 to 1930. See the annual reports of the treasurer in the *Indiana History Bulletin* for these years.

Together they were each able to undertake more than they could have done alone. The Society acquired, without having to pay for them, a secure headquarters in the IHC office and a part-time administrator and clerical staff. The IHC, later the Bureau, acquired the support of a thousand-member organization, a ready-made constituency available for generating ideas for new programs, for lobbying, and for undertaking historical work on a volunteer basis. Though the files and the financial records were kept scrupulously separate by the able and long-serving clerical staff, Helen C. Gray and Cleta Robinson, and though Coleman was usually careful to distinguish between the occasions when he was secretary of the Society and those when he was director of the IHC/IHB, in effect the organizations were unified.

It was an unusual arrangement. Although many other states had more than one statewide historical organization—Massachusetts, Pennsylvania, and New York, for instance, each had a congeries of private and public historical organizations with a statewide focus—, it was rare for two such institutions to be located in the same city and rarer still for them to share a staff. In the larger states of the Middle West, moreover, the usual pattern was a unified state historical program: Wisconsin, Minnesota, Ohio, and Illinois created centralized state historical agencies that had no rivals within the state. Only in Michigan, where the historical society joined forces with the Michigan Historical Commission, was there an arrangement that resembled the Society's.[6]

---

[6] Whitehill, *Independent Historical Societies*, pp. 31-33; Donna McDonald (comp. and ed.), *Directory of Historical Societies and Agencies in the United States and Canada* (11th ed. Nashville, Tenn.: American Association for State and Local History, 1978). For Michigan see *Michigan History Magazine*, I (1917), 76, 126; *Chronicle, The Magazine of the Historical Society of Michigan*, XIV (1979), 13. The Michigan society apparently linked up with the Michigan commission in 1917 and separated from it in 1963.

Almost the first task Coleman faced in the fall of 1924 was to preserve this collaboration, which was threatened by legislative demands for efficiency and economy. As early as 1923 it apparently had occurred to someone in the legislature that the Indiana Historical Commission should be consolidated with the State Library. Society officer Will E. English, who was then serving in the state senate, proposed a countermeasure, i.e., that the commission and the Society should consolidate instead. The point was to throw a bone to the efficiency-hounds in the legislature while protecting the historical work of the state.[7]

Charles Moores, then president of the Society, wrote to English of his agreement with the plan, adding his strong opinion

> that it would be a very serious mistake to tie the historical interests of the state up with the library interests in the way that has been suggested in some quarters. There is no logical connection between the two activities, and it might result in both the historical and library interests getting mixed up in politics, a thing greatly to be avoided.

Moores went on to suggest that any effort of the legislature to merge the "library interests and historical interests" might be opposed as unconstitutional since the merger might be construed as an

> attempt to curtail or modify the powers of the Historical Society, which operates under a private charter created by the state in 1830, and which under the authority of the Dartmouth College case can not be brought into politics or under state control, even with its own consent so long as it has trust funds to administer or trust obligations to carry out.[8]

With the help of a strenuous letter-writing campaign by the Society the threatened merger was defeated in 1923, but it was

---

[7] C. W. Moores to W. E. English, January 13, 1923, "Historical Commission Correspondence" folder, Box 3, Records of the IHC.
[8] *Ibid.*

clear that the legislature would insist on some kind of consolidation during the next session. A few months after Coleman took office the commission faced even a greater threat, that of removal from Indianapolis and from the State Library to be made an adjunct of the history department at Indiana University in Bloomington. The plan was proposed by Logan Esarey as part of the university's case for increased funding, and Esarey argued that the IHC's work could be done more cheaply in Bloomington. The planned co-operation between the Society and the commission would clearly have been greatly obstructed by such a move, and Coleman's appointment as IHC director would presumably have been rescinded, since the whole point of the proposal was to save the state the small cost of commission salaries. The IHC would have been run by a member of the Indiana University history staff, probably Logan Esarey, working part time.[9]

Faced with the alternative of this rather drastic curtailment of the commission, Coleman and the Society reluctantly accepted the previous plan to consolidate the library and the historical commission into a single department managed by a single board. The Library and Historical Department was created by the General Assembly on March 6, 1925. The commission was transformed thereby from an independent body working under a nine-member board, all of whom represented historical interests, into the Indiana Historical Bureau, a division of a department working under a five-member board, of whom only one would be recommended by historical interests.[10]

---

[9] "Historical Commission Correspondence" folder, *ibid.*; Indianapolis *News*, January 21, 1925; Indianapolis *Star*, February 4, 1925; J. M. Swan to all representatives and senators, Indiana General Assembly, February 10, 1925, "Marion County" (folder), IHS Papers.

[10] *Laws of Indiana*, 1925, pp. 190-201, especially 194-95; Christopher B. Coleman to Dr. A. R. Newsome, February 17, 1931, in "Historical Bureau 1931" folder, Box 4, Records of the IHB. The other four members of the State Library

Although Coleman reported several years later that the IHC was in some ways a more effective organizational form than the Bureau, he conceded that the consolidation of the historical and the library interests probably had enhanced their ability to secure regular appropriations from the legislature. And it certainly was responsible for the state's eventual willingness to provide a library and historical building.[11]

Acquiring a "Permanent" Home

When the Indiana Historical Society formally accepted the Delavan Smith bequest in December, 1924, it legally committed itself to finding an appropriate home for the William Henry Smith Memorial Library. The Society at this point lacked even an office of its own; its records were simply kept with those of the IHC (soon to become the Bureau) in its little room on the third floor of the State Capitol next door to the State Library. The State Library, which included the archives of the state, was so badly cramped in its quarters that large quantities of material were inaccessible to researchers, and the IHC's quarters, similarly cramped, featured the additional inconvenience of not even being indisputably its own. During each biennial session of the General Assembly the commission was required to remove itself entirely from "its" room and work in the hallway, while the room usually assigned to it was used by the staff that engrossed bills.[12]

---

and Historical Board represented the state board of education (one member), library interests (two members), and the governor (one member).

[11] Coleman to Newsome, February 17, 1931, in Records of the IHB.

[12] For a description of the Society headquarters see *Indiana History Bulletin*, IV (1926), 51-52; Louis J. Bailey, "A State Library and Historical Building," in *Proceedings of the Indiana State History Conference, 1926*, pp. 17-20. The Smith library was stored in boxes in a warehouse from 1925 to 1934.

The subject of a state historical building was one that had arisen, it will be recalled, on previous occasions. The territorial centennial commission in 1900 had recommended such a building; and the statehood centennial commission had, in a disorganized way, recommended some sort of building in 1913. By 1924 the state was about to build a large new public building as a memorial to Indiana's participation in what was then called "the World War." Not long before his death in 1923, Charles Moores had suggested that this building might appropriately house the Society's library. After consulting with lawyers about whether the terms of the bequest would allow such an arrangement, the Society decided to accept space in the World War Memorial Building as the bird in the hand, notwithstanding the disadvantages for the Society's staff of being separated either from the much more comprehensive collections of the State Library or, if it retained offices near the State Library, from its own library. Though planning to move the Smith Library into the War Memorial, the Society resolved also only a few months later at its annual meeting in December, 1925, that the "state should provide a suitable building for the library and historical department."[13]

For the next few years the Society made plans to move into the Memorial in late 1929 or early 1930 while at the same time its leaders lobbied vigorously for a State Library and Historical Building. Christopher Coleman urged both Republicans and Democrats to pledge support for the new building in their platforms. He also requested aid from influential Society members in lobbying for the building, and many of them responded. Woodburn wrote similar letters, and State Librarian Louis J.

---

[13] Indiana Historical Society Annual Report in *Proceedings of the Indiana State History Conference, 1925*, pp. 16-22; Minutes of IHS, October 28, 1924, March 30, April 24, 1925.

Bailey asked the entire membership of the Indiana Academy of Science for their support. Appealing directly to the public in a radio talk on WFBM, Coleman asked Hoosiers to instruct their senators and representatives to vote for the State Library and Historical Building.[14]

The efforts were successful. The General Assembly agreed in February, 1929, to impose a tax to raise funds for the structure. By 1931 the Society's leaders had decided to locate the Smith Library there instead of in the War Memorial. This meant a delay of several years in opening the library, since the War Memorial was almost ready for occupancy in 1931 and the State Library and Historical Building was just accepting bids from architects, but the advantages to the Society from the latter arrangement seemed great. First, as already mentioned, it was seen as a large convenience for the Society-Bureau staff to have ready access to the state's historical collections; second, under the original plan the State Library and Historical Board agreed not only to house the Smith Library but also to provide the services of the state librarian as director of the Smith Library and a full-time qualified librarian for the library, all at the expense of the State of Indiana (the latter measure was subject to confirmation by the legislature). In addition the state promised to transfer its own rare books to the Smith Library to enlarge the usefulness of the Society's collections. The plan was that the Smith Library would serve as a complement to the State Library: the former would specialize in rare books, the latter in more general ones.[15]

---

[14] Indiana Historical Society Annual Report in "Proceedings of the Indiana State History Conference, 1926," in *Indiana History Bulletin*, IV (1927), 255-84; Minutes of IHS, February 4, 1927, May 28, 1928; Christopher B. Coleman memorandum, May 29, 1928, "Library Building, 1928-1930" folder, Box 4, Records of the IHB; Louis J. Bailey to members of Indiana Academy of Science, December 17, 1928, *ibid.*; letters of James A. Woodburn and Christopher B. Coleman to various people, *ibid.*; text of Coleman's radio address on WFBM, *ibid.*

[15] Indiana *House Journal*, 1929, pp. 314, 843; Minutes of IHS, June 1, 1931.

It is ironic that when the state legislature finally authorized a building devoted at least partly to historical interests in early 1929 the country was on the brink of a major economic depression. By January, 1933, the first Democratic governor of Indiana in twenty years was installed in the State Capitol, the dynamic and highhanded Paul McNutt. As part of the traditional change-of-party housekeeping, and exacerbated by the impact of the country's emerging economic disaster, the plans for the new building were assailed by the McNutt administration. First Coleman and his allies were faced with the suggestion that the new building be divided so that part of it would house the state supreme court judges. The historical establishment defeated this proposal but was forced to accept the abrogation of the State Library and Historical Board's offer of a state-employed director and librarian for the Smith Library. The offer was invalidated when McNutt reorganized all state departments and simply eliminated the board. The Society reached a new agreement with the state, which now was represented by the Board of Buildings and Property. The changed sections provided that the Society would employ its own librarian and eliminated the provision that the state librarian would be the director of the Smith Library.[16] The provision for transfer of the State Library's rare books to the Smith Library was also never carried out.

The state government clearly was still in no mood to support the historical society. After a hundred years the Society could expect nothing more from the state than 2,000 square feet of floor space in a public building to house its rare book library and the part-time administrative and clerical services of the Indiana Historical Bureau.

Nevertheless the Society was wearily pleased in 1934 when its

---

[16] Minutes of IHS, December 8, 1933; Christopher B. Coleman to Lew O'Bannon and others, January, 1933, in "Library and Historical Building 1934-1954" folder, Box 4, Records of the IHB.

library room was completed. The William Henry Smith Memorial Library and the Indiana Historical Society had a "permanent" home—one that would serve them for forty-three years.

New Directions for Established Programs

Perhaps the first change instigated by Christopher Coleman that would have been noticed by a Society member in the period from October, 1924, to September, 1925, would have been the size of the *Indiana History Bulletin,* which appeared then, as now, monthly. It got much bigger. Volume I was composed of 159 pages; Volume II was 272 pages long.

Into these extra pages Coleman and his assistant editor, Nellie C. Armstrong, introduced a variety of new features: there were regular columns reporting on anniversary celebrations, historic places, museums, notices, and books and newspaper articles. Occasionally the *Bulletin* devoted a whole issue to a single subject like museums (April, 1925) or Abraham Lincoln's ancestry. Coleman regularly covered the progress of legislation affecting historical activities in the state, and he editorialized, as Cottman had done in the old *Indiana Quarterly Magazine of History,* frequently and vehemently urging legislative support of history. In addition the *Bulletin* began to provide useful reference lists, such as a list of local historical societies in Indiana and their addresses and officers (October, 1936); lists of works in progress on Indiana history (April, 1926); lists of college history teachers in Indiana (January, 1936; January, 1941); regular lists of all publications of the Society and the Bureau[17]; lists of Society committees and their members; and infrequent lists of all Indiana Historical Society members. Beginning in 1930 the *Bulletin* also

---

[17] Complete lists of Society publications appeared in the *Bulletin* in 1933, 1938, 1944, 1948, 1953, 1955, 1957, 1962, 1965, 1967, 1969, 1971, 1973, and 1977.

included the *Proceedings* of the annual Indiana History Conference.

There was a strong flavor of boosterism and self-congratulatory patriotism in Coleman's *Bulletin*. History, in this popular presentation, was always a source of pride, and the appropriate relationship of the public to history was as a grateful celebrant of the anniversaries of triumphant occasions. At first glance this approach seems smug and ill-conceived to a more self-critical generation, but a second glance inclines one to a more sympathetic view. Coleman was selling history as a source of pride during a period of state and national history when people were ashamed of their governments, broke, and confused. Indiana state politics, like U.S. national politics, was mired in scandal throughout most of the 1920s. Governor Warren T. McCray was elected, like Warren G. Harding, in 1920, but had to retire in 1923 to serve a term in a federal penitentiary for mail fraud. The next elected governor, Ed Jackson, was linked with D. C. Stephenson and the Ku Klux Klan. He was indicted for bribery during his term and was only acquitted under the statute of limitations. This decade of fast and loose politics was followed by a decade of severe economic depression, unprecedented governmental expansion, and the outbreak of World War II. Coleman's strategy of using history to boost morale, to remind his audience of their predecessors' triumphs in adversity, was understandable at least.

In addition to making changes in the *Bulletin* Coleman also had a considerable impact on the *Indiana Magazine of History*—more, in fact, than he had planned. Unexpectedly, he collided with the *Magazine*'s editor, Logan Esarey, soon after assuming the direction of the Bureau and the Society. Esarey (1872-1942) was a colorful and distinctive personality, very different in style from the urbane clubman, Coleman. Esarey's cracker-barrel rusticity, expressed in a Hoosier twang and rumpled, pioneer-like clothing, contrasted sharply with Coleman's Yale-Chicago-Columbia polish. Since Esarey was also disappointed that the university failed to bring the IHC to Bloomington for him to run, the combination of irritants led inevitably, perhaps, to conflict.[18]

From available records the issue leading to the disagreement had nothing to do with Esarey's management of the *Magazine*. The question was whether Coleman was to have editorial authority in publishing a manuscript of "The Messages and Papers of James B. Ray" prepared by Esarey for the *Indiana Historical Collections*, published by the Bureau. Esarey had apparently been granted a very free hand with the earlier volumes he had prepared in the series and was deeply offended by editorial changes made by editorial assistant Nellie Armstrong with Coleman's approval. Esarey essentially refused to allow any changes in his manuscript, and Coleman, with the backing of the Library and Historical Board, refused to publish the documents without changes. Esarey's manuscript was not published, and Esarey had harsh words for Coleman before they ceased to speak to one another entirely in 1927.[19]

In fact, Esarey, like most of the editors of the *Magazine* who succeeded him, was also dissatisfied with the financial arrangement for its publication. Indiana University and the Indiana Historical Society were both reluctant to support the venture generously, each feeling that the other ought to do more. The editors of the journal were often in the position of fending off creditors while the two supporting institutions "stonewalled" one an-

---

[18] For Esarey see the eloquent essay by Buley, "Logan Esarey, Hoosier," in *Indiana Magazine of History*, XXXVIII, 337-81, especially pp. 355-56, 375-76.

[19] The dispute began apparently in May, 1925, and continued through various stages, including the solicitation of a ruling on the ownership of the manuscript by the state attorney general in 1925, until the manuscript was finally returned to Esarey in 1927. See "Professor Logan Esarey" folder, Box 3, Records of the IHB.

other. It was not an arrangement designed to enhance the relationship between Esarey and Coleman to begin with, and the criticism of Esarey's work on the James B. Ray papers merely added fuel to a smoldering situation.

Esarey dropped the phrase "Published with the cooperation of the Indiana Historical Society" from the title page of the *Magazine* in 1925, soon after the beginning of the altercation with Coleman and after the executive committee of the Society voted in August to refuse to delegate more funds to the *Magazine*. Esarey was away from the university during the 1925-1926 academic year, and Coleman was asked to edit the *Magazine* in his stead. Esarey returned to edit the 1927 numbers of the *Magazine* and then retired from the editorship. He had attempted to break the journal entirely away from the Society on the grounds that the Society was not paying the cost of the publication anyway. The Society paid only one dollar per subscription after August, 1925, having decided to discontinue the additional subsidy of $200 per year which it had accorded until then. Esarey attempted to persuade the university that the magazine would make more money by simply selling its subscriptions directly at two dollars each, rather than acquiring subscribers from the Society at one dollar each. Instead, the university apparently decided that Esarey was the obstacle to obtaining a larger subvention from the Society and allowed him to resign.[20]

Hence in December, 1927, Logan Esarey edited his last issue of the *Indiana Magazine of History*. Esarey was an important figure in Indiana history. His work on the Indiana Historical Survey as a collector, editor, and research director; his own research and writing, especially his edition of the messages and

---

[20] Minutes of IHS, August 29, 1925; William Lowe Bryan to Christopher B. Coleman, September 28, 1925, "*Indiana Magazine of History—General—1925-29*" folder, IHS Papers; William O. Lynch to Coleman, December 21, 1929, *ibid.*

papers of William Henry Harrison and his two-volume history of Indiana; and his distinguished editorship of the *Magazine*, leading it to the forefront of state journals, were outstanding accomplishments. In retrospect the observer must feel sad that his connection with the *Magazine* and with the Society ended rancorously.

Esarey's successor, William O. Lynch, enjoyed essentially good relations with Coleman during his tenure as editor, 1928-1941. But neither Lynch nor President William Lowe Bryan of Indiana University was able to persuade the Society's executive committee that it should either raise the price of membership or grant regular subsidies to the *Magazine*. Even Coleman in fact attempted on several occasions to convince the committee to increase its support and was firmly rebuked for his pains. At least one reason for the Society's obstinacy on this point was the knowledge that if Indiana University would not publish the *Magazine* for a dollar a subscription some other school would. Indiana State's president, L. N. Hines, was a member of the executive committee, and he repeatedly offered to take the *Magazine* to his college.[21]

In fact Indiana University's department of history had done an outstanding job with the *Magazine,* and the university was by no means willing to see it assigned elsewhere. The words "owned by Indiana University" began to appear on the title page in 1930 to counter the threat of the *Magazine*'s removal from Bloomington.

Coleman's position throughout this period was that the Society should pay the cost of producing the *Magazine* except for editorial salaries, which the university, he believed, should pro-

---

[21] Minutes of IHS, December 13, 1929, March 13, 1930; Lynch to Coleman, April 18, 1929, Coleman to Lynch, April 16, 24, 1929, in *"Indiana Magazine of History*—General—1925-29" folder, IHS Papers.

vide. He was not able to persuade the executive committee on this issue, however, so that the hard feelings, though usually muted, tended to persist.[22]

Lynch opened his magazine to the Society in 1928, offering Coleman a regular column that usually ran one or two pages. Lynch was also friendly and tactful with nonprofessional contributors and enjoyed unusual success in attracting the work of local historians. Lynch's "solution" to the financial problem was a more or less continuous effort to get the Society to recruit more members. However, the Society was by no means ready to undertake large-scale recruitment, and the membership hovered around a thousand throughout Coleman's tenure as secretary.[23]

As is implicit from the foregoing account, the role of the Society's executive committee changed dramatically under Coleman's direction. In January, 1924, the executive committee met for the first time in two years. After Coleman took over in October, and with the strong support of Society President Woodburn, the committee began to meet several times a year in addition to registering its opinions by mailed votes in between times. Although Coleman no doubt found this arrangement clumsy at times, it secured the commitment and concern of the Society's officers in the important new areas into which he wished to lead it, such as supporting an archaeology program and public monuments.

The effectiveness of the committee was greatly enhanced by its stability. The same officers served faithfully for many years, and Indianapolis was strongly represented. Evans Woollen (1864-1942), president of the Society in 1931 and 1932, served

---

[22] Coleman to L. N. Hines, December 24, 1929, in "*Indiana Magazine of History*—General—1925-29" folder, IHS Papers.

[23] "Proceedings of the Indiana History Conference, 1929," in *Indiana History Bulletin*, VII (1930), 152.

Dorothy L. Riker

Indiana State Library

opposite, above, Indiana
Historical Bureau's room in the State
Capitol, circa 1930. Left to right,
Dorothy Riker, Helen Gray, Cleta
Robinson; *below,* Indiana State
Library and Historical Building

right, Lee Burns, executive committee,
1921-1945; *below,* Evans Woollen,
vice-president, 1924-1931, and
president, 1931-1932; John G. Rauch,
Society officer, 1931-1972

David V. Burns

Society Library

John G. Rauch, Jr.

Indiana State Library

Indiana State Library

Indiana State Library

above, Logan Esarey, editor of the *Indiana Magazine of History*, 1913-1927; William O. Lynch, editor of the *Magazine*, 1928-1941; *left*, James A. Woodburn, president of the Society, 1924-1930

opposite, above, Richard B. Wetherill, a Society vice-president, 1928-1939; Linnaeus N. Hines, executive committee, 1922-1933; *below*, Albert L. Kohlmeier, executive committee, 1936-1948; Cornelius O'Brien, executive committee, 1934-1948, and a vice-president, 1949-1953

Society Library

Society Library

above, October, 1927, pilgrimage to the J. F. D. Lanier mansion in Madison; *left*, George Rogers Clark Memorial under construction in Vincennes, February, 1933

opposite, Christopher B. Coleman, 1875-1944

relatively briefly, and at that he was an officer for eight years. The son of William Watson Woollen, longtime Society member, naturalist, and prominent lawyer, Evans Woollen inherited his father's public spirit. Among other things he was a staunch Presbyterian and president of the Indianapolis Art Association. The younger Woollen was also president of the Fletcher Trust Company, the Society's financial manager.[24] Eli Lilly became the Society's president in 1933 and served as an officer for the next forty-four years. He was president (1933-1946) for most of the years of Coleman's tenure as secretary, and attracting this man to the Society stands high among Coleman's many services to the institution. Lilly's central role in building the Society's archaeology program, described in a later chapter, was augmented by his close attention to all the Society's programs and his frequent willingness to fund new ventures.[25] Attorney John G. Rauch (1890-1976) served as Society treasurer from 1931 to 1945, first vice-president from 1949 to 1954, president from 1955 to 1956, and was chairman of the board of trustees until 1972. A graduate of Harvard College, the debonair and accomplished Rauch was also a stalwart supporter of the art association, the symphony, and the children's museum. He steered the Society through many legal tangles, including the purchase of the archaeologically important Angel Mounds group of properties in 1937 and the Society's unsuccessful attempt in the 1940s to get financial support for the publication of the Calvin Fletcher diary from the estate of Laura Fletcher Hodges.[26]

The Indianapolis contingent was balanced by a trio of outlanders. Martha Tucker Morris (1867-1948) of Salem served for twenty years on the executive committee (1925-1945) and for

---

[24] Indianapolis *Star*, May 20, 1942.

[25] For Lilly see below, Chapter VIII.

[26] Indianapolis *Star*, February 4, 1976.

fourteen years as second vice-president (1931-1945). She was the only woman officer for many years. Morris, the key figure in the Washington County Historical Society, had a national reputation as an expert genealogist and was the first editor of the Society's genealogy column in the *Indiana Magazine of History*.[27] Arthur G. Mitten (1866-1938), a retired railroad executive from Goodland, served as third vice-president from 1931 to 1938. Mitten was an important collector of rare books and manuscripts on United States and Indiana history. He was in a position to offer the Society excellent advice on acquisitions for the Smith Library, but his election to office probably also was inspired by the hope that he would give his superb personal collection to the Society. The hope proved to be a vain one, but the Society was able to purchase the major part of his historical library from his estate in 1939.[28] Richard B. Wetherill (1889-1940), first vice-president from 1931 to 1940, was a Lafayette physician and the mainstay of the Tippecanoe County Historical Society. Wetherill built a program in Tippecanoe County that has continued to thrive, but his primary personal interest in Indiana history was the site of Fort Ouiatanon, which he mistakenly believed he had discovered. Wetherill built a replica of the fort near South River Road, outside West Lafayette. He supported the Society's early archaeology program and, like Morris and Mitten, brought a useful "out-of-town" perspective to the Indianapolis-based group.[29]

The officers were automatically members of the executive committee, but there were in addition other members elected specifically to the committee. Lee Burns, as mentioned before, was a member of the committee and its chairman from 1924 to

---

[27] *Indiana History Bulletin*, XXVI (1949), 13-14.

[28] Indianapolis *Star*, November 25, 1938. See also below p. 243.

[29] *Indiana History Bulletin*, XVIII (1921), 54-55.

1945. Other long-serving members of the committee in this
period were Cornelius O'Brien (1883-1953), a Lawrenceburg
businessman who also served as trustee of Purdue University
and was active in Democratic party politics; Albert L. Kohlmeier
(1883-1964), Woodburn's successor as department chairman
at Indiana University; and Linnaeus N. Hines (1871-1936),
mentioned earlier, president of Indiana State Teachers College
at Terre Haute.[30]

The committee was truly an executive body. It undertook the
major responsibility for evaluating the Society's financial condition and reconsidering its investments from time to time. It explored the legal ramifications of various Society enterprises and
on occasion initiated lawsuits. It passed explicitly on every major
decision of a complex, active institution.

The executive committee, moreover, delegated its power to a
number of other important committees with executive responsibilities and significant budgets. The Smith Library was governed
by a committee, as were also the Society's publications program,
the archaeology program, and, later, the bibliography of Indiana
authors project. There were additionally special interest committees engaged in a wide variety of activities. In May,
1937, the following committees of the Society were listed in
the *Bulletin:*

Executive	Indian History
Archaeology	Indiana History Teachers' Association
College section	Legal history
Indiana History Conference	Old Mills
Covered Timber Bridges	Pioneer Cemeteries & Churches
Genealogy	Publications
High School	Roadside Planting
Historical Markers	Smith Library

---

[30] Cincinnati *Press,* July 16, 1953; Indianapolis *Star,* July 15, 1936, June 26,
1974.

These committees all met independently during the year and reported their activities at the annual meeting. Some were more active than others; some disappeared altogether after a few years, often to be replaced by others. But throughout the Coleman years the Society engaged the active participation of a significant number of members in running its affairs. Though no longer a gentlemen's club, it was still a member-run organization.

A further, though indirect, indication of the increased importance of members in the Society is the notice taken of their deaths. Beginning in 1924 the names of members who died during the year were read at the annual meeting, and by 1929 Coleman was presenting brief biographies of each. The annual history conference also reflected the increased participation of members in the Society's business. As Coleman put it in 1934, "The annual meeting is concerned chiefly with reports of what its [the Society's] committees are doing and what public sentiment may accomplish through the agency of the Society."[31]

The history conference changed, too, in other ways under Coleman's leadership. Participation broadened, so that, in addition to the local and state historical societies which had initiated the conference in 1919, twenty years later Coleman could list the following groups as regular participants: high school, college, and university teachers of history; junior county historical societies and high school clubs; archaeologists; and genealogists. Moreover, Coleman and the new participants broadened the range of discussion to cover a wide variety of historical topics. In 1928, for instance, the history and social science section heard lectures on Russia and "Our Neighbors Across the Seas."[32]

---

[31] Minutes of IHS, December 7, 1928; Christopher B. Coleman, "Indiana Historical Society," in *Indiana Magazine of History*, XXX (1934), 171.

[32] Coleman, "Indiana Historical Society," in *Indiana Magazine of History* XXXV (1939), 308; *Proceedings of the Indiana History Conference, 1928*, pp. 78, 80.

Coleman introduced a new level of prestige to the conference by bringing in national figures as speakers. In 1926, Carl Sandburg spoke to the Indiana History Conference on Abraham Lincoln, concluding his remarks with recitation from his own poems and a performance of folk songs, accompanying himself on his guitar. Other literary figures like Meredith Nicholson and Claude Bowers addressed the conference on several occasions, and prominent representatives of the American historical profession came year by year: Dixon Ryan Fox (1925), Milo Quaife (1927), James A. James and Allan Nevins (1928), to mention a few.[33]

Despite these signs of vigor, the Society did not grow much in numbers throughout the Coleman years. There were 1,002 members in December, 1924, and only 1,200 in 1945. To a considerable extent these numbers reflect the Society's policy of accepting members by invitation only. As Coleman explained in 1930, the Society would not solicit members generally because they wanted "to keep the Society representative of the very best citizenship of the state." Coleman's own estimate of how many people might comprise "the very best citizenship" was not very large. He apparently never aimed for more than two thousand members, a figure considerably below the five thousand *Magazine* editor Lynch wanted. Coleman did circularize for new members among those who already belonged to the Society and also sent circulars to teachers of Indiana history, members of federated women's clubs, the DAR, and similar groups. There is even a very polite letter from sex researcher Alfred Kinsey of Indiana University in the Society's files, explaining in response to a Society circular that his "own interests are not directly enough connected with the Society to warrant my joining with you."

---

[33] *Proceedings of the Indiana History Conference, 1926,* p. 41; *ibid., 1925,* pp. 7, 57, 101; *ibid., 1928,* pp. 60, 113.

More conservatively the Society also attempted to get mailing lists from banks and trust companies in order to find prospects for new members. And, more effectively, Coleman clung like grim death to all the members he already had, sending dues notice after dues notice to those who lapsed. As he often commented in these letters, which were very polite and graceful, "Biblical authority notwithstanding, there is more rejoicing in the Society over a hundred members paying dues now, than over one repentant paying delinquent dues next year."[34]

At Lynch's fervent urging the dubious executive committee employed a canvasser for memberships for a short time in 1940, but few members were acquired and the committee terminated the experiment with relief. The committee flatly rejected the idea of exchanging publications with other historical societies.[35]

Coleman's Society—the Society, too, of Woodburn and Eli Lilly, of Evans Woollen, and Lee Burns—was still, like the Society of Dunn, English, Howe, and Charles Moores, an elite society of active members, though both the number of members and the range of activities had widened dramatically.

New Programs

Not only did the Society's established programs change under Coleman, but a number of new ones also emerged under his leadership. These were basically of three different sorts: popular programs, scholarly projects, and projects designed to bridge the gap between amateur and scholar.

---

[34] *Indiana History Bulletin,* VII (1930), 100, 152; Coleman, "Indiana Historical Society," in *Indiana Magazine of History,* XXVII (1931), 131; "Circulars" folder, IHS Papers; Alfred Kinsey to Coleman, April 22, 1942, in *ibid.;* Minutes of IHS, March 3, 1931; Christopher B. Coleman circular letter, April 9, 1934, "Circulars" folder, IHS Papers.

[35] Minutes of IHS, April 17, 1926, March 28, 1940.

Coleman strongly believed in the importance of heroes, memorials, and anniversary celebrations. The historian, he explained,

> . . . knows that man's progress has been slow, painful, and even uncertain. But this is all the greater reason for commemorating those great men who surmounted the difficulties of the past. . . . Our own generation is facing problems whose solution we cannot easily find. . . . If from the illustrious dead we gain a renewal of their spirit, if in their commemoration we are dedicated to our tasks, we may with confidence look forward to the building, even out of mistakes and wrecks, of a better, happier future.

While Coleman despised smugness and provincialism, he cherished "the tradition of the greatness of our inheritance" because he believed it was "a source of moral strength, a constant incentive for us to achieve great things."[36]

Among Coleman's first accomplishments in support of these views was his persuading the legislature in 1925 to declare December 11 "Indiana Day" to be an annual observance of the anniversary of the state's admission to the union. Coleman worked persistently to make Indiana Day a success, but its observance does not seem to have survived him.[37]

More successful along these lines was his promotion of a George Rogers Clark sesquicentennial to celebrate the 150th anniversary of Clark's victory over the British at Vincennes in 1779. Coleman found little interest in the other states of the Old Northwest in erecting a monument to the capture of Fort Sackville, which not everyone considered as Coleman did the major factor in the United States' acquisition of the territory from the

---

[36] Christopher B. Coleman, *The Undying Past And Other Addresses* (Indianapolis: State Library and Historical Board & Indiana Historical Society, 1946), p. 13; Coleman, "Traditions of Indiana," in *ibid.*, p. 72.

[37] *Proceedings of the Indiana History Conference, 1925*, p. 17. The last mention of Indiana Day in the *Bulletin* appears in 1944.

British after the Revolution. But Coleman did arouse interest among people in the Vincennes area, where half a million dollars was raised to buy the site of the fort and build a boulevard to connect it with Grouseland, William Henry Harrison's home in Vincennes. The state eventually raised another $400,000 to help buy the Fort Sackville land, and the federal government appropriated $1 million for a monument.[38]

The Indiana Historical Society and its secretary took a leading role in all of this. Coleman even reduced his work schedule at the Bureau to half-time in order to direct the Clark project. The Society appropriated money to the commission to support its work in the early stages but only on condition "that the [Clark] Commission would use its best endeavor to securing life and sustaining memberships, and also annual members" for the Society.[39]

Appropriately, the Society celebrated its own centennial in 1930 with a gala three-day program. The shock of the economic depression and the severe drought were acknowledged by the centennial planners, but Coleman asserted that remembering "the spirit and the intelligence" of the pioneers would help the Hoosiers of 1930 to surmount their calamities. Professor James Woodburn, by now seventy-four years old, composed a brief history of the Society as a valedictory gift. He had been a member of the Society for thirty-five years, its president for seven, and thus was in a position to provide an insider's overview of the Society's accomplishments. He claimed that the Society had

---

[38] Coleman, "Rediscovery of the Old Northwest," in *Undying Past,* pp. 27-49; *Indiana History Bulletin,* IV (1927), 143.

[39] Coleman memorandum to State Library and Historical Board, May 21, 1929, "Library and Historical Department" folder, Box 5, Records of the IHB; *Indiana History Bulletin,* VII (1930), 168, 243; *ibid.,* IX (1932), 173. Coleman seems to have served the Clark commission until 1931. Minutes of IHS, April 17, 1926, February 4, 1927.

provided ten important services, of which the most important was keeping "alive the spirit of history and constantly [inculcating] a spirit of loyalty to the state and its achievements, past and present." He also included the Society's work in improving the State Library, supporting the IHC, cosponsoring the history conference, helping the *Indiana Magazine of History*, promoting archaeological work, leading the celebration of the George Rogers Clark sesquicentennial, and promoting Indiana history in the schools. To the annoyance of some Pioneers, Woodburn also claimed, inaccurately, that the Society was responsible for organizing the Society of Indiana Pioneers.[40]

The days of celebration included a reception at the governor's mansion by the Harry G. Leslies. Evarts Greene, president of the American Historical Association, addressed the meeting on "Our Pioneer Historical Societies," and eighty-two-year-old William Dudley Foulke spoke on Oliver P. Morton, Indiana's Civil War governor, whom he compared with Napoleon, Lincoln, Clay, Webster, and Homer.[41]

It was an exhilarating occasion, heightened no doubt by the victory the previous year of the bill to provide a State Library and Historical Building. Only six years after he had undertaken the Society-Bureau leadership, Coleman could point to an unprecedented level of activity in his historical organizations.

Coleman continued to work to establish memorials. He helped in the drive to have the state preserve the architecturally distinctive J. F. D. Lanier home in Madison (1925); he urged the executive committee to support a state memorial monument to Nancy

---

[40] *Indiana History Bulletin*, VII (1930), 243; Woodburn, "The Indiana Historical Society: A Hundred Years," in Coleman (ed.), *Centennial Handbook*, p. 38; "Proceedings of the Indiana History Conference, 1930," in *Indiana History Bulletin*, VIII (1931), 293-94.

[41] "Proceedings of the Indiana History Conference, 1930," in *Indiana History Bulletin*, VIII (1931), 374-87.

Hanks Lincoln (1927); and he worked to save the Shrewsbury house in Madison from demolition (1927). The Society's annual participation in pilgrimages with the Pioneers to visit many of these memorial sites in different parts of the state provided opportunities to demonstrate vividly the impact of historical monuments and places. Among Coleman's other pet projects were the restoration of the Whitewater Canal (1940-1941) and planting trees as memorials. He was especially enthusiastic about using trees to mark historic roads, and he also proposed reforestation with tulip trees. In connection with the latter project the Society sponsored a contest among Boy Scout troops in order to gather tulip tree seeds.[42]

The Society came up with other programs involving young people during the Coleman years. At the end of 1931 the High School Committee was created as a state clearinghouse for history clubs, junior county historical societies, and for those teaching Indiana history in high schools. Committee head Daniel W. Snepp of Bosse High School in Evansville also used the group to lobby against the legislature's reduction of social studies requirements in 1934. By December, 1937, at the suggestion of high school students Richard Simons and William Sell of the Grant County Junior Historical Society, the executive committee was exploring the idea of a state junior historical society, in which local clubs would have an institutional affiliation with the Society (rather than individual members having "junior memberships"). An organizational meeting was held in 1938 in Marion

---

[42] *Proceedings of the Indiana History Conference, 1925*, pp. 17-18; Minutes of IHS, February 4, June 10, 1927; *Indiana History Bulletin*, XVII (1940), 74-75; *ibid.*, XVIII (1941), 271, 358-59; *ibid.*, XIX (1942), 23-25. Eli Lilly and Company executive John S. Wright was the chairman of the Tulip Tree committee. He worked hard for the cause of reforestation with tulip trees and defrayed the costs of the project. See "Tulip Tree Committee" folder, IHS Papers. Wright also remembered the Society generously in his will. IHS Board of Trustees Minutes, November 1, 1963, May 18, October 29, 1964.

on Simons's initiative, and the Indiana Junior Historical Society was formed. It was the first state junior historical society in the country. The organization became inactive when World War II began, however, and was not revived until 1949.[43]

In December, 1935, the Society's executive committee, which included the enthusiastic genealogist Martha Morris of Salem, considered the question of issuing a genealogical magazine. Coleman urged the proposal before a session devoted to genealogy at the annual meeting. Committees were appointed by the Society and by the Pioneers to plan the publication, and at the meeting in 1936 a Genealogy Section of the Society joined the other committees in making its annual report. From this beginning the genealogy section, now known as the Family History and Genealogy Section, has grown to be the single most popular program of the Society.[44]

The Pioneers contributed $200 and the Society $100 toward the publication the first year, a sum so modest that the plan for a separate magazine had to be dropped. William Lynch of the *Indiana Magazine of History* was approached and agreed to give the genealogists space in the *Magazine* in return for payment of the extra printing costs. The section, edited by Mrs. Morris, was an instant success and continued to appear until 1961, when the Society's officers decided that member interest in genealogy was sufficiently widespread to justify publishing a separate magazine.

All of these projects—the memorials, the junior societies, the aids to genealogical research—were moves to popularize history

---

[43] Coleman to Daniel W. Snepp, December 24, 1931, "High School Committee" folder, IHS Papers; Snepp to committee members, April 5, 1934, *ibid.*; IHS Executive Committee Minutes, December 10, 1937, July 1, 1938; Horace Carroll, "The Junior Historian Movement in the Public Schools," in *Bulletins of the American Association for State and Local History*, I (1947), 335-36. Richard Simons became a member of the Society's Board of Trustees in 1976.

[44] F. B. Fowler, "Genealogy," in *Indiana History Bulletin*, XIV (1937), 43-44.

and all were reasonably successful. Coleman apparently saw no conflict between his policies of popularizing history and keeping the Society small and select, but his successors were to discover tensions in these goals.

The new scholarly projects initiated by the Society under Coleman's leadership were effective to varying degrees. The archaeology program was extremely important. Except perhaps for the library and the publications, the archaeology program has been the most important contribution the Society has made to Indiana history. Coleman devoted considerable care to nurturing the archaeology program, and it was partly his influence and personality that attracted the participation of the program's key figures, Eli Lilly and Glenn Black.

Coleman also tried to establish an architectural archive in order to preserve the memory of buildings that could not be preserved physically and to provide the basis for a history of midwestern architecture. This plan was supplemented by the Society's support of the Historic American Buildings Survey, a New Deal program to employ architects and at the same time locate historic buildings. Although Coleman's proposed architectural archive did not thrive during his own time, it was revived in 1978 and promises to become an important Society program in years to come.[45]

Another area of history that Coleman thought was important and tried to promote was business history. In 1942 he urged Society volunteers to investigate early industries and building methods. There was little response to this call.[46] However, folklorists did come forward in the 1940s, welcomed by Coleman. The Society's folklore section reported for the first time at the annual meeting in December, 1943, with the important folklor-

---

[45] *Indiana History Bulletin*, IX (1932), 484-85; IHS Executive Committee Minutes, December 8, 1934.
[46] *Indiana History Bulletin*, XIX (1942), 159-61.

ist Stith Thompson of Indiana University as chairman. The section went on to publish *Hoosier Folklore* for several years, representing a useful collaboration between professional scholars and amateurs.[47]

Building links between professionals and history-minded amateurs was, according to Coleman, what historical societies were for. As he put it in 1933 in a paper he read before the American Association of Museums at Chicago,

> ... historical societies are primarily a means to an end, not an end in themselves. . . . [The end] may be expressed as the cultivation of intellectual activity of adult citizens along historical lines.

It was a very broad goal. He argued that professional and amateur historians needed one another.

> Historical societies need the guidance of professional historians and the colleges and universities need contacts with the outside world to keep their faculties from becoming academic and even pedantic. The object of history is to give an understanding of society and its institutions.

To achieve this, Coleman insisted, "requires the co-operation of an intelligent people—amateurs and professionals."[48]

These were not mere sentiments with Coleman. Under his leadership and with the strong support of President Woodburn, the professional historians of the state were drawn into the affairs and activities of the Society to an unprecedented extent. Beginning in December, 1924, and continuing until 1957 many years after Coleman's death, the annual Indiana History Conference featured a special breakfast for college teachers. The break-

---

[47] *Ibid.,* XXI (1944), 49-51; *Hoosier Folklore,* I (1942).

[48] Coleman, "The State and the Local Historical Society," in *Undying Past,* p. 83; Coleman, "Indiana Historical Society," in *Indiana Magazine of History,* XXXVII (1941), 62.

fast provided a forum for professionals to meet one another and discuss problems of mutual interest. It also provided recognition that the Society valued the participation of professional historians in its own meetings.

Coleman reached out regularly and persuasively to this group. The professionals were valued qua historians, not only for contributions to Indiana history. Coleman said again and again in the columns of the *Magazine* that "The word 'Indiana' in the name of the Society ought to be construed geographically rather than topically." Even Society publications were not to be limited entirely to works on Indiana history but could make room for more general pieces.

> Historians might well regard this as a medium for the preliminary publication of work which they have in hand and which they plan to develop into more extensive, permanent contributions to historical knowledge.[49]

All this encouragement did not meet with indifference. Indiana college history teachers participated widely in the Society's affairs—as members of important committees and officers of the Society, as policymakers, as authors of publications, and as speakers at the annual conferences. To a considerable degree Coleman succeeded in bringing together all elements of the adult population that were actively interested in history.

Conclusion

Coleman presided over the expansion of the Society from small club to modern historical society. He obviated for the time being the question of relationships between historical institutions by pulling them together under his leadership. Not only

---

[49] Coleman, "Indiana Historical Society," in *Indiana Magazine of History,* XXVIII (1932), 191; *ibid.,* XXXIII (1937), 201.

did he "unite" the Bureau and the Society but for six years he also acted as the director of the State Library, taking over the position in 1936 during a period of intense politicization of all state offices and preserving the library's integrity under extremely trying circumstances. In fact these were all challenging jobs, and attempting to perform them all at one time was a strain for Coleman, as the Bureau-Society position was increasingly to prove a strain for his next two successors.

Coleman provided continuity with the Society's heritage in these years of change. A gentleman himself, a man of independent means, he maintained the Society's sense of itself as an elite organization. At the same time he drew to the organization the professional historians needed to give substantive meaning to the elite "image." He also promoted and popularized history with memorials and booster rhetoric, in the conviction that history should offer popular comfort and inspiration, as well as food for more sophisticated analyses.

More than his predecessors by far, Coleman brought the Indiana Historical Society into the national forum. As an important member of the national historical establishment Coleman's voice was heard in organizations like the American Historical Association, the Conference of Historical Societies, the American Association for State and Local History, the Society of American Archivists, and in projects like the publication of the Territorial Papers of the United States. His abilities were widely respected. In 1940 Coleman was invited to edit the *Mississippi Valley Historical Review*, with the understanding that the Society would underwrite the journal. The Society was not willing to assume the financial obligation, and Coleman was not willing to accept the position anyway, but he was justly flattered by the proposal.[50]

---

[50] Coleman to J. D. Hicks, September 16, 1940, "Out of State 1940-47" folder, IHS Papers.

The Smith Library was organized and opened in the Coleman years. Though a review of its history is to be found in a later chapter, one can say here that Coleman was a daily advisor and supervisor of its growth. The Society's publications and its archaeology program, both to be treated in later chapters, also reflected Coleman's constant attention.

But Coleman's greatest contribution to the Society was effective leadership, that is, the kind of leadership that inspires and allows other capable people to offer their services. Coleman's tactful diffidence and graceful encouragement left room for persons like Woodburn, Lilly, Black, Caroline Dunn, Nellie Armstrong, Lee Burns, and a long list of other important members and staff to make strong contributions of their own to the Society. Without impressive financial resources Coleman built a vital historical movement in the state, at the same time keeping faith with the traditional values of the Society.

VI

Years
of Growth

1945-1976

Indiana State Library

Jack Householder

Howard H. Peckham
Secretary 1945-1953

Hubert H. Hawkins
Secretary 1953-1976

VI

*"The Society needs its own physical headquarters, it needs its
own staff, it needs its own administrator."*
Hubert Hawkins, 1964

Christopher Coleman died suddenly of a heart attack at age
sixty-nine in June, 1944. His colleague Dorothy Riker, a
person not given to exaggeration, wrote a few days later that
"It has been a terrible shock to us all." Thirty-five years later
she speculated that his six-year service as director of the State
Library (1936-1942) had simply worn him out. The job had
been made a patronage position by the McNutt administration,
as had all the State Library appointments; Coleman, a Democrat, took over in order to protect the library and its staff as
much as possible from the consequences of the spoils system.
It was not an enviable task. His successor Harold Brigham later
described Coleman's ordeal:

> Without benefit of a board of control, and in the face of constant
> difficulties and discouragement, he managed through six telling years
> to maintain the organization and services of the State Library in-
> tact. . . .

Caroline Dunn described it more succinctly: "He saved the State
Library."[1]

---

[1] Dorothy Riker to Jacob Blanck, June 30, 1944, in "Out of State, 1943-1944"
folder, IHS Papers; interviews with Riker, Thornbrough, Dunn; *Indiana His-*

Most of Coleman's staff and fellow officers continued to serve for many years after his death. An exception was Nellie Armstrong, editor of both Bureau and Society publications throughout Coleman's tenure, who resigned in 1947.[2] But Lee Burns, for instance, though he resigned from the chairmanship of the executive committee in 1945, served in other offices until 1956. Eli Lilly, elected president for the first time in 1933, retired from the office at the end of 1947 and stayed on, first on the executive committee and then on the board of trustees, until his death thirty-one years later. And, similarly, John Rauch resigned as treasurer at the end of 1945, having served since 1931, but he too continued in other offices until his death in 1976. Hence the Society was able to benefit from the services of its three senior officers throughout most of the period of growth and change from 1945 to 1976.

They were joined by a variety of newcomers, many of whom would carry on the tradition of long and active service as officers: for example, John D. Barnhart (1895-1967), editor of the *Indiana Magazine of History* from 1941 to 1955, who served from 1949 to 1967;[3] Herbert Heimlich (1897-1975), a Lafayette newspaper editor, who served from 1950 to 1966;[4] John P. Goodwin (1880-1972), a Brookville banker and former member of the State Library and Historical Board, who served from 1953 to 1972;[5] and, more recently, Hester Adams, Columbia

---

tory Bulletin, XXI (1944), 370-71. In his anxiety to persuade someone younger and equally capable to take over the library, Coleman had finally taken the unusual step of urging the Society's executive committee to pay Brigham's personal moving expenses from Louisville to Indianapolis, which the Society agreed to do. IHS Minutes of Executive Committee, August 27, 1942.

[2] *Indiana History Bulletin,* XXIV (1947), 131.

[3] Indianapolis *Star,* December 26, 1967.

[4] *Ibid.,* May 1, 1975.

[5] *Ibid.,* August 6, 1972.

City newspaper publisher;[6] John Wilhelm, a Hammond banker;[7] Thomas S. Emison, a Vincennes lawyer and scion of an historic Vincennes family;[8] and David V. Burns, like his father an Indianapolis architect and faithful officer of the Society.[9] These last four officers began to serve in the early 1960s and all continue to serve in 1980.

Coleman's death precipitated a new challenge to the linkage between the Bureau and the Society. Indiana University made another bid to acquire the Bureau. Indiana University President Herman B Wells wrote to the chairman of the State Library and Historical Board on July 5, 1944, only a few weeks after Coleman's death, proposing that a member of the history faculty should direct the Bureau. The board deferred a decision until it could consult with the Society. Executive committee member and chairman of the Indiana University history department Albert L. Kohlmeier argued in favor of the proposal before the Society's executive committee at the end of August. University affiliation, he said, would give the director more professional influence and would provide access to graduate student labor. The university did not expect the Bureau to move from Indianapolis to Bloomington; the director therefore would be an absentee one, with a separate base of operations in Bloomington.[10]

It was not a proposal likely to be embraced enthusiastically by the Indiana Historical Society. For twenty years the Bureau director had also been the Society's secretary; the jobs seemed to them to be two halves of one job. An absentee director seemed to threaten the stability only recently achieved by the Society:

---

[6] Columbia City *Post,* July 13, 1978.

[7] Hubert H. Hawkins and Robert R. McClarren, *Indiana Lives* (Hopkinsville, Ky.: Historical Record Association, [1967]), p. 84.

[8] *Indiana Legal Directory,* 1976 edition, s.v. "Emison, Thomas."

[9] *Who's Who in the Midwest,* 10th edition, s.v. "Burns, David Vawter."

[10] Minutes of IHS, August 31, 1944.

the Smith Library had been established in Indianapolis only a decade earlier.

The executive committee quickly rejected the idea. Although the committee agreed that the Society should consult with the university's history department about editing and publishing material in Indiana history, members immediately raised questions about the Bureau director's problems of serving two masters if he were associated with the university (forgetting perhaps that the Bureau director already served two masters—the Bureau and the Society—so that the problem would have become three masters instead of two). The committee was also skeptical that a university professor would be enthusiastic about dealing with amateur historians, an important part of the post. It was perhaps a testimony to Coleman's tact that they seemed to have forgotten that he at least had once been a university professor. The committee "after a full discussion decided that the wider historical interests of the state would best be served by continuing the Historical Bureau with its independent status." The vote was 5 to 2.[11]

Any other decision would really have been unthinkable. Both the Bureau and the Society would have been diminished by removing their director from the staff in Indianapolis, substituting a part-time leader for a full-time one, and handing their leadership over to one state university, to provoke the wrath of the other university and the ambitious state colleges. Moreover, although the Society had cultivated the participation of college teachers, its executive committee probably did not wish to surrender its governance to them. The Society had been a citizens' organization, then a gentlemen's club, then a coalition of interests. The gentlemen who ran the Society in 1944 had no intention of allowing it to become a professors' club, or worse, a small part of the university structure.

---

[11] *Ibid.*, September 29, 1944.

The Howard Peckham Years, 1945-1953

Having decided that the head of the Society and the Bureau should stay in Indianapolis and should not be a university professor, the executive committee approved the selection of a man with strong credentials both in library work and in editing. Howard Peckham was only thirty-four years old in February, 1945, when he began his tenure with the Society/Bureau. Born and educated in Michigan, Peckham was curator of manuscripts at the University of Michigan's William L. Clements Library of American History from 1936 to 1944. He also had edited three books before coming to Indiana. A man both scholarly and energetic, he was an active member of the national historical establishment. He was, for instance, a founding member of the Society of American Archivists and a longtime officer of the American Association for State and Local History (which he would serve as president from 1954 to 1956).[12]

Under Peckham's leadership two of what would become the most significant policies of the next thirty years were undertaken: popularization and expansion of membership.

The first of these policies was not explicitly an Indiana Historical Society policy; it was a Bureau policy, intended to affect primarily Bureau publications. Peckham proposed, and the State Library and Historical Board agreed, to have the Bureau publish material intended for the general public, not just for scholars. Peckham did not intend to abolish the Bureau's more scholarly work but planned instead to supplement it with more popular publications, like an historical almanac.[13]

In connection with the intended widening of scope, Peckham wished also to expand the *Bulletin*'s readership to include state

---

[12] *Indiana History Bulletin*, XXII (1945), 67-68; *Who's Who in the Midwest*, 12th edition, s.v. "Peckham, Howard."

[13] *Indiana History Bulletin*, XXII (1945), 120-21.

legislators, state officers, and county historical societies. He also wanted to reach schoolchildren, with illustrated leaflets on topics in Indiana history, and schoolteachers, with a Bureau-prepared outline of Indiana history for the fourth grade.[14]

Peckham implemented all of these plans, and additionally he changed the tone of the *Bulletin* significantly. Coleman had frequently been the booster of Indiana history; Peckham was the cheerleader. The new editor used his newspaper experience to produce breezy headlines like "Grandma Had a Signal for It," "State Song Humming," "The Magical Month of June," and wrote articles in the bright, slangy style of a feature writer. He also incorporated a column in the *Bulletin* common in Indiana newspapers, the "100 Years Ago" section.[15]

In the same vein Peckham was responsible for providing a new cover for the *Indiana Magazine of History* in 1947. The new emphasis on popularization was also perhaps responsible for the disappearance of the Society's column in *IMH*, one of its traditional links with the academic community, soon after Peckham arrived. This is somewhat ironic because Peckham himself was a fine professional historian who published a very well-received monograph on Pontiac soon after he took charge of the Society. His appearances in *IMH* during his years with the Society are almost all as a book reviewer or as the subject of a review, not as a spokesman for the Indiana Historical Society. As part of the general move to brighten the Society publications during Peckham's tenure, the publications committee asked permission to change the traditional somber grey covers to something more colorful, and the executive committee rather reluctantly consented.[16]

---

[14] *Ibid.*

[15] *Ibid.*, p. 208.

[16] *Indiana Magazine of History*, XLIII (1947), 62; IHS Executive Committee Minutes, December 5, 1952, September 24, 1953.

Peckham's enthusiasm for popularization of local history expressed itself in Society programs as well. He and the education committee tried on several occasions to produce a radio program on Indiana history but found the technical problems insuperable for amateurs working part time on the project. Under his leadership the Society inaugurated in 1947 a semiannual meeting to be held each year in a different place so that the Society would reach out to more of its members. The Society also introduced a program called Centennial Family Farms to reward Indiana families that had farmed the same acreage for a hundred years or more. This explicit appeal to "old" families in Indiana was an unusual policy for the Society, which always emphasized that there were no lineage requirements for membership. The Old Families emphasis had historically been left to the Society of Indiana Pioneers. But the program was popular, and the Society rewarded a large number of farmers with bronze medals.[17]

Peckham also originated a Spring History Workshop in 1951, a Bureau project cosponsored by the State Library and the State Conservation Department. The workshop appealed to local historical societies, offering experts from all over the state to consult with local historians, genealogists, and local society managers. The same was true of another program cosponsored by the Bureau, the Hoosier Historical Institutes, a series of weekend pilgrimages organized by Ross F. Lockridge in 1947. The program was set up in co-operation with the state universities and colleges and the state departments of commerce, public relations, and education. Participants could earn extension credit at Indiana State Teachers College. *History News*, the magazine of the American Association for State and Local History, described the program as a pioneering one and urged other states to emulate it. Though the Society did not formally

---

[17] *Indiana History Bulletin*, XXIII (1946), 133; *ibid.*, XXIV (1947), 3-4, 6, 127, 132; Minutes of IHS, June 8, 1951, June 3, 1952.

participate for many years, Society members were enthusiastic participants from the beginning.[18]

The Society also reached out again to young people. Peckham, with the assistance of the now grown-up Richard Simons, worked diligently to revive the Indiana Junior Historical Society and the individual high school history clubs. The Bureau offered a prize to the most active junior club, and Peckham himself spoke before many of the clubs around the state. By 1949 the state junior historical society was active again. Indiana University offered two scholarships to senior club members, one to be from the northern, the other from the southern half of the state, and the Bureau published a monthly newsletter for the group. The Society also worked with Boy Scouts in Indiana, sponsoring an annual "Lincoln Trail Hike." The scouts were encouraged to read a book on Lincoln and then to walk from Lincoln State Park to Anderson Ferry Park near Troy, a route that Lincoln was known often to have traveled during his youth in Indiana. The Society offered a bronze medal to each scout who participated between 1949 and 1956.[19]

As a concomitant of Peckham's concern to broaden the appeal of the Society's activities, he also in effect changed the membership policy of the Society. In May, 1945, Peckham announced in the *Bulletin* that "Everyone with an interest in history is invited to join" the Society, and by July, 1946, the formerly staid, elite Society was taking memberships from a booth at the State Fair. This was not quite the revolution that it might seem since the Society continued to circularize more elite organizations like the Indiana Society of Chicago, the Sons of Indiana, and the American Association of University Women,

---

[18] *Indiana History Bulletin*, XXVIII (1951), 27-28; *History News*, IV (1947), 7-8.

[19] *Indiana History Bulletin*, XXIV (1947), 62, 143; *ibid.*, XXVI (1949), 92-93.

along with sending circulars to everyone listed in the lawyer's directory. Nevertheless, the new membership policy as well as the folksier style of the *Bulletin* seem to have had an effect. The Society numbered 1,171 members at the end of December, 1944. At the end of 1953, the year Peckham left the Society, the membership had nearly doubled—2,044.[20]

It is not altogether clear who these one thousand new members were: were they county historical society members, responding to Peckham's assiduous efforts to help them reorganize their societies after the war? Were they mostly members of other clubs responding to the Society's many circulars? Were they members of Old Families, joining the Society to bolster their sense of community leadership in the face of rapid social changes after World War II? Were they persons prompted to join by the urgent patriotism engendered by the Cold War and its threat to American values?

All of these factors may have had some influence on the growth in membership. But it should also be remembered that the Society published some magnificent volumes in these years and offered them free to members. During Peckham's tenure members received *The Journals and Indian Paintings of George Winter, 1837-1839* (1948) and *The Old Northwest: Pioneer Period, 1815-1840,* by R. Carlyle Buley (1950). The former publication was elegantly printed and bound and contained exquisite full-color reproductions of Winter's paintings. The latter publication won the Pulitzer Prize for history. Unquestionably these volumes, along with the less spectacular but reliably interesting and well-produced regular *Publications* of the Society, attracted some new members.

---

[20] *Ibid.,* XXII (1945), 145; *ibid.,* XXIII (1946), 236; Howard H. Peckham circulars addressed to members of Indiana Society of Chicago, April, 1946, and Sons of Indiana, August, 1946, in "Circulars" folder, IHS Papers; IHS Executive Committee Minutes, June 3, 1952.

Ironically the great increase in membership greatly strained the Society's budget, since every $2.00 membership represented a loss. The organization's services and publications cost the Society more than $2.00 per member. Hence the success in the membership drive led to an increase in membership dues to $3.00 in 1950, the first increase in thirty-seven years. In addition the Society circularized its members asking them to become sustaining members at $10.00 annually.[21]

The increase in dues in 1951 put a temporary halt to expansion of membership, which stabilized around two thousand for a decade. The increase also brought the editor of the *IMH* around to point out again that the Society was by no means paying for its share of the magazine. John D. Barnhart asked for half of the dues increase, so that the Society dues would continue to be divided equally between the Society and the *Magazine*. After some hesitation the executive committee agreed.[22]

The Society was by no means prosperous in these years and for many thereafter. The situation remained essentially the same from 1924 until the Society received its first significant addition to its general endowment funds with the $20,000 Howe bequest in 1957. The Delavan Smith fund, which could only be used for the library's operations, generated enough money to run the library extremely frugally but not enough to hire staff to catalog the library's possessions. This condition was alleviated somewhat during the period from 1946 to 1955 by contributions amounting to $93,000 from J. K. Lilly, Jr., a member of the library committee, through the Lilly Endowment. This income was used for library expenses instead of the Smith income and thereby allowed the Smith fund nearly to double in value. Sim-

---

[21] Minutes of IHS, February 15, 1950, December 13, 1946.

[22] *Ibid.*, September 19, 1950, February 19, 1951.

ilarly the Lilly brothers Eli and J. K., Jr., between them supported the Society's most ambitious programs with yearly contributions. Eli Lilly contributed $25,500 to archaeology, for instance, in 1953; the bibliography fund, provided by J. K. Lilly, spent $20,000 to print *Bibliographical Studies of Seven Authors of Crawfordsville, Indiana,* the same year, and he also contributed $6,525 that year to the Smith Library.[23]

Although it never was so identified in the Society's reports, the Lilly Endowment also began to pay the secretary a salary— $200 per month—for the first time in 1946. Howard Peckham protested the executive committee's move, which changed his status from that of a gentleman officer to a paid professional. Unlike Coleman, whose independent means obscured his status as a professional, Peckham made his living as an historical administrator. This change in 1946 foreshadowed another important aspect of the Society's development in these years, the professionalization of the Society's management.[24]

The actual administration of the rest of the Society's program —the regular publications, the Society's conferences, encouraging local societies and junior societies, lobbying for memorials and historical interests generally—was accomplished on nickels and dimes. The entire non-Lilly, non-library budget for 1953, for example, was $7,044, including *IMH* subscriptions ($3,043.75), Boy Scout Lincoln Trail medals ($1,500), publications, postage, and editorial work.

The part of the Society's work that was closest to Peckham's heart was building the collections of the Smith Library. Co-author of a volume on book collecting and a former manuscripts

---

[23] These figures are reflected in the Society's annual reports at the Indiana History Conference, published in the *Indiana History Bulletin* during this period. See also Librarian's Report, 1954-1955, IHS Papers.

[24] Minutes of IHS, January 31, 1946.

curator, Peckham brought both enthusiasm and expertise to his library responsibilities. Peckham shared these interests with J. K. Lilly, Jr., with whom he worked closely to build the Society's collections in these years. Among other things, Peckham was responsible for the innovation of separately published annual library reports, attractively printed, which described the items collected and suggested their historical significance.

When his alma mater offered him the directorship of the Clements Library in 1953, Peckham found "the opportunity to engage directly in educational work with professors and students, to move in a campus atmosphere, and to live in a small city" irresistible. Regretfully the executive committee accepted his resignation and wished him well. Peckham has maintained his friendship with staff members over the years and has served as a sort of unofficial advisor and Friend of the Society.[25]

The Hubert Hawkins Years, 1953-1976

When the State Library and Historical Board set out to find a successor to Howard Peckham, they were anxious to provide someone who could be expected to remain with the Bureau for a long time. Secretaries of the Indiana Historical Society before Peckham had remained on the job for lengthy periods: Dillon was secretary for twenty years, Dunn for thirty-eight, Coleman for twenty. The board, hoping to find a similarly dedicated officer for the Bureau, tried to find a person whose first loyalties belonged to Indiana. "Every effort was made," the board reported, "to find a native Hoosier for the job."[26]

---

[25] *Ibid.*, June 25, 1953. In December, 1979, Peckham responded generously to a letter from the author inquiring about his own sense of the accomplishments and problems of the Society during his secretaryship.

[26] *Indiana History Bulletin*, XXX (1953), 127.

In Hubert Hawkins they found not only a native Hoosier, born in Marion County in 1916, but a DePauw graduate, teaching at Butler University, working on a dissertation in Indiana history. Though the dissertation was to fall by the wayside in his efforts to carry on more urgent tasks, Hawkins's research in Indiana history gave him the background for nearly a thousand talks on Indiana history and the Indiana Historical Society that he delivered in his twenty-three years as Bureau director and Society secretary.[27]

Hawkins was thirty-seven years old in 1953. He was a World War II veteran, having served two years in Europe with the Education and Information Service. He had received his master's degree in history from Western Reserve University and had worked briefly both for the Western Reserve Historical Society and for the *Mississippi Valley Historical Review*. A Harrison Fellow at the University of Pennsylvania, he finished the requirements for the doctorate except the dissertation and went on to teaching positions at Buffalo State and Butler University.

Except for the participation of Howard Peckham in the board's work, the Indiana Historical Society had no direct hand in Hawkins's selection. As Hawkins describes it, he was simply presented to the Society as a fait accompli, and the executive committee dutifully elected him the Society's secretary.

A tall, gangling, disarming person with an open, friendly manner and a perennially almost lighted pipe, Hawkins, far more than his predecessors, had what is sometimes called "the common touch." Though somewhat professorial in style, he made himself readily available for friendly conversation with all sorts of people. He showed none of the austerity of manner that seems often to go along with intellectual interests. In addi-

---

[27] *Ibid.*, pp. 127-28. Hawkins estimated the number of talks he delivered during twenty-three years as secretary in an interview with the author, December 7, 1979.

tion to his personal aptitude for making friends for the Society, Hawkins was convinced that the Society needed a greatly expanded membership. As he pointed out in his first annual report in December, 1953,

> While it is probably true that we will never reach and ought not to aspire to a mass membership, it would be the height of intellectual snobbery to assume that there are but two thousand Hoosiers who are qualified for membership.

Hawkins went on to point out that four thousand members would be better than two thousand: "To consider but one aspect, the unit costs on our publications would be considerably reduced on a press run of 4500 as compared to the 2800 ordered for our current issue."[28] Hawkins also believed that a larger historical society would have a better chance to influence the state legislature to support historical interests.

Although the Society's two increases in dues, first in 1950 to $3.00 and in 1955 to $5.00 per year, discouraged increases in membership for most of the 1950s, in the 1960s the Society nearly doubled in size. There were 2,488 members in December, 1960; there were 4,607 in December, 1970. The membership stabilized around 5,000 in the 1970s.

Much of this growth can be attributed to Hawkins himself. He was extremely generous with his time. He estimated that he drove twenty to thirty thousand miles a year to visit local societies, delivering forty to fifty talks a year. He addressed school groups, service organizations, and patriotic clubs in addition to local historical societies. "I was," he said in 1979, "very disappointed if I did not bring home a few new memberships from each trip."

---

[28] *Indiana History Bulletin*, XXXI (1954), 15.

But in addition to these personal appearances of Hawkins's, the Society acquired other techniques for presenting itself to potential members. Hawkins began to use the *Bulletin* to drum up memberships soon after he arrived. In 1960 he designed a promotional brochure and a pamphlet quoting reviews of Society publications, both of which were used in direct mailings. The staff also began to make up packages of books and membership brochures to send to meetings that Hawkins could not himself attend, and these efforts sometimes were successful.[29]

Hawkins stressed that Society membership was a bargain and emphasized that members received from the Society publications worth more than their membership cost them. Many of the new members probably were persons persuaded by this argument.

The largest increment of new members came from the ranks of the genealogists, who were attracted to the Society by its lively and well organized Genealogy Section (renamed Family History and Genealogy Section in 1978). Beginning in January, 1961, the section initiated a bimonthly magazine called *Hoosier Genealogist* to replace the "Genealogy" column in the *Indiana Magazine of History*. Confining themselves to Indiana materials, the magazine's editors published a wealth of local history records. Compiled by guest editors the first year, *Hoosier Genealogist* has since been edited by Nell Reeser of West Lafayette (1962-1965), Dorothy Riker of the Bureau and the Society staffs (1965-September 1978), and Rebah Fraustein (December 1978 to the present).

The Genealogy Section offered special sessions at the Spring History Workshops and the annual history conferences; they originated regional training courses in genealogy throughout the

---

[29] *Ibid.*, p. 167; *ibid.*, XXXVII (1960), 158-59.

state. A special spring symposium on genealogy was initiated in 1968 and attracted 250 interested individuals; later ones have been equally popular. In 1963 the first of a series of genealogical source books was published by the Society, Volume I of Willard Heiss's *Abstracts of the Records of the Society of Friends in Indiana*. Heiss served as chairman of the Society's section after 1968; in 1973 he issued the first number of *Genealogy*, a magazine that appears eight times a year, to supplement *Hoosier Genealogist*, which then began to appear quarterly. *Genealogy* specializes in news, queries, and book reviews, while *Hoosier Genealogist* publishes local records.[30]

This rich program attracted thousands of participants in the Society's genealogical program. Approximately three thousand Society members receive genealogical publications. Although many of these members are also interested in other Society activities, it is probably true that the historical interests of most are centered in their own family's history.

In addition to the factors already mentioned—Hawkins's personal campaign for support, the new advertising brochure and direct mailings, the packaged materials for meetings, the expanded genealogy program—probably another influence should be acknowledged in analyzing the reasons for the Society's expansion in the 1960s: the state and the nation were embarked on an unprecedented series of celebrations of historic events. Indiana celebrated the Civil War Centennial 1961-1965, and the statehood sesquicentennial in 1966, followed by the national Bicentennial in 1976. However hectic and demoralizing the 1960s and 1970s have sometimes seemed to contemporaries, the decades were clearly times of acute historical consciousness. Popular awareness of history has been sometimes dramatically

---

[30] The best published source on the Society's genealogy program is *Hoosier Genealogist*.

high as in the instance of *Roots* and the Watergate hearings on national television, *Patton, Coming Home,* and *The Deer Hunter* in films, and *All the President's Men* in journalism. Historical societies appealed to many people as a medium for expressing concerned interest in their own history.

The impressive expansion of the Society membership brought the benefits Hawkins had envisioned and some problems as well. As usual, more members meant more pressure on the Society's budget, and again in 1965, ten years after the last increase, annual dues were doubled. The new dues schedule was $10 per year for "annual" members, $25 per year for "sustaining," and $50 per year for "contributing." As usual the increase in the Society's dues triggered a response from the *Magazine.* After some considerable jockeying the Society agreed early in 1969 to pay the actual costs of the manufacture of the *Magazine* plus the postage, an arrangement which still basically continues.[31]

Along with expanded membership the Society undertook a number of important new projects during Hawkins's tenure as secretary. Perhaps the most ambitious and consequential of these projects was the planned five-volume history of Indiana to celebrate the statehood sesquicentennial in 1966 to be published jointly with the Bureau. Initially proposed by R. C. Buley, the undertaking was planned in 1956 for publication a decade later. Only three of the proposed five volumes have appeared so far— Emma Lou Thornbrough's *Indiana in the Civil War Era* (1965), Clifton Phillips's *Indiana in Transition . . . 1880-1920* (1968), and Dorothy L. Riker and John Barnhart's *Indiana to 1816* (1971), and they have been extremely well received.[32]

---

[31] IHS Board of Trustees Minutes, February 25, 1969.

[32] IHS Executive Committee Minutes, October 24, 1956; interview with Hubert Hawkins, December 7, 1979.

Indianapolis *Star*

Indiana State Library

Tippecanoe County
Historical Association

Library Occurrent

Richard Simons, Indianapolis *Star*

opposite, above, Eli Lilly and John Rauch, shown here at the 1941 history conference, continued to serve as officers into the 1970s; John D. Barnhart, officer 1949-1967; *below,* Herbert Heimlich, officer 1950-1966; John P. Goodwin, officer 1953-1972

above, new 1947 cover of *Indiana Magazine of History;* Howard Peckham and Indiana Junior Historical Society officers and club sponsors from Beech Grove, Decatur Central, and Indianapolis Tech, 1950; *left,* Roy Samuelson played William Conner and Lila Stuart sang the role of Mekinges, his Delaware wife, in the 1966 premier production of Walter Kauffman's *A Hoosier Tale,* commissioned by the Society

opposite, above, Society Board of Trustees and staff members at a meeting in 1969; clockwise from left, John G. Rauch, John F. Wilhelm, Gayle Thornbrough, Eli Lilly, Herman B Wells, Hubert Hawkins, Mrs. George W. Blair, Elsie Sweeney, Mrs. John Quincy Adams, David V. Burns, and William E. Wilson; *below,* Willard Heiss, chairman of the Family History and Genealogy section since 1968; Donald F. Carmony, editor of the *Indiana Magazine of History,* 1955-1975

right, Hubert Hawkins and Caroline Dunn were surrounded by manuscripts in this 1964 news photograph taken in the library; *below,* By 1973 many materials were in storage, but the library was still crowded.

right, Jameson Woollen was the Society's treasurer 1966-1979; *below*, the State Library and Historical Building Expansion Commission at the groundbreaking ceremony June 30, 1975. L. to r., Marcelle K. Foote, state librarian; John F. Wilhelm, chairman of the Society's Board of Trustees; John E. Horner, president of the Indiana Library and Historical Board; William C. Floyd, office of the governor; David V. Burns, Commission chairman

opposite, *above*, the new building under construction; *below*, The building was complete in 1976.

Jack Householder

Indianapolis *Star*

Jack Householder

In 1962 Society board member Elsie Sweeney of Columbus proposed the most striking of the Society's large projects in these years: she arranged for the Society to cosponsor an opera with the Indiana University School of Music. The opera would deal with an episode in Indiana history and would appear as a celebration of the state sesquicentennial in 1966. The university was enthusiastic, and Sweeney, a knowledgeable and experienced music patron, underwrote the opera's composition. *A Hoosier Tale* by Walter Kauffman explored the theme of Indian-white relationships in the life of pioneer William Conner. Conner's Indian wife and their children left Indiana with the Delawares in their tragic exodus in the 1820s and Conner rejoined the white society he had earlier rejected. Though by no means an unqualified success, the opera was an imaginative and appropriate celebration of the 150th anniversary of statehood and an interesting historical society venture into patronage of the arts.[33]

The Society was less fortunate with a project it undertook in 1955 to administer a grant to finance a history of the Panhandle Eastern Pipe Line Company. The project was to be a model for a series on Indiana business history, but unfortunately, like many pilot studies, it failed. Despite the efforts of several researchers, editors, and a supervisory board, the difficulties of the task proved insurmountable.[34]

Another large project undertaken by the Society was a two-year manuscript collection venture. In 1967 the Lilly Endowment granted $35,000 to the Society to hire William E. Wilson,

---

[33] IHS Executive Committee Minutes, October 25, 1962; "Opera" folder, IHS Papers. As is often the case most local critics were harsher than the one from New York. The New York *Times* critic, Allen Hughes, found much to praise and concluded that "The state should be proud of this contribution to its celebration." New York *Times*, July 29, 1966.

[34] IHS Executive Committee Minutes, December 9, 1955.

former state superintendent of public instruction, to search out historically significant manuscripts in the field and acquire them for the Society's library.[35] Though reasonably successful, the project underscored a major space problem with which the Society soon found it could no longer avoid dealing.

The Indiana Historical Society was badly cramped in its small quarters in the State Library and Historical Building. Moreover, not only were its own space needs not met by the situation but also the Society was increasingly seen as an unwanted guest by those who had to contend with the growing space needs of the State Library and the archives. Although Hawkins requested and received permission from the executive committee to support a drive for a separate state archives building in 1954, that building and hence that solution to the problem failed to materialize. Already by 1959 Hawkins was raising hard questions about the Society's future, questions prompted by the Society's need for space.[36]

In 1961 the executive committee approved a planning committee to consider the Society's future needs and early in 1962, prompted by the availability of the old Indianapolis City Hall Building, Hawkins discussed the Society's needs and problems in a six-page mimeographed letter to the executive committee. The key to his analysis of the Society's needs was his sense that it was crucial to separate the Society from the Indiana Historical Bureau.

"The Indiana Historical Society," Hawkins argued, "projects a blurred and unsatisfactory image." Most people mistook the Society for a government agency, Hawkins reported, and "Many who might become members are reluctant to give even annual dues to a state agency." Hawkins's proposed solution

---

[35] *Ibid.,* May 3, 1967.

[36] *Ibid.,* October 6, 1954, November 3, 1959.

was to remove the Society physically from the Bureau and from the State Library. A new headquarters could provide both the space needs of the Society and an identity independent of the state agencies.[37]

In the course of the next ten years Hawkins was to suggest a variety of new locations for the Society: the City Hall Building, into which the state museum was eventually to move; the John Rauch family mansion at 30th and North Meridian; a site on the Indiana University-Purdue University Indianapolis campus at New York and West streets. In the early 1960s Hawkins even suggested to board members that the Society should move outside the city limits to Conner Prairie to protect the Smith Library from destruction in case of nuclear attack![38]

For some of the senior officers and staff the idea of the physical separation of the Society from the State Library was an insuperable stumbling block to the acceptance of Hawkins's plans. Remembering Coleman's struggle to get the state to build a State Library and Historical Building only thirty years before, there was deep reluctance to remove the Society from it. Moreover the Smith Library had been organized as a specialized, supplementary library; it was feared that its value as a research library might be reduced by taking it away from the larger collections of the State Library.

Eli Lilly, in particular, was unhappy at the prospect of removing the Society from the State Library. The role of a "merchant prince" who chooses to be active in the affairs of a nonprofit organization is in all cases likely to be an extremely important one; hence it is perhaps especially noteworthy among the many

---

[37] Hubert H. Hawkins to Board of Trustees, February 7, 1962, in "Board of Trustees correspondence" folder, IHS Papers.

[38] *Ibid.*; Hawkins to B. K. Trippet, March 15, 1962, *ibid.*; IHS Executive Committee Minutes, February 11, May 5, 1972.

notable aspects of Eli Lilly's participation in the Indiana Historical Society that he exercised his considerable influence with gentleness and reticence. Although deeply interested in the projects he supported personally—the archaeology survey and extensive digs at Angel Mounds and the special publications, to mention the most notable—, Lilly rarely allowed himself the indulgence of interfering with their management. As Gayle Thornbrough remembers it, "he let people alone to do their work."

Eli Lilly was a modest, hardworking man with simple tastes and a passion for excellence. Born in Indianapolis on April 1, 1885, only nine years after his grandfather founded Eli Lilly & Company, "Mr." Eli began to work weekends for Colonel Eli when the former was only ten years old. After graduating from Shortridge High School he was sent, as his father J. K. Lilly, Sr., had been, to the Philadelphia College of Pharmacy and Science and entered the family business immediately upon graduation as a pharmacist in 1907. Like his father and grandfather, Eli Lilly was deeply loyal to his business, his fellow workers, his community, and his state.[39]

He had been drawn to the Indiana Historical Society by his interest in archaeology, and, when he discovered the talented young Glenn Black, Lilly essentially arranged to underwrite the archaeologist's work through the Society. Lilly's own capable and attractively written work on archaeology found an appreciative audience in the Society, which also, moreover, offered him a group of colleagues whom he respected and whose company he enjoyed.

Mr. Lilly maintained a strong interest in the Society throughout the years when he was president (1932-1948) and chairman of the board (1948-1961) of Eli Lilly and Co. Although he was

---

[39] New York *Times*, January 25, 1977.

the head of a successful international business, Lilly found time
to take an active part in running the Society. His presidency of
the Society (1933-1947) coincided almost exactly with his years
as president of the family business, but he appeared at almost
all Society executive committee meetings and took a leading,
though by no means dominating, part in discussions and decisions.

Eli Lilly's role in the decision of how and when to provide new
quarters for the Society was, however, a dominant one. By the
middle 1960s, when the question was being urgently debated,
Lilly had been a dedicated officer of the Society for thirty years.
Even had he not also been the Society's major financial resource
for thirty years, his years of service would have given him the
senior place in decision making. Although the Society's Planning and Development Committee, composed of Eli Lilly,
Thomas Emison, Elsie Sweeney, David Burns, and Hubert Hawkins, reported to the board of trustees in November, 1966, that
they had agreed to raise an endowment of $2.5 million,
$900,000 of which would be used for a separate building, Lilly
and others had second thoughts about the plan. After consulting
with Governor Roger Branigin, among others, Lilly announced
to board chairman John Rauch that he had changed his mind.
He believed that it was overridingly important that the Society
remain associated with the State Library. "The Governor,"
Rauch then reported to the board by way of mitigation, "had
expressed his interest in helping to solve the space problems of
the Society." With this, the board acceded to Lilly's judgment
and reversed its earlier decision to raise money to acquire a separate building.[40]

The decision reflected Eli Lilly's commitment to the tradi-

---

[40] Interviews with Hubert H. Hawkins and Gayle Thornbrough, fall and winter, 1979; IHS Board of Trustees Minutes, May 3, 1967.

tional heritage of the Society, that is, to its mission to collect and disseminate the materials of Indiana history. If the Society was to remain a publishing society, its staff needed constant and ready access to the unique research collections of the State Library. Moreover the decision reflected the traditional sense that the State Library and the Smith Library were supplementary to one another, that each collection made sense best in the context of ready access to the other. Since this decision meant that the State Library would continue to benefit from public access to the Society's library, Lilly also believed that the state should contribute to the project of expanding the State Library and Historical Building (and the quarters of the Indiana Historical Society).

It was at this point during the lengthy debate on the housing question that the Society suffered a significant staffing loss, one that led to a temporary reorganization of the Society's administrative structure and an outside evaluation of the overall condition of the Society.

Gayle Thornbrough resigned as editor in 1967 to accept a position as curator of manuscripts with the Library of Congress. In her thirty years with the Society, Thornbrough had acquired a national reputation as an historical editor. For the *Indiana Historical Collections* published by the Bureau, Thornbrough, along with her colleague Dorothy Riker, had compiled and edited *Journals of the General Assembly of Indiana Territory, 1805-1815* (1950); *Indiana Election Returns, 1816-1851* (1960); and several volumes of the *Messages and Papers of the Governors of Indiana* series, including those of James Brown Ray (1954), Noah Noble (1958), and Samuel Bigger (1964). For the Society, in addition to all of the *Prehistory Research Series* she produced *The Journals and Indian Paintings of George Winter, 1837-1839* (1948); *The Buffalo Trace* (1950), based on George R. Wilson's 1936 report on behalf of the Buffalo Trace Commission;

Outpost on the Wabash, 1781-1791, Letters of Brigadier General Josiah Harmar and Major John Francis Hamtramck (1957); *Letter Book of the Indian Agency at Fort Wayne, 1809-1815* (1961); and *Correspondence of John Badollet and Albert Gallatin, 1804-1836*; and with Holman Hamilton *Indianapolis in the "Gay Nineties": High School Diaries of Claude G. Bowers* (1964). In addition to these 'visible' works, she had prepared essentially all of the Society's books for publication, generally assisted by Dorothy Riker, from *The Old Northwest* (1950) to *Angel Site* (1967). (She did not work on the special bibliographies published separately by the committee on bibliography, which hired its own staff [1944-1952].) The high level of the Society's publications since 1937 is in large part due to the contribution of Gayle Thornbrough. Other institutions had sought to employ her talents from time to time—the Society's executive committee raised her salary to meet an offer from the University of Minnesota Press in 1948, for instance—, but until the invitation from the Library of Congress, in recognition of her work with documents, Thornbrough's interests and loyalties had kept her in Indianapolis.[41]

Here then was a crisis. Hubert Hawkins had been arguing for years that the Society needed a larger staff and its own, separate administrator, as well as new, larger quarters. Now the Society had to face not only its impossibly cramped physical quarters but also a critical staffing loss. Impending also was a major transition as Caroline Dunn, the Society's librarian, approached retirement. Moreover, fifty-hour weeks and efforts to lead expanded programs both for the Bureau and the Society were wearing away at Hawkins's stamina.

Thornbrough's resignation led to a temporary revision of the Society's administrative structure in recognition of all these pressures. Since the Society was not yet ready to separate from

---

[41] IHS Executive Committee Minutes, October 12, 1948.

the Bureau, it separated its own administrative responsibilities instead, dividing them into two jobs: executive secretary and a newly created position, the Director of Publications and the Library.[42]

It took the Society six months, sending out seventy-five letters of inquiry and sorting through nearly thirty applications, to decide that by far the best candidate for the new position was Gayle Thornbrough. She accepted the Society's offer in January, to begin in August, 1968.[43]

In May, 1968, chairman John Rauch wrote to the Board of Trustees on another matter with profound consequences for the Society's future. Mr. Lilly, now eighty-three years old and concerned about the future of the institution, had given twenty thousand shares of Eli Lilly & Co. stock to the Indiana Historical Society as an unrestricted gift. In money, that turned out to be something more than $2.5 million, the amount the erstwhile Planning Committee had decided upon in 1966, when the proposed separate building had been first considered.[44]

Major resources create major options. The jolt of the Lilly gift provoked the Society to an unprecedented effort of self-evaluation. To aid themselves in this task, the board, at the prompting of Hubert Hawkins, secured the services of an expert on American historical societies, William T. Alderson, Jr., director of the American Association for State and Local History. Alderson spent three days at the Society in September and wrote a thirty-five page report describing his findings and recommendations.

---

[42] IHS Board of Trustees Minutes, May 3, 1967.

[43] *Ibid.*, January 17, 1968.

[44] John Rauch to Board of Trustees, May 20, 1968, "Board of Trustees" folder, IHS Papers. When the author asked Dorothy Riker in December, 1979, whether people had known in 1968 that Eli Lilly had made this gift, she replied in surprise, "I didn't know it *now.*" The gift was kept secret as he wished.

He was, for the most part, sanguine about the Society's prospects: "The Indiana Historical Society is a basically healthy institution with a larger than usual membership among state historical societies, a respected library program, a record of distinguished work in the field of archaeology, and an acknowledged high-quality publications program." The problems that he saw were, by and large, the ones that Hawkins had been stressing for years: the confusion of identity between the Society and the Bureau; the handicap of inadequate space; too few and underpaid librarians; a large backlog of uncataloged books and manuscripts. In addition Alderson found some technical shortcomings in the Society's executive machinery and then recommended the following amendments: a) overlapping terms for the trustees, to insure continuity of leadership; and b) removing the executive secretary from the board of trustees, to make a clear separation between trustee and administrative responsibilities.

Alderson also felt the Society should continue the arrangement with Indiana University whereby the Society bought from the university enough copies of the *Indiana Magazine of History* to supply its membership. This arrangement has continued, with the *Magazine* being under the able editorships of Donald F. Carmony, 1955-1975, and presently James H. Madison.[45]

Perhaps the most important of Alderson's recommendations was that the Society not use the Lilly gift of more than $2 million to attempt a building program. "If the Lilly gift should be diverted to the building project," he continued, "the Society could very well wind up with adequate building and crippled program. . . ." There was no help for it, in his view; the Society must seek yet more funds for a new building and resist

---

[45] William T. Alderson, Jr., "Report on the Organization and Operation of the Indiana Historical Society," September 21, 1968, "Board of Trustees" folder, IHS Papers.

the temptation to divert the Lilly gift from the budget program.[46]

On the whole the Society accepted Alderson's advice. By October, 1968, when the new Director of Publications and the Library made her first report to the board, many of the detailed recommendations had been implemented and/or augmented. Thornbrough brought a new burst of energy to the rescue of the small library staff, which had been nearly buried under a mass of books and manuscripts. In order to clear the tables in the reading room, she rented space as a short-term solution to store seldom-used material; she purchased vertical files for more efficient storage of manuscripts; and she removed both the periodicals and cataloging operation from the reading room. What she added was a cataloger.[47]

With the Society's new resources, both financial and administrative, the Society's programs were strengthened and augmented in the transitional years from 1968 to 1976. The changes were reported annually in the handsome new report the Society began sending to its members, beginning with the *Annual Report, 1969-1970*. A lecture series featuring nationally respected scholars was inaugurated (or, more strictly, since Coleman had initiated a series in 1941, the lectures were revived) in 1969, with the results published and distributed to members. Also, two important, long-term documentary projects were undertaken by the Society in 1969: the Calvin Fletcher diary, long considered an invaluable source for nineteenth-century Indiana history, and a documentary history of the Harmony Society of George Rapp, covering the decade the German community lived in Indiana.

The question of what to do with the archaeological artifacts assembled by Glenn A. Black in his nearly thirty years as So-

---

[46] *Ibid.*

[47] IHS Board of Trustees Minutes, October 23, 1968, February 25, 1969.

ciety archaeologist was resolved in this period. The Lilly Endowment subsidized the construction of the Glenn A. Black Laboratory of Archaeology at Indiana University. In addition the Endowment provided for the continuing usefulness of the Angel Mounds site by providing an "interpretive center" to be used both to explain the site to visitors and to work as a research station for the Indiana University archaeology department.[48]

The Society received a $30,000 grant in 1972 from the Lilly Endowment to support the Junior Historical Society. New "sections" were formed in 1974 to provide separate publications and more activities for members with special interests. Dr. Charles A. Bonsett of Indianapolis, the founder of the Indiana Medical History Museum, acted as chairman of the new Medical History Committee. The committee works with the Indiana State Medical Society to develop the museum and also publishes the *Indiana Medical History Quarterly*. The Military History Section was also organized in 1974, with Thomas M. Joyce of Plainfield as chairman. Richard M. Clutter of Indiana Central University edits the section's quarterly *Indiana Military History Journal*, and the section sponsors a diverse program of special activities to preserve and promote military history. Both groups sponsor special sessions at the Society's conferences.[49]

The Society was growing and prospering with its expanded income and augmented leadership, but the more it grew the more it was squeezed by its small quarters. Each year Hawkins reported, "The Society badly needs additional space to accommodate its growing collections, store its publications, and house its staff efficiently."[50]

---

[48] Indianapolis *Star*, June 5, 1970; Indianapolis *News*, November 29, 1972.

[49] IHS *Annual Report, 1971-1972*, p. 5; ibid., 1975-1976, pp. 21-24; IHS Board of Trustees Minutes, May 5, 1972.

[50] IHS *Annual Report, 1971-1972*, p. 5.

Governor Branigin's hopes for a new supreme court building to provide space for the Society had not been realized during his administration, and by 1972 State Librarian Marcelle Foote believed, as her predecessor had believed, that the Society should remove its library from the State Library building to make room for the state's own holdings. The Society attempted to interest the legislature in building an addition to the State Library, but the prospects did not look promising. Before the Society's housing committee and the State Library and Historical Board were to meet with Governor Otis Bowen early in January, 1973, to request support for the bill, Secretary Hawkins visited Mr. Lilly and reported that the effort was likely to fail. When asked for a suggested remedy, Hawkins proposed that the Society offer to bear a significant part of the cost of the expansion project, for instance a million dollars.[51]

Lilly agreed to this suggestion and appeared at the meeting with the Society committee, the State Library and Historical Board, and the governor. All were amazed, including Hawkins, when Eli Lilly proposed that the Society bear not one million dollars of the proposed cost, but *two* million. "He looked at me with that puckish grin he sometimes had and repeated it carefully, 'two million dollars,' " Hawkins recalled. Lilly then offered to provide one million dollars personally, the other million to come from the Society's endowment. The state legislature, heartened by the prospect of having a public building subsidized by private funds, passed the bill.[52]

Under the heroic chairmanship of Society trustee David Burns, a respected architect, the building expansion commission supervised the completion of a four-story structure in time for an official dedication in October, 1976, though the Society did

---

[51] IHS Board of Trustees Minutes, May 5, 1972; Hubert Hawkins interview, December 7, 1979.

[52] Hubert Hawkins interview, December 7, 1979; *Laws of Indiana*, 1972-1973, pp. 42-47.

not receive its full complement of furniture until a year later. The "open house" celebration in November, 1977, attracted a large number of friends of the Society.[53]

The new building was a fitting tribute to the persistence of Hubert Hawkins and the special vision of Eli Lilly. It provided the space and distinctive image that Hawkins had urged for so long, while it also retained access to the research collections Lilly had perceived as essential to the Society's scholarly mission.

When the building was well underway in 1975, Hubert Hawkins announced his resignation, effective March 31, 1976, to the Society's board. He was tired and ill. In his twenty-odd years with the Society he had accomplished many of his objectives, and the most urgent goal, that of a larger, permanent home for the Society, was essentially in hand. Eli Lilly summarized the feelings of the Society's friends in a personal letter to Hawkins:

> You have done many, many great jobs for the Society during your term of office, and we will all regret your departure both from a Society and a personal standpoint. Needless to say, you have a strong position in our minds and hearts, and our good wishes are yours forever and ever, amen.[54]

Hawkins made two further recommendations as he took his leave, both of which were accepted by the Society's board of trustees: first, that the Society's secretary should *not* also be the Bureau director, and second, that his colleague Gayle Thornbrough should be his successor as executive secretary. Also on Hawkins' recommendation Bureau editor Pamela J. Bennett became director of the Bureau. Much of his program achieved, Hubert Hawkins then retired to tend his garden and restore his health, leaving the Society on the threshold of the next phase of its development.

---

[53] Building Expansion Commission files, IHS Papers; IHS *Annual Report, 1976-1977*, p. 3.

[54] IHS Board of Trustees Minutes, May 19, 1975; Eli Lilly to Hubert H. Hawkins, September 26, 1975, "Board of Trustees" folder, IHS Papers.

VII

The Society as Custodian of History: Publications and the Library

John Giles

The Calvin Fletcher diary and manuscripts are representative examples both of the Society's manuscript holdings and the publications program.

VII

"The establishment of safe depositories for the keeping of natural curiosities, manuscripts, public documents, etc. in the custody of intelligent guardians . . . has ever been found promotive to the public good and auxiliary to the advancement of science and literature. . . ."
John H. Farnham, 1830

The main object of any historical society is to collect and preserve historical materials. The Indiana Historical Society struggled for more than a century with the problems of attempting to carry out this purpose without adequate quarters. The Society did not open its library to the public and begin serious collecting until 1934, and by the late 1950s it discovered that the quarters, won with such difficulty a few decades before, were neither permanently available nor sufficiently large. Only in 1977 did the Society move its collections into a "permanent" home—in a part of a building for which the Society holds a ninety-nine-year lease—with a generous space allotment.

Most of the history of the Society's efforts to fulfill its mission is, therefore, a story of adversities. The extent of the adversity is, however, unknown. Though it is clear that much that had been collected before the 1920s was lost, it is not clear how much material was involved, or, for the most part, what it was. Occasionally there is evidence of a specific painful loss. The Indianapolis *Journal* of January 23, 1833, for instance, reported that former governor William Henry Harrison, who was in Indianapolis for a public dinner honoring him, had handed over "the original correspondence of the Territorial Executive with the federal government" to John H. Farnham as a gift to the Indiana Historical Society. If the newspaper report was correct and Harrison did give this material to the Society, it has been lost. Certainly this material forms no part now of the Society's manuscript collections. In addition there are tantalizing reports of questionnaires collected by John B. Dillon from a large number of volunteers from the various counties reporting on the early history and settlers of each place. These, too, are gone. What remains from the early library are a small collection of law books presented to the Society by John H. Farnham and a number of books reported as acquisitions in the early minutes, most of which became part of the State Library collections either during the period before 1934, when the Society had no quarters for its library, or after 1934, when the Society's collecting policy narrowed and many of the older books no longer suited the new collecting objectives.

Before 1934, then, the society had books but no library. The Smith bequest in 1922 gave the Society a quite distinguished collection of books and a modest income for increasing and maintaining the collection, but the books were stored in a warehouse. The Society still had no library until the state provided one in 1934.

Did the Society then fail completely to fulfill its obligation to collect the materials of Indiana history before it acquired a library in 1934? A negative judgment would be unjust. Although the Society failed to collect in the most obvious sense, it collected the materials of Indiana history in another way. Through the publications program the Society preserved and collected much that was otherwise in danger of permanent loss. Hence to speak of the Society's "collections" in the period from 1830 to 1934 is to speak of Indiana Historical Society *Publications*.[1]

Publications

Before 1886 there was, of course, very little, and it was extremely fugitive. Still, the early pamphlets represent very well the kinds of history the Society has published for the past 150 years: documents, biography, reminiscences, monographs, archaeology, and essays.

The Society's first publication was a document, a letter written by Nathan Dane in response to an inquiry by John H. Farnham, explaining Dane's part in the framing of the Ordinance of 1787. Except for monographs, the Society has published more documents than any other kind of material. Before 1934 the Society issued the following edited documents: *Proceedings of the Indiana Historical Society, 1830-1886* (1897); *Loughery's Defeat and Pigeon Roost Massacre* (1888); *Documents Relating to the French Settlements on the Wabash* (1894); *Slavery Petitions and Papers* (1894); *Executive Journal of Indiana Territory, 1800-1816* (1900); *Diary of William Owen from November 10, 1824, to April 20, 1825* (1906); *Names and Persons Enumerated in Marion County, Indiana, At the Fifth Census, 1830* (1908); *Lockerbie's Assessment List of Indianapolis, 1835* (1909); *Journal of Thomas Dean, A Voyage to Indiana in 1817* (1918); *Minutes of the Indiana Historical Society, 1886-1918* (1919); *Early Indianapolis* [quotations from Sarah Fletcher's Diary, 1820s-1830s] [1919?]; *Fort Wayne in 1790* [journal of Henry Hay]

---

[1] For a complete list of all Indiana Historical Society publications see Appendix, below, pp. 339-50.

(1921); *Indiana's First War* [reports on the war between the French and the Chickasaws dated 1736, printed both in French and English translation, from the French National Archives] (1924); *The Journey of Lewis David von Schweinitz to Goshen, Bartholomew County, in 1831* (1927); and *Unedited Letters of Jonathan Jennings* (1932). The Society also printed a facsimile of the Patrick Henry instructions to George Rogers Clark of January 2, 1778 (1859).[2]

Like the Society's manuscript and book collecting program after 1934, the pre-1934 publications stressed pre-Civil War documents. The Society's monographs in the *Publications* series also emphasized the early period. Except for Dillon's *The National Decline of the Miami Indians* (1848), there was little that focused on Indians. But the Society published more on the French period and on Indian wars.[3] Most of the early monographs described aspects of pioneer life such as the legal system,[4] transportation,[5] pioneer freemasons,[6] the term "hoosier,"[7] public health,[8] arts and handicrafts,[9] architecture,[10] building specific

---

[2] For the Patrick Henry instructions see above p. 64.

[3] *Ouiatanon, a Study in Indiana History* (1893); *Sieur de Vincennes, the Founder of Indiana's Oldest Town* (1897); *The Mission to the Ouabache* (1902); *Sieur de Vincennes Identified* (1919); *Life in Old Vincennes* (1929); *The Vincennes Donation Lands* (1949); *At the Headwaters of the Maumee. A History of the Forts of Fort Wayne* (1971).

[4] *The Laws and Courts of Northwest and Indiana Territories* (1886).

[5] *Internal Improvements in Early Indiana* (1912); *The National Road in Indiana* (1919); *Early Navigation of the St. Joseph River* (1925); *The Village at the End of the Road, A Chapter in Early Indiana Railroad History* (1938); *The Buffalo Trace* (1946).

[6] *A History of Early Indianapolis Masonry and of Center Lodge* (1895).

[7] *The Word "Hoosier"* (1907).

[8] *One Hundred Years in Public Health in Indiana* (1921).

[9] *The Search for Henry Cross* [early tombstone carver] (1966); *Portraits and Painters of the Governors of Indiana, 1800-1943* (1944); *Indiana Coverlets and Coverlet Weavers* (1928); *Furniture Makers of Indiana, 1793 to 1850* (1972).

[10] *Early Architects and Builders of Indiana* (1935); *Harmonist Construction* (1964).

communities,[11] the social and ethnic backgrounds of the pioneers,[12] and folkways.[13]

But there were some standard political histories: *The Acquisition of Louisiana* (1887), *William Henry Harrison's Administration of Indiana Territory* (1907), and *The Northern Boundary of
Indiana* (1928). A few monographs deal with the Civil War[14]
and with the histories of specific institutions.[15] *The Circle, "The
Center of Our Universe"* (1957) and *English's Opera House*
(1960) describe the history of famous landmarks.

In keeping with the objective of preserving the material for
the history of early Indiana, the Society also published more
than a dozen each of reminiscences and biographical studies in
the *Publications* series. Among the reminiscences some of the
more outstanding were Nathaniel Bolton on early Indianapolis
(1853); Robert Duncan on central Indiana in the 1820s and
1830s (written 1879, published by the Society in 1894); George
W. Sloan on his fifty years in pharmacy (written 1898, published
1903); John H. Holliday on early Indianapolis and the Civil War
(1911); Joseph T. Elliott on the explosion of the steamboat
Sultana in April, 1865, carrying the Union survivors of the Con-
federate prison camps at Andersonville and Cahaba and killing

---

[11] *Making a Capital in the Wilderness* (1908); *An Indiana Village—New
Harmony* (1914); *Pioneer Sketches of the Upper Whitewater Valley, Quaker
Stronghold of the West* (1945).

[12] *Some Elements of Indiana's Population; of Roads West and Their Early
Travelers* (1900); *Planting Corn Belt Culture: The Impress of the Upland
Southerner and Yankee in the Old Northwest* (1953).

[13] Leah Jackson Wolford's *The Play-Party in Indiana* (1959).

[14] *Lincoln's Body Guard, the Union Light Guard of Ohio, with Some Personal
Recollections of Abraham Lincoln* (1911); *Morgan's Raid in Indiana* (1919);
Washington County Giants (1921); *Evansville's Channels of Trade and the
Secession Movement, 1850-1865* (1928); *Camp Morton, Indianapolis, 1861-
1865, Indianapolis Prison Camp* (1940).

[15] *The Scotch-Irish Presbyterians in Monroe County, Indiana* (1910); *Centennial Handbook, Indiana Historical Society, 1830-1930* (1930); *Our Pioneer
Historical Societies* (1931); *A History of Spiceland Academy, 1826 to 1921*
(1934).

approximately 1,900 people (1913); William Watson Woollen on the early Marion County bar (1919); Harrison Burns on his childhood in Jefferson and Jennings counties, his youth working on steamboats and at odd jobs along the Ohio River, his career as a lawyer, and his adventures in the Montana gold fields (1975). Perhaps the most successful of the reminiscences is *A Home in the Woods: Oliver Johnson's Reminiscences of Early Marion County*, originally published by the Society in 1951, reprinted in 1971, and published by the Indiana University Press in a new edition in 1976.

The Society's biographical studies cover a wide variety of persons. They include reformer and antislavery pioneer Lucius B. Swift; jurists Joseph G. Marshall and James Lockhart; political figures John Law and Jesse D. Bright; an Indian family, the Pokagans; Civil War General Robert S. Foster; and a flock of pioneers, of whom the Conner family of Noblesville are perhaps the most striking. There is also an interesting study of Abraham Lincoln's career as a lawyer, written by the Society's president, Charles W. Moores, and originally delivered to the American Bar Association in 1910.

These early publications were issued first in pamphlet form. They were often printed on inferior paper and always were bound in an austere grey wrapper. After there were a sufficient number of pamphlets to make a 500-page volume, they were bound in dark blue cloth. Then the title Indiana Historical Society Publications was stamped in gold on the cover. Since the Society never attempted to do more than "break even" on the cost of printing them, the *Publications* have always been a bargain. There are now twenty-five full volumes of *Publications*, and they retain their usefulness to researchers although they lack a cumulative index.

Before 1940 the overwhelming majority of the *Publications* were authored by amateur historians who were members of the

Society. After 1940 the Society tended more to use its own professionally trained staff and submissions from professional historians, even if they were not Society members.

In addition to the *Publications* series, the Society began in the 1930s to publish a series of pamphlets on prehistory. There are now five volumes in the *Prehistory Research Series*. The first volume presented research on Indiana languages, including five numbers on Jacob Piatt Dunn's work on the Miami language. Most of the succeeding volumes are archaeological studies, many directly related to sites in Indiana.[16]

In 1937 the Society published *Prehistoric Antiquities of Indiana*, a volume that was and remains an impressively beautiful and ambitious work. It was made possible by a large donation to the Society from its author, Eli Lilly. As an object, an example of graphic design and the printer's art, the volume has become so valuable that its usefulness as text has been largely overshadowed. There were only about a thousand copies printed for distribution to the Society's members, and thus it has also become a rare book.

It was a boon for those members who received the volume free, as a membership premium, and whose possession now commands $50 to $75 in the open market. Lilly's book deserved wider circulation than it has attained, for it is generally considered the best introduction to Indiana prehistory. It was enthusiastically reviewed, and the experience encouraged Lilly and his brother J. K. Lilly, Jr., to subsidize other special publications for the Society.[17]

In May, 1938, J. K. Lilly, Jr., an astute book collector, wrote to Christopher Coleman, inquiring whether there was available

---

[16] For a complete list of *Prehistory Research Series* titles see below, pp. 348-50. Most are out of print.

[17] See "Prehistoric Antiquities" folder, IHS Papers.

"a listing of all writers born in Indiana." If not, he wanted one drawn up, at his expense. From this modest inquiry resulted a project that lasted more than a decade and produced four award-winning bibliographies.[18]

By February, 1939, J.K. Lilly, Jr., had planned the project sufficiently to present it to the Society's executive committee: the Lilly Endowment would grant not less than $6,000 per year for five years to the Society for bibliographical studies of Indiana authors. The Society accepted eagerly and, as usual, appointed a committee to oversee the project: J.K. Lilly, Jr., Benjamin D. Hitz, Coleman, and Albert Rabb. At Lilly's suggestion the bibliographers were to be Indianapolis rare book dealers Anthony J. Russo and his wife Dorothy Ritter Russo. The Russos began on March 1, 1939, working in the Smith Library on a "noiseless" typewriter. The committee wrestled with the problem of how to define the project—how to define an "Indiana author"—for several months, but by May Lilly had hit upon the strategy that would be followed. Coleman noted after a meeting at the Smith Library in May,

> J. K. Lilly . . . stated he had about concluded that the best procedure . . . would be to concentrate on a complete, and as nearly as possible perfect, bibliography of James Whitcomb Riley, with a view to publication, and to collect information about all books of authors who had any connection of consequence with Indiana, i.e., were born here or lived here any length of time.[19]

The Riley project was hampered by the sudden, unexpected death of Anthony Russo in June, 1940, and the committee

---

[18] J. K. Lilly, Jr., to Christopher B. Coleman, May 2, 1938, "Indiana Authors, Bibliography of" folder, IHS Papers.

[19] Coleman to J. K. Lilly, Jr., February 24, 1939; Coleman to Benjamin D. Hitz, February 27, 1939; Coleman note on Bibliography Committee meeting in Smith Library, May 23, 1939, in "Indiana Authors, Bibliography of" folder, IHS Papers.

searched for some time for a replacement. Jacob Blanck (1906-1974) of the Library of Congress, an expert in American first editions, oversaw the final preparation of the Riley manuscript throughout 1943. The bibliography was greatly aided by the availability of J. K. Lilly's superb collection of Rileyana. As Dorothy Russo wrote of Lilly in the preface to the Riley volume in 1944, "the fullest credit belongs to him."[20]

Dorothy Russo continued on the bibliographies, compiling *A Bibliography of George Ade* in 1947. With Thelma Lois Sullivan she also turned out the Booth Tarkington bibliography in 1949 and the volume on Crawfordsville writers in 1952.[21]

The original five-year project lengthened to nearly fourteen years and cost more than $120,000. The resulting four extremely handsome volumes were well received by reviewers. Designed by the Lakeside Press, two of the books—the Riley and the Crawfordsville authors bibliographies—won typographical awards in national competitions. The project ended when Dorothy Russo retired in 1952. The volumes remain useful to libraries and to collectors of rare books.[22]

---

[20] "Anthony J. Russo," undated mss. in "Indiana Authors, Bibliography of" folder, IHS Papers; *A B Bookman's Yearbook, 1975*, s.v. "Blanck, Jacob Nathaniel"; Anthony J. Russo and Dorothy R. Russo, *Bibliography of James Whitcomb Riley* (Indianapolis: Indiana Historical Society, 1944), p. xviii.

[21] The committee was undecided for a while about what to do after the Tarkington work. In a letter to the committee Lilly teased fellow member Benjamin Hitz (who very much disliked Theodore Dreiser):

> Still another idea is to do a thorough piece of work on Theodore Dreiser. I am sure my colleague Mr. Benjamin Hitz would feel this would be a grand undertaking and we might even include brother Paul in the book and give it some such title as "Sons of _____ of Terre Haute."

J. K. Lilly, Jr., to Committee Members, September 21, 1948, "Indiana Authors, Bibliography of" folder, IHS Papers.

[22] Howard H. Peckham to Harold English, Society of Typographic Arts, April 6, 1945; Certificate, Chicago Book Clinic, award for *Seven Authors of Crawfordsville*, March 15, 1953; Certificate 1953, Society of Typographic Arts, all in IHS Papers.

J. K. Lilly, Jr.'s idea of a single book listing outstanding Indiana authors was not realized. After wrestling unsuccessfully with definitions of Indiana authors for several years, he concluded in 1943, in a rueful letter to Coleman that, "there are not enough Indiana authors who are worth while, to wad a 16 gauge shotgun with and, that being the case, the project of a volume of leading Indiana authors probably should be abandoned. . . ." A more general list of *Indiana Authors and Their Books 1816-1916* was published by Wabash College in 1949, under the editorial direction of Lilly, Peckham, Hitz, and Richard E. Banta, hence the original project Lilly had in mind was completed by someone other than the Society's bibliographers.[23]

Along with the beautiful bibliographies published at the instigation of J. K. Lilly, Jr., the Society also published several more volumes in this period sponsored by Eli Lilly or the Lilly Endowment. They were *The Journals and Indian Paintings of George Winter* (1948), *The Old Northwest: Pioneer Period, 1815-1840* (1950), and *Walam Olum or Red Score: The Migration Legend of the Lenni Lenape or Delaware Indians* (1954).

The Winter volume was a collaborative effort. Winter's descendant Cable G. Ball of Lafayette and the Tippecanoe County Historical Association authorized the Society's use of the original drawings, paintings, and journals made by the artist as he observed Potawatomi and Miami Indians in northern Indiana. Art historian Wilbur D. Peat evaluated the paintings as art; Howard Peckham placed Winter in his American context; and Gayle Thornbrough wrote a biographical sketch, based primarily on careful use of Winter's own writings. Lakeside Press again produced a lavish book, with unusually fine reproductions of

---

[23] J. K. Lilly, Jr., to Coleman, December 7, 1943, "Indiana Authors, Riley Bibliography" folder, IHS Papers. A follow-up volume, *Indiana Authors and Their Books 1917-1966*, was compiled by Donald E. Thompson and published by Wabash College in 1974.

watercolor paintings. Like the other special publications it was distributed free to members who indicated they wanted one.[24]

This lovely volume was followed in 1950 by another Lilly-sponsored publication, the most famous of the Society's publications. R. Carlyle Buley (1893-1968) was an Indiana author by every estimate. Born in Georgetown, Indiana, educated at Indiana University, he spent forty years (1925-1964) teaching American history at Indiana University. Only the few years he spent earning a doctorate and teaching in Madison at the University of Wisconsin, a brief period teaching high school in Illinois, and a stint in the army in World War I, took him away from the state. In 1949 the Lilly Endowment agreed to fund the Society's publication of Buley's magnum opus, *The Old Northwest: Pioneer Period, 1815-1840*. He had worked on the book for twenty years. "Publication of my manuscript," he reported to Peckham, "long since ceased to be a question of financial remuneration or even academic prestige; it had become a question of preserving my morale. . . ." He had tried to find a publisher for five years, and none had been willing to take on his massive manuscript.[25]

The Society undertook the project to celebrate the territorial sesquicentennial in 1950. Buley watched over his lifework in every stage of publication, involving himself so deeply in planning the typography and graphic design as to provoke sometimes the exasperation of his editors. However, at the end of the project, just as the author and editors were recovering from their ordeal, the Pulitzer Award Committee gave the prize for

---

[24] Some of the beautiful color prints of the Winter paintings were reproduced in *American Heritage*, II (1950), 34-39.

[25] *Indiana History Bulletin*, XXVI (1949), 11-12; R. C. Buley to Peckham, April 20, 1949, in "Buley's Old Northwest" folder, Publication files, IHS Papers. For Buley see "Memorial Tribute to R. Carlyle Buley," in *Indiana Magazine of History*, LXIV (1968), 323-26.

1951 to their efforts. It was the first and until now (1980) the only Pulitzer prize ever awarded to a book published by an historical society.[26]

Walam Olum was a collaborative effort. Many scholars joined together to unravel the puzzle of a copy made by Constantine Rafinesque in 1833 of Indian pictographs recording the migration legend of the Delawares. Linguistic, archaeological, ethnological, historical, physical, anthropological, and speculative implications were explored in the Society's *Walam Olum*, which accepted the pictographs as authentic clues to Delaware history. The resulting volume was both beautifully crafted and intriguing, and it was generally well received by scholars.[27]

By the 1950s the Society had established a tradition of publishing books that were both beautiful and useful. The tradition reflected not only the resources and values of the Lilly brothers, but also the taste and expertise of officers like Lee Burns, Benjamin Hitz, and Howard Peckham, some of whom were themselves book collectors. The tradition continues, though the economics of printing discourages the level of lavishness represented by some of the early books. But the beautiful published edition of the Calvin Fletcher diary is clearly representative of the tradition as have been the recent book on steamboat building, *Indiana Houses of the Nineteenth Century*, the T. C. Steele biography, and even the softbound *Chronicle of the Overbeck Pottery*, to mention only a few.

---

[26] Correspondence in "Buley's Old Northwest" folder, Publications files, IHS Papers. The Society had been rather cautious in printing the book—only 2,919 copies were published, and these were sold fairly quickly by Society standards. Graciously the executive committee turned over the plates to Buley to arrange as he would for reprinting with a publisher who could offer him royalties. The book was reprinted by Indiana University Press in 1951 and is now, unfortunately, again out of print. Minutes of IHS, December 8, 1950, June 8, 1951.

[27] See also below, pp. 288-89.

Glenn Black's *Angel Site*, always described as monumental because there is nothing else to call it (1967, two volumes), was the most recent of the very large, elegant books published by the Society. Its publication was a work reflecting the Society's deep affection for Black, who died in September, 1964, having completed most of the manuscript of the report on his twenty-odd years work with the Angel site in southwestern Indiana. His student and successor, Dr. James H. Kellar, prepared the few sections Black had not completed, and Gayle Thornbrough undertook the extremely complex task of pulling the work together. The project was endangered in the fall of 1966 by the theft of 420 illustrative photographs, keyed to the dummy; they were stolen from the automobile trunk of the Lakeside Press representative. Replacing the pictures and figuring out where they belonged in the book was an enormous task. But as Thornbrough wrote at the time, it could have been worse. Black's drawings had not been lost: "If the drawings had been taken, I think we would have [had] to call the whole thing off." The book was published in 1967 and met with unambiguous acclaim. *Ethnohistory* called it "a landmark in New World archaeology"; the *Journal of American History* described it as "monumental"; and *Archaeology* paid tribute to "the consummate archaeological craftsmanship and warm personality of its author."[28]

The Society's largest publishing project began in 1968, when Gayle Thornbrough rejoined the Society staff as Director of Publications and the Library. The subject of publishing the Calvin Fletcher diary first came up in 1923, when Laura Fletcher Hodges's will was made public, with its proviso that her estate should publish her grandfather's work. Fletcher, an Indianapolis

---

[28] Gayle Thornbrough to Peckham, October 17, 1966, "Angel Site Correspondence" folder, Publications files, IHS Papers; *Ethnohistory*, XVIII (1972), 81; *Journal of American History*, LV (1968), 375-76; *Archaeology*, XXIII (1970), 265.

city father of broad interests, high intelligence, and astonishing
energy, kept a detailed diary during most of the years from 1817
to 1866. In it Fletcher reported on everything that interested
him—from the state of his own soul to that of his wide business
interests, from politics to charity, from his children to his old
friends, from the latest issue of the *Atlantic Monthly* to the latest visiting lecturer. Fletcher knew everyone and had an opinion
about everything. He was an important man in Indiana, and his
diary was immediately recognized as an important historical
document.

The redoubtable Lucy Elliott, then assistant secretary and
treasurer of the Society, wrote to Dr. Fletcher Hodges, the
executor of the estate, offering to publish the Calvin Fletcher
diary "free of cost." Hodges does not appear to have responded
to the offer, which was just as well. At the time Elliott made the
proposal the Society could not have afforded to publish even one
of the thirteen manuscript volumes. However, Hodges did deposit the diaries with the State Library with the understanding
that a librarian would transcribe the diary whenever there was
time available from other chores. In 1925 the executive committee discussed publishing the diaries and referred the matter to
a committee. Coleman raised the question again in 1931, and
the committee sought a legal opinion about whether Delavan
Smith money could be used to publish the diaries. Meanwhile, in
1931 and 1932 the Society paid $1,892.95 for the preparation
of a typed copy of the diary, which elicited a demand from Dr.
Hodges that the Society disclaim any right to the title of the papers. The matter then lay dormant for almost a decade, reflecting perhaps the unpromising economic picture in the larger
community. But the Society again took up its cudgels to secure
publication of the diary in 1940. For the next decade the Society
attempted to get the Hodges estate to publish the diary, at first
through persuasion and later resorting to legal action. This

phase of the diary's publication history ended in 1949, when the Indiana Supreme Court ruled in favor of the Hodges's estate's claim that Laura Hodges's will directing the publication of the diaries did not constitute a public, charitable trust.[29]

At this point the Society had custody of the diaries but did not own them. When the 1968 Lilly gift enabled the Society to undertake, among other things, the publication of the Calvin Fletcher diary, among the Society's first acts was to acquire legal title to the diary from the Hodges's estate heirs. Once secured the Society proceeded with the work of editing the long-awaited diary. Gayle Thornbrough reported to the board in 1968 that the project would require ten volumes of approximately 600 pages each. This was, of course, an unusual undertaking. There are few ten-volume diaries published, fewer still whose authors are private citizens in midwestern cities.[30]

To a great extent Fletcher's diary chronicled the history of Indianapolis and of Indiana. His references were most often to persons known locally, and the editors of his diary attempted to identify everyone Fletcher mentioned and to amplify every cryptic comment he made. The annotated diary is, therefore, the single richest source for Indianapolis and Indiana history for the period from 1821 to 1866. In addition, the diary is a powerful contribution to an understanding of the psychohistory of the early nineteenth-century Midwest, for Calvin Fletcher was an introspective, highly expressive "self-made" man. He was the nineteenth-century hero par excellance: virtuous, rich, indus-

---

[29] L. M. Elliott to Fletcher Hodges, October 22, November 13, 1923, "Marion" folder, Box 7, Records of the Indiana Historical Commission; Minutes of IHS, April 24, 1925, March 3, 1931, May 19, 1932, March 28, December 13, 1940, December 11, 1943, June 8, 1944, June 8, 1945, December 16, 1947; *Indiana Supreme Court Decisions*, May Term, 1949, pp. 571-98 (June 8, 1949); see also "Fletcher Lawsuit" folder, IHS Papers; IHS Library Committee Minutes, June 17, 1940, October 12, 1943.

[30] IHS Board of Trustees Minutes, December 11, 1968.

trious, patriarchal. Rarely in American letters has an essentially unschooled writer found so much to say, so vividly and compellingly.

Editing this massive work has been a demanding undertaking. Thornbrough began it, designing a basic approach that has been followed throughout the work by her coeditors Dorothy Riker and Paula Corpuz. They have worked their way meticulously through all relevant local sources and sought out remote sources in extensive correspondence. Critics have found the editing consistently awe-inspiring in its thoroughness.[31]

The standard of editing throughout the Society's publications has been good, but the level achieved by its professional editors has been very high indeed. Christopher Coleman brought Nellie Armstrong with him to the Bureau and the Society when he came in 1924. Armstrong, born in Pardee, Kansas, was educated at Knox College and the University of Illinois (M.A. 1919). She learned historical editing under Theodore Pease of the Illinois Historical Collections in the early 1920s. She worked for the Society as an intrinsic part of her Bureau responsibilities, editing Society publications like *Lucius B. Swift*; *New Harmony, An Adventure in Happiness: Papers of Thomas and Sarah Pears*; *The Schramm Letters*; *Indiana Imprints, 1804-1849*; *Sons of the Wilderness: John and William Conner*; and *Camp Morton, 1861-1865*. Armstrong, a small, handsome woman with style and dignity, was a respected colleague of Coleman's, and her voice was also heard in determining what the Society would publish, along with the voices of the various Publications Committee members.[32]

Armstrong in turn trained Dorothy L. Riker, who came to

---

[31] See for example *Journal of American History*, LXIII (1976), 415, LXI (1975), 1100; *The Old Northwest*, I (1975), 204; *Indiana Magazine of History*, LXX (1974), 180.

[32] *Indiana History Bulletin*, XXIV (1947), 131; Knox College Archives; interview with Dorothy L. Riker. In 1942 Armstrong married Paul H. Robertson.

the Bureau in 1929 and, like her mentor, worked to prepare Society publications as a normal part of her job. Riker, a native of Elwood, Indiana, took a B.A. at Indiana University in 1926, and, after a brief period teaching history and government at Frankton High School, returned to the university for an M.A., which she received in 1928. Recognized immediately as "a find" by Coleman, Riker stayed with the Bureau until 1971, serving as editor of the *Collections* after Armstrong left in 1947. In 1971 she retired from the Bureau and came to work directly for the Society to help with the Fletcher diary, and she continued that work throughout the decade, finally retiring at the end of 1979, her fiftieth year as an Indiana historian.[33]

Professionally, Riker's career is represented by several inches of entry cards in the file of any major library, most identifying books she wrote or edited for the Bureau. Except for the publication she prepared on Jonathan Jennings's previously uncollected letters (1931) and *The Diary of Calvin Fletcher*, for which she was coeditor on volumes II through VII, Riker's work for the Society was mostly invisible. That is, she checked footnotes, proofread, polished prose, and prepared indexes for Society publications. Her career in Indiana history is a larger story than that of her work for the Society, but the same dedication to the truth, apparently endless energy, and imaginative strategies to seek out elusive facts characterize her work for the Society as characterized the rest of her life in history.

Gayle Thornbrough was the first full-time Indiana Historical Society employee. She came to the Society in 1937, immediately after her graduation from Butler University. Born in Hendricks County, Thornbrough grew up in Indianapolis in a history-oriented home, was secretary of the junior history club at Short-

---

[33] *Directory of American Scholars*, 7th edition, Volume I, s.v. "Riker, Dorothy Lois"; Christopher B. Coleman to Charles N. Thompson, October 18, 1930, "Library and Historical Department" folder, Box 5, Records of the Indiana Historical Bureau.

Mrs. H. W. Rhodehamel

Indiana Magazine of History

opposite, above, J. K. Lilly, Jr., sponsored the Society's bibliographies of
Indiana authors and was a longtime
library committee member; Dorothy
Ritter Russo, Society bibliographer;
below, Both Benjamin D. Hitz (left)
and W.J. Holliday (right) were book
collectors and dedicated members of
the library committee.

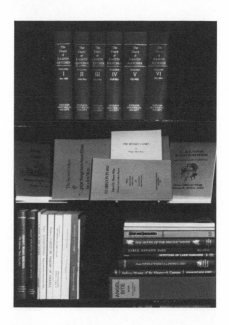

above, R.C. Buley, author of Pulitzer
prize winning *The Old Northwest,*
published by the Society in 1950;
right, an assortment of Society publications

Society Library

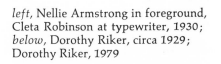

left, Nellie Armstrong in foreground,
Cleta Robinson at typewriter, 1930;
below, Dorothy Riker, circa 1929;
Dorothy Riker, 1979

Richard Simons Indianapolis *Star*

above, Hubert H. Hawkins, Society secretary, and Gayle Thornbrough, Society editor, in 1954; *right,* Gayle Thornbrough, Society president John Rauch, and the Claude Bowers diary, 1964

left, Caroline Dunn, Society librarian, 1939 to 1973; *below*, quarters of the William Henry Smith Memorial Library of the Indiana Historical Society from 1934 to 1976, reading room and library cases

opposite, Society library since 1976; *above*, reading room, and a section of the stacks showing compact shelving, *below*

Indianapolis *Star*

Indiana State Library

ridge High School, and studied history at Butler. A person with wide cultural and intellectual interests, Thornbrough was hired to edit the new and highly technical *Prehistory Research Series*, as well as to help with the Society's other special publications and the regular *Publications*. She took most of a year off in 1941-1942 to take a master's degree at the University of Michigan, where faculty members encouraged her to stay and complete a Ph.D. in history. Coleman advised her against it unless she wanted to give up historical editing for college teaching. She chose research and editing.[34]

In 1947, after Nellie Armstrong left, Thornbrough joined the Bureau staff and became jointly Bureau-Society editor, the only person to hold such an appointment. As mentioned, she left the Society and the Bureau at the end of 1966 to accept an appointment with the Library of Congress in recognition of her reputation as a documents editor. When Thornbrough returned in the summer of 1968, she was given major administrative responsibility for both the library and the publications program, and in 1976 she became, in addition, executive secretary, the chief administrative officer of the Society.

Despite the significant enlargement of her responsibilities, Thornbrough has not abandoned editing. The Fletcher diary project has remained under her close supervision, though she has had to assign to others much of the legwork she would previously have undertaken herself. In addition, she was primarily responsible for overseeing Volume I of the Harmony Society documents, the beautiful Overbeck Pottery book, and the *Publications* on Harrison Burns and the Robert Dale Owen

---

[34] *Indiana History Bulletin*, IX (1932), 420; Gayle Thornbrough to Christopher B. Coleman, [March, 1942], Coleman to Thornbrough, March 7, 1942, in "Out-of-State 1940-42" folder, IHS Papers.

Her sister Emma Lou Thornbrough chose teaching and has enjoyed an outstanding academic career at Butler University.

travel diary, to mention only a few projects from the years after she received heavy administrative assignments.

Thornbrough and Riker have also undertaken to train younger editors. Paula Corpuz, an Indianapolis native and St. Agnes High School graduate, came to the Society as an editorial assistant in 1970, soon after graduation from Marian College. Corpuz completed a master's degree in history at Butler in 1978 and has served as editor since 1977. A skilled copy editor and researcher, Corpuz has lent a hand for nearly every editorial project undertaken since she came in 1970, but her major work has been the Fletcher diary. In 1975 the Society hired Lana Ruegamer as part-time editor. Ruegamer, a doctoral candidate in history at Indiana University, had served as editorial assistant on the *Journal of American History* (1973-1975). She was assigned primary responsibility for Volume II of the Harmony Society documentary history and subsequently worked on the Elwood Haynes biography, the *Portraits and Painters of the Governors of Indiana 1800-1978*, the Society lectures and American Revolution Bicentennial Symposia, among others. Lisa Nowak joined the staff as editorial assistant in 1977 after receiving a B.A. in 1976 and acquiring an M.A. in English in 1977 from Butler University. Nowak worked on the massive index for Volume II of the Harmony Society documents and has had heavy research responsibilities for the present volume, among other assignments.

The Society's genealogical publications, edited by members of the Family History and Genealogy Section, most often by the longtime chairman Willard Heiss, have likewise established a tradition of excellence. From the seven volumes of Quaker records to the periodicals *Hoosier Genealogist* and *Genealogy*, the publications of the Society's genealogists have won wide acclaim.[35]

---

[35] For a full list of genealogical publications see below pp. 347-48.

The *Indiana Military History Journal* produced by the Society's Military History Committee and its editor, Professor Richard M. Clutter, publishes scholarly articles, book reviews, and annotated historical documents. The *Indiana Medical History Quarterly* is edited by Dr. Charles Bonsett, chairman of the Society's Medical History Committee, recently assisted by the Society's historian of medicine, Professor Ann Carmichael of Indiana University. The journal, which has formerly consisted primarily of memoirs, extracts from physicians' journals, and reprints from medical books of historical interest, is expanding its scope to include scholarly articles.

The Library

It has, of course, been many years since the Society's publications were required to "substitute" for more traditional collections of historical material. When the William Henry Smith Memorial Library opened its doors on February 1, 1934, the Indiana Historical Society owned approximately 6,000 volumes from the Delavan Smith bequest and 3,000 to 5,000 more volumes from the Marion County Library Association. However, by the time these collections had been sorted and the desired volumes were selected for the library, the actual size of the Society's collection was only about 3,000 books. Less than half of the Smith collection and a much smaller number of the Marion County books donated to the library turned out to be the type of books that the Society wished to collect.[36]

---

[36] IHS Library Committee Minutes, 1934-1936.

For information on the library the author is indebted to Eric Pumroy, Leona Alig, Thomas Rumer, and Caroline Dunn, in addition to sources mentioned.

What kind of a library, then, is the Society's collection? So far as books are concerned, the answer has been fairly closely defined since 1934: it is a library that specializes in the early history of Indiana and the Old Northwest. By definition, then, it is largely a collection of rare books, and the book collectors who have served on the Library Committee have usually sought to acquire especially fine first editions of relevant books. After Howard Peckham became involved in collecting for the library, the policy became even more explicit: the Society's library was "primarily to preserve and conserve, secondarily to use."[37]

Having defined its collecting policy narrowly, the Society succeeded to an admirable degree in acquiring the books that fitted the policy. William Henry Smith had already collected a significant part of the material the Society wished to own, and the Society was able to purchase much of the rest. The annual $10,000 gifts made to the library by J. K. Lilly, Jr., during the years Howard Peckham was secretary enabled the Society to acquire an impressive array of seventeenth- and eighteenth-century French, English, and American volumes that had hitherto remained beyond the Society's reach. The library thus contains nearly a complete collection of published source material on the early history of the Ohio Valley, the Old Northwest, and Indiana. It includes a fine collection of travel guides, travel journals, Jesuit relations, campaign diaries, and early Indiana imprints. These are supplemented by a fairly extensive collection of related maps and broadsides.[38]

The library's manuscript collection has never been so nar-

---

[37] IHS Library Committee Minutes, November 26, 1945.

[38] See the Society's published *Library Reports*, 1944 to 1953, for specific acquisitions in this period. See also the *Library Report* for 1968-1969, with a special review of acquisitions from 1954-1965 and subsequent reports in the IHS *Annual Report* since 1969.

rowly defined as its book library. This is partly due to the fact
that the library's "role" vis à vis the State Library in collecting
manuscripts was never so clearly spelled out as it was for books.
Perhaps no one ever imagined that the Society would collect
manuscripts extensively. In any event, the Smith Library included a rather diverse collection of documents in 1934 and has
not significantly narrowed its focus since then.

The Society acquired, of course, the William Henry Smith papers with the Delavan Smith bequest in 1922. This collection
reflects Smith's extensive concern with Republican party politics
and his close relationships with important politicians in the post-
Civil War period. It is a rich collection but does not fit any particular pattern of collecting associated with the Society, hence
it has not yet been used very much.

In 1932 the Society received part of the important William H.
English Collection. The former president of the Society had collected a large number of documents on the Old Northwest and
the territorial period, in addition to his own political correspondence. He left his collection to his son Will E. English in 1896,
with instructions to complete the planned history of Indiana
from his notes. Will E. did not accomplish this task himself, but
he gave a significant part of his father's collection to Willoughby
G. Walling, his nephew, with the request that Walling complete the work. Walling deposited the collection in the University of Chicago Library in 1924. In Will E. English's will, he
left all the remaining manuscripts in his father's collection to
Walling while the books were bequeathed to English's wife,
Helen Orr English. In 1928 Mrs. English promised to give the
Society the manuscripts that remained in her possession (despite
Walling's apparent right to them), but she died in 1932, having
married Frank Prince. Although her will directed Prince to give
the manuscripts to various historical societies, he attempted instead to sell them. After some negotiation, and with the con-

sent of Willoughby Walling, the Society purchased the English papers in November, 1932, for $1,000.[39]

The third major manuscript collection the Society acquired was the Arthur Mitten collection, purchased in 1939 for $9,000. Mitten, a railroad executive from Goodland, Indiana, had assembled an impressive, though diverse, collection of books and manuscripts. Among his chief interests were William Henry Harrison and the Old Northwest, autographs of the presidents of the United States and the signers of the Declaration of Independence, Indiana political figures, Andrew Jackson, Abraham Lincoln, and cabinet officers in the administrations of the latter two figures, among others.

Mitten's and English's manuscripts on Harrison and the Old Northwest contribute significantly to the Society's present collections classified under those names. Except for the core of documents on Harrison and on the Old Northwest acquired from English and Mitten, the Society's Harrison and Old Northwest collections have been assembled piece by piece over the past forty years. They now form important research collections composed of approximately 500 to 600 pieces each. Other Society collections from the colonial and territorial periods include the John Armstrong Papers (1755-1867, 5,000 pieces), Thomas Posey Papers (1776-1839, 87 pieces including a Revolutionary War journal), Francis Vigo Papers (1751-1841, 483 pieces), and a small collection of Anthony Wayne Papers.

For the early statehood period, i.e., pre-Civil War, the Society's major collections include the Calvin Fletcher Papers

---

[39] See "William H. English" folder, Library files, IHS Papers. The Society also purchased a duplicate of the original 1816 Indiana Constitution from Prince in 1933.

In 1956 the University of Chicago generously deposited English's collection of biographical material on Indiana legislators, 26 boxes of material, with the Society as an indefinite loan. The material is an outstanding source for state and local history and is used constantly.

(1817-1866, 2,000 pieces including diary 1817-1866), the Samuel Merrill Papers (1812-1908, 1,700 pieces), Elihu Stout Papers (1780-1902, 950 pieces), Samuel Vance Papers (1797-1868, 2,000 pieces), and a small New Harmony Collection, including 75 pieces of Owen family papers and 200 pieces from the Owen period. These collections are significant in their own rights, but when considered in conjunction with those of the Indiana Division of the State Library, which include the papers of the Noble and Ewing brothers and John Tipton, to mention only a few important collections, they are considerably amplified.

Important political figures represented in the Society's major collections for the period after 1850 are Conrad Baker, Noble C. Butler (a close associate of Walter Q. Gresham), Charles Warren Fairbanks, William H. English, Henry Smith Lane, the earlier mentioned William Henry Smith, and also his son Delavan Smith, the Meredith Nicholson-Carleton McCulloch correspondence, Stephen Marion Reynolds (a close friend of Eugene Debs and fellow Socialist), William R. Holloway and Oliver P. Morton in a jointly-named collection, and Lew Wallace. The William H. English collection of biographical material on Indiana legislators (1816-1896), on indefinite loan from the University of Chicago, is another rich source for Indiana political figures.

In addition to these traditional sources for political history the Society library contains important sources for midwestern social and economic history. There are, for example, large collections of family papers, like the John M. Judah family papers (1820-1936), the Worthington B. Williams family papers (1837-1866), the Hutchings-Koehler-Zulauf family papers (1790-1916), and dozens of smaller collections, casting light on the values, careers, and lifestyles of a wide variety of people at different times and places in Indiana.

Similarly, the Society's collection of diaries is a rich source, both for local history and for nineteenth-century social history.

Some of the outstanding diaries in the Smith Library include the aforementioned Calvin Fletcher diary (1817-1866), supplemented by family letters and the diary of his granddaughter Emily (1866-1872); the Lyle King diary, giving a vivid account of Madison, Indiana, 1842 to 1874; the August Schramm "day books," 1851 to 1908, giving a detailed factual account of daily farming in Hancock County (the diaries before 1857 are written in German, most in the old script, and seem to have been at first a writing exercise); and the Maria Graham Grant diary, describing her life in New Albany and Muncie, 1854 to 1921. The library contains approximately 150 manuscript diaries, covering the period from 1790 to 1920.

Account books from early businesses provide a wide variety of information, from prices and credit practices to products handled or manufactured and names and numbers of customers. The Smith Library contains hundreds of account books. Among others are the books of Nicholas McCarty, a pioneer Indianapolis merchant (35 books, 1824-1849); Attica pork packer James D. McDonald (7 volumes, 1836-1855); John Elder, pioneer Indianapolis architect and contractor (1830-1847); and Indianapolis realtor John S. Spann (14 volumes, 1865-1949). The Society also owns 43 account books for Indiana and Kentucky mills (1782-1920). Other important business records in the collections include papers from the Indianapolis Stockyards and from the Indianapolis Commercial Club, the latter the predecessor of the Chamber of Commerce.

Civil War diaries and letters show nineteenth-century men and women dealing with crises and hardships. Consequently, one learns from them not only the politics, strategy, and suffering of war but also something of the lives the war interrupted. The Civil War, among other things, provided occasions for persons never before separated from their loved ones to write about their daily lives. Men and women who had never before and would never again compose a letter wrote to their families and friends during the war. The Society began to collect Civil War manuscripts during the centennial of the war and now has extensive holdings, much of which is on microfilm, acquired through the Indiana Civil War Centennial Commission manuscript project.

In the past decade the Society has been the recipient of the records of several charitable organizations, resulting in an interesting social welfare collection. Included in the group are records of the following agencies: Indianapolis Free Kindergarten and Children's Aid Society (1851-1950); Widows and Orphans Friends Society/Indianapolis Orphans Asylum (1850-1923); Indianapolis Asylum for Friendless Colored Children (1871-1922), established by the Society of Friends; and the Family Service Association of Indianapolis (1879-1971).

The Society also holds scattered records of religious groups in Indiana. Its collection of Indiana Quaker records, by way of contrast, is nearly complete, including about fifty volumes of original records and more than a hundred reels of microfilm.

In the past few years the Society has inaugurated new collecting programs. The library seeks to collect documents reflecting the wide range of ethnic groups that have settled at various times in Indiana; records of architectural firms; and documents in Indiana black history. It is hoped that these areas will become strong parts of the library's collection.

The manuscript collections contain about 150,000 pieces. About one third of the collection is still unprocessed. For the past decade the library has been attempting to catch up with its collections after nearly forty years of having been understaffed, crowded, and short of funds.

The Smith Library staff from 1934 to 1961 usually consisted of one librarian, one or two clerk typists, and a volunteer worker. The duties of the librarian were to evaluate, sort, catalog, and conserve all of the materials that came to the library as a gift; to keep abreast of the market in rare books and manuscripts and, with the advice of the library committee, to bid for and purchase all appropriate material; to train and supervise the clerk typists and any volunteers; and last, but by no means least, to help scholars find and use the materials in the Society's collections.

None of the library assistants were professional librarians, though some extremely capable people performed much more than clerical chores. Richard C. Smith, for example, came to the library directly from high school in 1936 and remained until 1941, working with special effectiveness on the Society's collection of covered bridges and water-powered mills. A few years after leaving the library Smith went to college and graduate school and became a professor of philosophy. Martha Wilson Willis, who worked in the library from 1948 to 1950, responded adeptly to written queries and, though not a trained librarian, performed a wide variety of library tasks, as did Martha Norman, secretary for the library from 1956 to 1970 and Mary Studebaker, secretary from 1952 to 1971. Martha Schaaf was hired to calendar the Lew Wallace Papers on a part-time basis, and Gayle Thornbrough was occasionally loaned to the library for calendaring in the 1940s. Before 1962, however, when Leona Alig joined the staff, the Smith Library's budget provided for the employment of only one professional librarian.

The Society's first two librarians, therefore, were called upon to perform miracles, to work as though they were several persons, and they struggled heroically to create a fine library on a shoestring. Florence Venn (1883-1939) was the first librarian of the William Henry Smith Memorial Library. A native of Indianapolis, Venn was educated at Shortridge High School and Wellesley College, receiving her B.A. in 1905. After working for a few years in the reference division of the Indiana State

Library, Venn spent the summer of 1908 studying at the New York Library School in Albany. When she returned to the State Library in the fall she was named head of reference, a post she occupied until 1933. After twenty-nine years of service, Venn, a Republican, was simply fired by Paul McNutt one afternoon as part of the overall move to politicize the State Library. She packed up her desk and left. The State Library's loss was the Society's gain. Coleman and the library committee soon hired her to head the Smith Library.[40]

Venn's successor described her as "a charming, quiet person, very competent. . . ." Together with Christopher Coleman and the members of the library committee, Venn constructed the policies for the new library. She and Benjamin Hitz sorted out the Smith books that seemed more appropriate for the State Library collection and loaned them to the state. There were relatively few research queries in the early days of the library, and Venn was able to spend most of her time organizing the collections and cataloging them. Although the library committee originally was consulted on every purchase, this method became cumbersome and resulted in the Society's losing opportunities to purchase desirable material. Early in 1938 Venn and Coleman were authorized to use their own judgment on purchasing books and manuscripts "of moderate price."[41]

Venn's major acquisition for the library was the cream of the Arthur G. Mitten collection, the purchase of which she carefully negotiated for the Society. The purchase was an important one, and it can be credited to Venn's tact and good judgment. She died in August, 1939, after a brief illness, only fifty-six

---

[40] Indianapolis *News*, August 23, 1939; Indianapolis *Star*, May 30, June 1, 1933, January 24, 1934.

[41] Caroline Dunn interview, December 31, 1979; IHS Library Committee Minutes, February 9, 1938. Hitz and Venn turned over 555 books with the Smith bookplate to the State Library in May, 1934. *Ibid.*, June 5, 1934.

years old. The Indianapolis *News* praised her as "a true librarian
—not the keeper of a storehouse but the bearer of light."[42]

Her successor was twenty years younger than Venn but still
a highly qualified and experienced librarian. Moreover, as the
daughter of Jacob Piatt Dunn, Caroline Dunn brought to her
office both an historic association and a family tradition of outstanding service to the Indiana Historical Society. Between them
the two Dunns devoted seventy-two years to the Society. Caroline Dunn was educated at Butler University (B.A. 1923) and
the Columbia University School of Library Service (B.S. 1928).
Her library experience included four years with the Indianapolis
Public Library (1923-1927), eight years with the Connersville
Public Library (1928-1936), and three years as reference librarian in the Indiana Division of the State Library—one of only
two nonpatronage employees in the library in those years.[43]

The Society's library committee in offering her the Smith Library position stressed their hope that she would consider the
job "as at least relatively permanent." Coleman went on to say,

> We believe that the Historical Society library will be of constantly in-
> creasing importance and value and that its development may well be
> regarded as a worthy life work.

It may be said unequivocally that Dunn fulfilled the committee's
hopes. She served from 1939 to 1973 and was awarded an honorary doctorate from Indiana University in 1970 in recognition

---

[42] Indianapolis *News,* August 23, 1939.

[43] Caroline Dunn's story of being hired in those times of political pressure is a
fascinating one. She was taken by Esther McNitt, the head of the Indiana Division, in a taxicab to the home of Christopher Coleman, then acting head of
the State Library. She was interviewed, offered the job, and promised that she
would not have to contribute to the two percent club, all without setting foot
in the library. Much later she discovered that the leader of the Fayette County
Democrats had been asked to write a letter supporting her appointment.

of her tireless efforts in "extending resources of this reference library to a large and varied clientele. . . ." She was a fine researcher and conscientiously responded at length to a constant stream of queries from scholars all over the country. She was also diligent in acquiring new materials for the library.[44]

The pressure of correspondence and handling new materials prevented Dunn from maintaining the catalog, and the library committee attempted from time to time to find funds for an assistant to help with cataloging. The J. K. Lilly, Jr., annual gifts of $10,000 to the library for acquisitions from 1946 to 1954 enabled the Delavan Smith Fund to accumulate, generating a greater income. Even so, the salary the Society was able to offer for many years for a cataloger simply was not adequate to attract a qualified person.[45]

The Society was fortunate in attracting the services of a volunteer, Ralph Henderson, in 1953, who stayed for more than a decade, calendaring manuscripts, attracting members and donations, and making himself generally useful.[46]

In 1967 the Society received a two-year grant of $35,000 from the Lilly Endowment to collect manuscripts, and former state superintendent of public instruction William E. Wilson was engaged as the Society's agent. Wilson acquired a wide range of local materials, much of it loaned to the Society for copying. This was the Society's first effort to seek out historical documents through an agent working in the field. With its new resources the Society again in 1980 has fielded an agent to look for documents that would be appropriate acquisitions for the

---

[44] Coleman to Caroline Dunn, September 22, 1939, "Smith Library 1936-1945" folder, IHS Papers; IHS *Annual Report, 1972-1973*, p. 22.

[45] See IHS Library Committee Minutes, November 30, 1944, May 11, 1945, October 19, 1950; Benjamin Hitz to Eli Lilly, May 18, 1945, "Smith Library 1936-1945" folder, IHS Papers.

[46] Caroline Dunn interview, December 31, 1979; IHS *Library Report 1953*.

Society. James Leachman, newly appointed field librarian, will also work closely with local libraries to assist them in developing their local history collections.[47]

After the Lilly gift of 1968 the Society was finally able to begin a significant expansion of library staff. Caroline Dunn, nearing retirement, relinquished administrative responsibility for the expanding library staff to the new Director of Publications and the Library. By the end of 1969 the staff had been expanded to four professional librarians, two full-time and one part-time clerical workers, and the task of processing and cataloging the Society's collections of books, pamphlets, and manuscripts was undertaken in earnest. Leona Alig worked with the manuscripts from 1962 to 1978 and still contributes on a part-time basis. Ruth Dorrel made great inroads on the backlog of uncataloged books from 1969 to 1971; she was succeeded by Edna Miller, former librarian of Indiana Central College, who retired in 1978, having eliminated the backlog. IdaMae Good Miller joined the staff in February, 1973, to catalog the Society's collection of some 10,000 pamphlets and continues in that work. In 1977 Jeffery Gunderson was appointed reference librarian and Pamela Najar conservator. In 1978 Eric Pumroy was appointed manuscript librarian with the responsibility of preparing a guide to the Society's manuscript collection.[48]

Thomas A. Rumer, a native of Hardin County, Ohio, and graduate of Ball State University (B.A. 1966, M.A. 1971), and Indiana University Library School (1973), was hired as reference librarian in 1973. In addition to his reference duties, Rumer represented the Society in the Midwest Map Cataloging Project funded by the National Endowment for the Humanities in 1975-

---

[47] IHS Board of Trustees Minutes, May 3, 1967; IHS *Newsletter*, December, 1979.

[48] IHS Board of Trustees Minutes, November 7, 1969. A full listing of the library staff, with periods of service, appears in an appendix below.

1976 in searching out pre-1900 printed maps of Indiana. A graceful spokesman for the library, Rumer was named librarian in January, 1979, the third person and first male to hold the office. He presently directs a staff of fourteen.

Through the years much of the library's effectiveness can be attributed to the work of the Society's library committee, members appointed because of special areas of interest and expertise to oversee the long-term interests of the library. They served generously and intelligently. Benjamin D. Hitz (1890-1949), for example, was chairman from 1934 when the library opened until his death in 1949. His son, Benjamin D. Hitz, Jr., served in the same office from 1955 to 1971. Alan T. Nolan, who served from 1964 to 1976, contributed valuable advice and legal assistance. To mention only a few of the distinguished collectors who have served on the committee, J. K. Lilly, Jr., and W. J. Holliday both served long terms: Lilly from 1936 to 1954; Holliday from 1945 to 1967. Committee members have worked to acquire manuscript and book collections, both by gift and by purchase; they have wrestled with thorny questions of how to spend the limited income the Smith fund generated and how to decide what parts of gifts to keep. The librarians did not always agree with their decisions, but their collective wisdom undoubtedly brought a larger perspective than any single officer could have supplied.[49]

Although most of the library's book collection has been acquired by purchase, the greatest part of its manuscripts collections has been acquired by gifts. It is important to realize and to acknowledge the dependence of this library in the past and in the future on the patronage of responsible donors. If it were not for their desire to preserve historic documents and their willingness to place family and business papers in an historical library, the Society's collections would be considerably diminished.

---

[49] A full list of library committee members appears below on p. 336.

Conclusion

For the first hundred years the Society fulfilled its mission to collect and preserve the materials for a history of the state through its *Publications* series (and, indirectly, through its support of the *Indiana Magazine of History* after 1907). Except for a small collection, never perhaps exceeding 2,000 books, the Society had no library. Indeed, for many years after its reorganization in 1886 the Society did not even seem to aspire to a library, for it spent much of its energies working instead to improve the State Library. Without the dramatic and unexpected bequest from Delavan Smith in 1922, there is reason to wonder whether the Society would ever have acquired a library. With the William Henry Smith Memorial Library, the Society was able to begin in 1934—rather late for this kind of collection—to assemble the unique library it holds today.

The Smith Library is an important research source for anyone working in the topics of the Old Northwest and Indiana. The library's usefulness is greatly enhanced by its apposition to the larger and more general collections of the State Library, especially the Indiana Division, the Newspaper Division, and the Genealogy Division, and the Archives Division of the Commission on Public Records.

The Smith Library, moreover, is to a great extent unexplored by researchers. The absence of a catalog for most of the manuscripts for many years may have discouraged scholars from attempting to use the collections, and likewise, the absence of regular reports to historical journals on the library's acquisitions has tended to keep the Society's collections something of a secret. The planned guide to the Society's manuscript collections will do much to introduce the scholarly community to the unique resources of the Smith Library. Taken together with its new collecting programs, these steps suggest a period of greatly expanded usefulness for the library's future.

It is through its unusual publications program that throughout most of its history the Society has primarily achieved its goal of collecting and preserving history. It has been a publishing society from the beginning, though as we have seen regular publications did not begin until 1886. Overall the scope, volume, and quality of the Society's publications bear comparison with those of any other historical society in the country.

VIII

Eli Lilly, Glenn Black, and Indiana Archaeology

Eli Lilly   Glenn A. Black

VIII

"[Eli Lilly is] the one person essentially responsible for what has been achieved in the field of prehistory through the Indiana Historical Society during the last three decades."
Glenn A. Black, 1960

"Indiana archaeology depends on you, as I see it."
Eli Lilly to Glenn Black, 1932

In 1930 the fledgling archaeological program of the Indiana Historical Society attracted the independent interest of two men who would, through the agency of the Society, make important contributions to New World archaeology. The men were Eli Lilly, a forty-five-year-old business executive with a keen mind and a romantic curiosity about the mysteries of Indian prehistory, and Glenn Black, a thirty-year-old "estimating engineer" for a manufacturing company and former salesman and bandleader. Neither man was university trained, yet both would be recognized and honored during the next three decades as founders of professional archaeology in Indiana.

An Indianapolis native, Glenn A. Black was born August 15, 1900, to Emma K. and John A. Black. His father, a clerk in a wholesale grocer's firm, died when Glenn was about twelve years old. Black attended public schools and was graduated from Arsenal Technical High School in 1916. For a while after high school Black played the drums and led the Sacramento Syncopators, a band that played engagements around the Great

Lakes. He had returned to Indianapolis by 1918 to help care for his mother and worked the next dozen years for various firms, starting off as a salesman and by 1926 establishing himself as a cost estimator for Fairbanks Morse, a company that manufactured industrial scales. His work required a regular schedule of travel around the state, and he found himself many evenings stranded in unfamiliar towns and cities.[1] The serious-minded Black quickly developed ways to spend his time profitably, foremost among which was reading in the local public library. With the help of these libraries he immersed himself in the literature of archaeology. Describing this period of his self-education as an archaeologist, Black wrote

> I have read and reread the works of Mills, Shetrone, Thruston, C. C. Jones, Moore, Fowke, Funkhouser and Webb, Squier and Davis, and Putnam on the works in the Mississippi Valley and Skinner, Heye and Hetherington on the eastern coastal Algonkian and Iroquois works. I have almost memorized the works of Moorehead on artifact classification. . . .[2]

By October, 1930, the young amateur had attracted the attention of the Indiana Historical Society's summer survey director, a University of Chicago graduate student in archaeology named Fred Eggan. Eggan urged Christopher Coleman to encourage Black to help locate sites and collections. Fairbanks Morse was already slowing down production in response to the

---

[1] Information on Glenn Black's parents derived from Indianapolis city directories, 1911-1917; Arsenal Technical High School Yearbook, 1916. Glenn Black's older brother James T. Black apparently helped to support the family as Glenn was growing up. James Kellar interview, January, 1980; Dorothy Riker interview, January 23, 1980; Cleta Robinson interview, January 23, 1980.

The best description of Glenn Black's personality and career is James H. Kellar, "Glenn A. Black, 1900-1964," in *American Antiquity*, XXXI (1966), 402-405.

[2] Glenn A. Black to Eli Lilly, September 24, 1931, Lilly Papers, Glenn A. Black Laboratory of Archaeology, Indiana University, Bloomington.

business depression, and Black was working only three days a week. With a significant block of free time at his disposal Black offered his services at no cost to the Society in a rather moving handwritten letter in November, 1930:

> I have often wanted to broach the question as to whether or not you would accept my services in the survey work if they were offered gratis. As you know I am always scouting around for my own pleasure and diversion and if I could I would like to put my time and efforts to some real worth while work. I feel sure that I am capable of doing survey work as it was carried on by Mr. Setzler and Mr. Eggan. I have a sufficiently large knowledge of geology for the purpose and I believe my knowledge of archaeology is as thorough as anybody's who has not specialized in the subject in a university. I have had a great deal of experience in photography and understand thoroughly the workings of the camera you use. It just seemed to me that the coming months when the weather is unsuited for field work would be ideal for recording collections and locating persons who would later be of value in the survey. Work of this sort would give me great pleasure and I feel sure would be of value to you if for no other reason than time saved later on. I have made an intensive study of all present and past writers on the subject both as to sites, mounds, earthworks, and artifacts. To thoroughly familiarize myself with artifacts I have made a pen and ink sketch book containing over two thousand sketches of almost every conceivable form, class, and shape of artifact. My services should they be acceptable, would cost you nothing above the expense of operating the camera. Please consider this seriously and let me know by return mail. . . .[3]

Meanwhile, in the summer of 1930, in the course of his annual vacation at Lake Wawasee, Eli Lilly took his daughter and his niece to visit an elderly neighbor who had a collection of Indian relics. The neighbor, J. P. Dolan (1849-1934) of Syracuse, was an inspired teacher and had been principal of the high school

---

[3] Fred Eggan to Christopher B. Coleman, October 2, 1930, "Archaeology—June 1930" folder, IHS Papers; Cleta Robinson interview, January 23, 1980; Black to Coleman, November 19, 1930, "Archaeology—June 1930" folder, IHS Papers.

for many years. The combination of Dolan and his collection was an irresistible one for Lilly.[4] He had been working very hard at his family business for nearly all his life; he would continue to do so for another forty-seven years. But in 1930 he discovered the avocation that would hold his interest and challenge his abilities for many years.

Lilly quickly sought out other collectors and began himself to collect Indian artifacts through Thomas A. Hendricks (1875-1955) of Indianapolis, a noted collector. He was also anxious to learn and visited the Ohio State Museum, an important research center, in the fall. By October a pleased Christopher Coleman was writing to Dr. Carl Guthe, director of the University of Michigan Museum of Anthropology and chairman of the National Research Council's committee on state archaeological surveys, "Eli Lilly . . . has become interested and may possibly finance an excavation next year. If there is any publication, or group of publications, which can be sent to him and which might develop his interest, will you please put him on the mailing list?" In November Lilly visited the Smithsonian Institution and impressed the assistant curator for archaeology, Frank Setzler (the Indiana Historical Society's former surveyor), who reported to Coleman,

> I think the [archaeology] committee will be very fortunate to have
> such a man working with it. He seemed earnestly interested in the
> work and willing to learn all there is to know. I hope he will become
> enrolled in the American Anthropological Association, which will
> bring him the information he desired.

---

[4] Eli Lilly, *Prehistoric Antiquities of Indiana* (Indianapolis: Indiana Historical Society, 1937), p. vi; James B. Griffin, "A Commentary on an Unusual Research Program in American Anthropology," in untitled dedication booklet for the Glenn A. Black Laboratory of Archaeology, April 21, 1971, Indiana University Publications.

With unconscious understatement Setzler added, "More men of his type will certainly boost archaeology in Indiana."[5]

Lilly joined a handful of Indiana Historical Society members in December, 1930, to pay for bringing Dr. Warren King Moorehead, the dean of North American archaeology, to speak to the Society. Moorehead and Lilly each immediately recognized in the other an important resource and struck up a friendship as well.[6]

Thus, while Glenn Black was establishing himself as a useful advance man for the Society's archaeological surveys, Lilly was preparing to become a patron of the Society's archaeological program. What the Indiana Historical Society had done to attract the services of these two men was to begin to undertake serious research in archaeology.

Archaeology was a rather new enterprise in North America in 1930. Although serious-minded students had been digging in Ohio Valley mounds since the early nineteenth century—Charles Alexandre Lesueur, for instance, had excavated in Posey County around 1826—there was no formal university program for training archaeologists in the Midwest until the late 1920s and early 1930s, when Fay-Cooper Cole established one at the University of Chicago. The proliferation of mounds and earthworks in neighboring Ohio had attracted early attention, and some of the earliest studies of prehistoric remains focused on these sites. But pioneer archaeologists like Frederick Ward Putnam, Cyrus Thomas, Gerard Fowke, Moorehead, Clifford Anderson, and a pair of Rockport teenagers—Clarence H. Kennedy

[5] Griffin, "A Commentary on an Unusual Research Program in American Anthropology," in Black Laboratory dedication booklet; Coleman to Carl Guthe, October 29, 1930, Frank Setzler to Coleman, November 23, 1930, "Archaeology—June 1930" folder, IHS Papers.

[6] Griffin, "A Commentary on an Unusual Research Program in American Anthropology," in Black Laboratory dedication booklet.

and Arthur C. Veatch—also explored various sites in Indiana between 1870 and the turn of the century and left records of their work. Even so, compared with those of Ohio, Indiana's archaeological monuments were little explored. The Ohio State Archaeological and Historical Society founded in 1885 had worked diligently to support exploration of Ohio's prehistory, and by 1930 the Ohio State Museum was an important national research center.[7]

For much of North America, however, the archaeological record was extremely spotty, and the Indiana record was skimpier than most. Hence when the National Research Council's (NRC) Division of Anthropology and Psychology appointed a committee on state archaeological surveys in 1920, one of its targeted survey areas was Indiana. After committee chairman Clark Wissler conferred in the spring with likely individuals and organizations to carry out the survey, the committee prepared a proposal for systematic county-by-county surveys, which Amos W. Butler then presented to the Indiana Academy of Science at its annual meeting in December, 1920. A few days later the same proposal was also presented to the second annual Indiana History Conference. In response, Society secretary Jacob Piatt Dunn, long concerned with Indian history, moved that the conference support the survey; he also urged that the project "should be undertaken by a trained person under the direction of the Conservation Commission" and that a committee be appointed to lobby for archaeological appropriations from the General Assembly.[8]

---

[7] Glenn A. Black, ". . . that what is past may not be forever lost. . . ," paper read at Annual Indiana History Conference, December 10, 1960, in *Indiana History Bulletin*, XXXVIII (1961), 52-61; James H. Kellar interview, January, 1980; Whitehill, *Independent Historical Societies*, p. 282.

[8] Harlow Lindley's introduction to E. Y. Guernsey, "Archaeological Survey of Lawrence County," extra number, *Indiana History Bulletin*, I (1924), 5; *Proceedings of the Indiana Academy of Science* (1920), pp. 79-81; *Proceedings of the Indiana History Conference, 1920*, pp. 21-24.

For the next several years the Indiana Historical Commission took the lead in the project to survey the state county by county. In co-operation with the geology division of the Conservation Department, the IHC printed special maps of each of the counties so that volunteer surveyors could identify archaeological sites on them and supplied printed questionnaires, which were prepared by Butler and John W. Oliver with the help of Clark Wissler. Unfortunately the project was hampered in several ways. First, there was no budget allotted to the survey. Then, too, the commission was also pushing for a simultaneous historical survey, and the combined task probably frightened away many would-be local volunteers. The state geologists were somewhat reluctant to help, citing as an explanation that curiosity seekers tended to follow them around and ruin the sites they located. Although the commission worked hard at the annual history conferences to drum up volunteers for the archaeological survey —in 1923, for instance, they brought in William C. Mills of the Ohio State Archaeological and Historical Society to give a pep talk on prehistory and display Ohio's archaeological atlas—, by the time Christopher Coleman took over in 1924 as IHC director and Society secretary this approach had clearly failed. The two "surveys" published by the Commission/Bureau as models—on Lawrence County (1924) and Parke County (1927)—were skimpy, incomplete, and amateurish.[9]

Coleman decided to encourage the better-qualified amateurs to do more thorough work, in fact to undertake mound excavation. By June, 1925, he had assembled a group of volunteer archaeologists with good scientific training: Amos Butler, an ornithologist and founder of the Indiana Academy of Science; Henry L. Bruner, Butler University professor of biology and

---

[9] *Proceedings of the Indiana History Conference, 1922*, pp. 20-22; Amos W. Butler, "Notes on Franklin County Archaeology," in "Archaeology—June 1930" folder, IHS Papers; *Proceedings of the Indiana History Conference, 1923*, pp. 21, 30-31.

geology; J. Arthur MacLean, director of the John Herron Art Institute, who had done fieldwork with Dr. Mills and Dr. Shetrone of the Ohio State Museum; Dr. W. N. Logan, the state geologist; and E. Y. Guernsey, a Lawrence County legislator with training in geology and natural history. Of this group Coleman considered MacLean and Guernsey the best prospects for doing extensive archaeological work. The plan was to raise money for digs by private subscription and then send in the "expert archeologists" to whichever county the experts decided upon.[10]

The drive for $1,000 in subscriptions to finance excavations failed in 1925. Undaunted, seventeen interested men met on March 2, 1926, with Amos Butler in the chair, to plan another fund-raising drive. This time they determined to ask pledges from the county historical societies, and Coleman reminded *Bulletin* readers that eventually the state should pay for this work, after its value had been demonstrated by private initiative.[11]

In fact, the 1926 mound exploration was financed primarily by Bureau funds ($217.70) and by five individual contributors of $100 each, including Eli Lilly's father, J. K. Lilly. The work itself was directed by MacLean, who donated his two-week summer vacations in 1926 and 1927 to the task, and brought along his children to help. The mound selected for "the first thorough and scientific excavation of a large aboriginal mound in Indiana" was the Albee Mound, in Sullivan County. It had been

---

[10] *Indiana History Bulletin*, II (1925), 195-96; Christopher B. Coleman, "Introduction," in J. Arthur MacLean, "Excavation of Albee Mound," in extra number, *Indiana History Bulletin*, IX (1931); Coleman to Grafton Johnson, June 16, 1925, in "Archaeology 1925-June, 1927" folder, Box 3, Records of the IHB; Lew M. O'Bannon to E. Y. Guernsey, August 7, 1925, in "Archaeology—1928-1936" folder, IHS Papers; Coleman, Report for 1925, "Historical Bureau Director's Reports" folder, Box 4, Records of the IHB.

[11] *Indiana History Bulletin*, III (1926), 135.

briefly explored in 1916 by archaeology committee member William Ross Teel, an Indianapolis stockbroker originally from Terre Haute.[12]

The expedition was successful in heightening the interest of the volunteers. By the time of the history conference in December, the members were ready to form a special archaeology section within the Indiana Historical Society. (Glenn Black, in an historical review of Indiana archaeology presented to the Society's annual meeting in 1960, pointed out that 1926 marked "the centennial of archaeology in Indiana," counting Lesueur's digs in 1826 as the beginning.) In February, the executive committee appointed as officers for the section, Teel, chairman; Rabbi Morris M. Feuerlicht, secretary; and Leo Rappaport, treasurer.[13]

In May, 1927, two hundred people attended a lecture at the Columbia Club by the Ohio State Archaeological and Historical Society's archaeologist Dr. H. C. Shetrone, sponsored jointly by the Society and the Columbia Club. Despite the enthusiasm displayed, few apparently were moved to contribute to the archaeology fund. Indiana Historical Bureau records show that the state agency allotted even more in 1927 ($511.82) than it had in 1926.[14]

The archaeology program in Indiana was underway. Mac-

---

[12] Coleman to William Dearing, May 24, 1932, "Library and Historical Department, 1931-1932" folder, Box 5, Records of the IHB; "Contributions to Mound Exploration Work," May 27, 1926, in "Archaeology, Beginning June 11, 1928" folder, Box 1, *ibid.*; William Ross Teel, "Mounds near Terre Haute," in *Indiana History Bulletin,* III (1926), 95-96.

[13] *Proceedings of the Indiana History Conference, 1926,* p. 29; Black, ". . . that what is past may not be forever lost. . . . ," in *Indiana History Bulletin,* XXXVIII (1961), 62; Minutes of IHS, February 4, 1927.

[14] *Indiana History Bulletin,* IV (1927), 203-205; Coleman to Dearing, May 24, 1932, "Library and Historical Department, 1931-1932" folder, Box 5, Records of the IHB.

Lean's work was respectable for its time, and it generated real enthusiasm, since his report was readily available and he himself spoke about the work at the annual history conferences in 1925 and 1926. But MacLean left Indiana in 1927, and Coleman, ever the professional, used the opportunity to secure a university-trained archaeologist as MacLean's successor.

Frank M. Setzler (1902-1975) represented both the strong archaeology programs of Columbus, Ohio, and of Chicago. A native Ohioan, he spent his first three years in college at Ohio State, using the program of the Ohio State Museum to learn archaeology, then transferred to the University of Chicago for graduate training under Fay-Cooper Cole. Cole, whose research interest earlier had been ethnology, began to lecture in anthropology at the University of Chicago in 1924. In 1925, inspired by the NRC's committee on state archaeological surveys begun a few years earlier, Cole began a statewide archaeological survey. The University of Chicago was one of the few schools in the country at the time to offer academic training in the field, and Setzler was one of the early products of the new program.[15]

Perhaps it was the impact of Setzler's credentials, or the cumulative effect of two successful previous excavations, or both; in any event the Society's archaeological section secured pledges for about $900 from private contributions in 1928. The Society itself donated $150 in 1928, while the Bureau gave $833.65. Setzler was paid $200 a month plus expenses.[16]

The new tone of professionalism was clear from the start.

---

[15] *American Men of Science*: Volume III, *The Social and Behavioral Sciences,* 9th edition, 1956, s.v. "Setzler, Frank M." The University of Chicago established a Department of Anthropology in 1929. For information on Fay-Cooper Cole and the program at the University of Chicago the author is indebted to Professor James H. Kellar.

[16] Of the pledged $900, $525 was actually subscribed in 1928. Not all of this money was needed for the 1928 work, which cost only $1,557.73, so the balance was added to the Smithsonian's subvention of $627.07 and applied to the archaeology budget for 1929. *Proceedings of the Indiana History Confer-*

The plans for Setzler's work were made carefully. Shetrone of Ohio was called in to consult with Setzler later in May on where the summer's work should be done, and they agreed Setzler should concentrate on the Whitewater Valley. NRC's new chairman of the committee on state archaeological surveys, Dr. Carl Guthe, stopped in Indianapolis in late June to lend his support to the archaeology section. "Archaeologists of the country," he reported, "are looking with deep interest to your survey." He also urged collectors both to list their collections and to keep careful records of where their artifacts were found.[17]

Early in June, before the excavations began, Setzler wrote to Coleman passing along information from Cole, that Congress had appropriated funds to support archaeological work and urging Coleman to apply to the Smithsonian Institution for the funds. The Smithsonian officers agreed to provide one half the cost of the survey, and in fact contributed $627.07 in 1928, $1,000 in 1929, and $616.70 in 1930. After 1930 the Depression-stunned Congress failed to renew the appropriations, and the Society was again forced to rely entirely on its own resources. Despite the Society's frequent urging and various calls for a state archaeologist, the state legislature showed no inclination to support the archaeology survey. Of course, indirectly the state was supporting the project, since Coleman regularly allocated Bureau funds for archaeology, but even this was challenged in 1932 by the State Library and Historical Board member William Dearing.[18] For reasons which will soon be apparent, the issue was obviated by 1932.

---

ence, 1928, pp. 23-24; "Contributions, May 27, 1928," in "Archaeology, Beginning June 11, 1928" folder, Box 1, Records of the IHB; Coleman to Dearing, May 24, 1932, "Library and Historical Department, 1931-1932" folder, Box 5, *ibid.*; Minutes of IHS, January 7, May 28, 1928.

[17] Archaeological Section Minutes, May 9, 1928, "Archaeology 1928-1936" folder, IHS Papers; Indianapolis *Star*, June 26, 1928.

[18] Frank M. Setzler to Coleman, June 5, 1928, "Archaeology, Beginning June

Setzler, with considerable assistance from collectors, surveyed the Whitewater Valley and excavated several mounds in the summers of 1928 and 1929. In 1930 he surveyed Randolph County. His reports of this work were printed in the *Bulletin* in September, 1930, and October, 1931. The Society was very pleased with his work, and the interest generated by Setzler's survey was responsible to some extent for the creation in 1929 of Mounds State Park near Anderson.[19] Setzler's work was also observed by Glenn Black, who learned from the experience.

Setzler was a young man on the way up in the archaeology profession. He was offered a position with the Smithsonian in August, 1930, and with the Society's blessings resigned in the middle of his survey of the west fork of the White River. Setzler went on to become the head curator of the Smithsonian's department of anthropology, a position he was to hold from 1935 to 1960, and he would continue to be a friend of the Society throughout his career.[20] His work for the Society was continued in 1930 by another University of Chicago graduate student, Fred Eggan.

In late November, 1930, the Society received letters from two applicants asking to carry on the survey work—one a suggestion from Setzler himself that he carry on the work part-time in 1931, with the co-operation of the Smithsonian, the other from the very humble Glenn Black. Coleman offered the

---

11, 1928" folder, Box 1, Records of the IHB; *Proceedings of the Indiana History Conference, 1929,* pp. 168-69; *ibid., 1930,* p. 272; Minutes of IHS, December 7, 1928; Coleman to Dearing, May 24, 1932, "Library and Historical Department, 1931-1932" folder, Box 5, Records of the IHB.

[19] A member of the IHS executive committee, Charles Sansberry, was also president of the Madison County Historical Society, which bought the Mounds and presented the land to the state. *Indiana History Bulletin,* VI (1929), 74.

[20] Setzler retired in 1960 to Culver, Indiana, and was awarded an honorary doctorate by Indiana University in 1971. *Proceedings of the Indiana Academy of Science,* LXXXV (1975), 47-48.

position on December 2 to another Fay-Cooper Cole student, Thorne Deuel, probably before he had received Setzler's letter. He also responded in a friendly, though noncommittal way, to Glenn Black; "I am sure," he wrote, "that you can be of assistance in the archaeological work next summer in one way or another." With Teel's approval, Coleman wrote to Setzler December 3, urging him to explore the possibilities with the Smithsonian.[21]

The year 1930 was, of course, a milestone for the Society, its centennial year, and the month of December featured a variety of celebratory occasions. Among them was a visit from Warren King Moorehead, who delivered an illustrated lecture on the mound builders to a large audience on December 3, followed by an informal discussion. Among the audience and among the supporters of the lecture was Eli Lilly.

Lilly and Black, then, both turned to the Society at a time when their services were uniquely valuable. The Society was in between archaeologists, and government funds for archaeology were just about to be shut off temporarily. They were attracted by a newly established program that had demonstrated both seriousness and competence. But, separately, it is not clear how much each would have been able or willing to make a long-term investment in the Society's archaeology program. Together, they were to stay on the job for thirty-four (Black) and forty-seven (Lilly) years.

Setzler's proposal that the Smithsonian continue to support the Indiana survey by contributing his services in the summer months of 1931, did not, apparently, meet with the approval

---

[21] Setzler to Coleman, November 23, 1930, "Archaeology—June 1930" folder, IHS Papers; Glenn A. Black to Coleman, November 17, 1930, *ibid.*; Coleman to Deuel, December 2, 1930, *ibid.*; Coleman to Black, December 2, 1930, "Indiana Historical Bureau, 1931" folder, Black Papers, Glenn A. Black Laboratory of Archaeology, Indiana University, Bloomington.

of his employers. Lacking federal support, the archaeology section did not plan to do any excavating in the summer of 1931. The section did invite Moorehead to return to the state in May to make a fairly extensive, eleven-day tour of the most important known sites. The Society accepted Black's services as a guide for Moorehead, and Eli Lilly, along with several other section members, was a frequent member of the little group that accompanied Moorehead around the state.

These were extremely important days for the future of Indiana archaeology. Lilly was impressed by sixty-five-year-old Moorehead—"that kindly gentleman of the old school," Lilly would describe him in 1937—and he would support a number of the archaeologist's projects in the coming years. Moorehead expressed special enthusiasm for the Angel Mounds near Evansville, urging strongly that the site should be taken over by the state and suggesting that Lilly purchase that land to safeguard the mounds until the state was ready to take it over. Lilly would echo Moorehead's concern in 1937 in his *Prehistoric Antiquities of Indiana:*

> Here, baked in the glaring summer sun, frozen under winter snows, gradually wasting away under the plow and the harrow, is a site that the State of Indiana should rescue from oblivion, and so save to posterity another of our pre-Columbian heritages.[22]

Both of the older men, Lilly and Moorehead, were impressed by Glenn Black, the autodidact, although superficially he was

---

[22] Lilly, *Prehistoric Antiquities of Indiana,* pp. v, 47-48; Moorehead to Lilly, May 20, 1931, "Moorehead" folder, Lilly Papers. Moorehead returned Lilly's esteem. He was responsible for sending back to Indiana the material he had excavated from the Bone Bank on the Wabash River, turning it over to Lilly as an indefinite loan in June, 1931. These important artifacts are now in the Glenn A. Black Laboratory of Archaeology. Eli Lilly to Coleman, June 25, 1931, "Archaeology 1928-1936" folder, IHS Papers.

not especially imposing. Thirty years old, slender, with a sinewy build that might be described as scrawny, he had a very earnest manner, a bushy shock of curly hair, and ears that stuck out. His grammar was not altogether reliable, though he showed a gift for writing and spoke well. He was a year or two too young to have served in the war, and hence lacked the glamour of the veteran, and he had not been a success before the Depression set in. Nevertheless, it was soon apparent to these two men, as it would be apparent to many others in the years to come, that Glenn Black was someone to watch.

With Moorehead's approval Lilly hired Black to do archaeological work beginning June 15, 1931, at $225 a month plus expenses. Lilly funneled $150 of the salary for 1931 through the Society's archaeology fund and paid the balance to Black directly. There is no doubt that Eli Lilly could have employed a better trained archaeologist. By any reckoning, investing in Glenn Black was something of a gamble for Lilly, an exercise in judging character and intellectual potential. It is true that Lilly had Moorehead's moral support in this venture: Moorehead wrote to Lilly only a few days after Black was hired to say that "Mr. Black is an intelligent and willing worker and I am certain will make good. I predict a future for him." The old-fashioned Moorehead went on to say, perhaps revealing a pique toward the new generation of academic archaeologists, "We need practical, interested field workers and collectors today more than additional Doctors of Philosophy of which there are a super abundance!" And it is perhaps also true that Lilly, who had not himself been given a college education but was instead sent directly to pharmacy school after he graduated from Shortridge High School, took a certain quiet pleasure in supporting a person whose achievements would come from independent studies. It is certainly true that without Lilly's support there is no reason at all to believe that Glenn Black would ever have had an op-

portunity to become a professional archaeologist. To see his potential and invest in it was an act of real imagination. Winning
his bet on Glenn Black gave Eli Lilly more pleasure than anything else in his life.[23]

At the beginning there was some question whether the Society's archaeology section and the NRC's committee on state
archaeological surveys would accept Black's services, even as a
gift from Eli Lilly. Moorehead reported to Lilly in May, before
Black was hired, that he had discussed the question with NRC's
committee chairman Dr. Guthe. Guthe had insisted on "a
trained man" for the 1931 summer survey, but, Moorehead
went on,

> in view of the hard times and lack of a regular department or organi-
> zation in Indiana, after listening to my rather long story he thought it
> would be possible to train young Black so that he could handle field
> operations next year.[24]

The members of the Society's archaeology section were hesi-
tant primarily on the grounds that they feared their survey
would lack credibility if their field director lacked formal credentials. They were especially sensitive to the opinion of the
nearby Dr. Cole, who was, after all, turning out trained archae-

---

[23] Moorehead to Lilly, May 20, 1931, "Moorehead" folder, Lilly Papers; Coleman to Black, July 28, 1931, Black Papers; *Proceedings of the Indiana History
Conference, 1931*, p. 152; *Indiana History Bulletin*, IX (1932); Copy, Moorehead to Lilly, June 17, 1931, "Eli Lilly 1931" folder, Black Papers. Eli Lilly
was heard to remark in response to his brother's statement that the Lilly Library at Indiana University was the most rewarding thing in his life, that
"The most rewarding thing in my life is knowing Glenn Black." Interview with
Professor Kellar, January, 1980.

[24] Moorehead to Lilly, May 20, 1931, "Moorehead" folder, Lilly Papers. Professor Kellar noted that Black, "though he began as a serious amateur, tended
to divorce himself from other collectors throughout his professional life. To
be sure, there were a few amateurs that he encouraged and he gave dozens
of talks to groups throughout the state, but he never seriously encouraged
avocational archaeologists." Kellar to author, March 11, 1980.

ologists and placing them in just such positions as the Society could offer. Teel and Coleman compromised in 1931 by engaging both Black and a Cole student, J. Gilbert McAllister, to carry out the survey. Hence they were in a position from the beginning to compare Black's work with that of a university-trained man. McAllister worked in Porter County, while Black surveyed Greene County.[25]

Greene County was especially rich in archaeological remains, and Moorehead had strongly urged that the 1931 survey begin there. The state geologist W. N. Logan had done some exploratory work in the county in 1927, and two collectors, Fred Dyer and Judge Oscar Bland, were planning to excavate the Schaffer Cemetery site south of Worthington in June, 1931. Dyer and Bland invited the Bureau to advise them and record their findings, and this was Black's first assignment. Later in the summer he surveyed Greene County and then excavated a number of key sites.[26]

Although Dorothy Riker recalls that Black worried that he had made a number of errors in his Greene County excavations, on the whole Coleman and Teel were impressed with his work—impressed enough to want to give Black some credentials. Lilly described the situation to Moorehead in August, 1931:

> Our good friends Coleman and Teel, and I must say I join them a little bit, wish to avoid the scorn of one Dr. Cole in case he would say, "Black, Black, who is this man Black?" So Mr. Teel is trying to make arrangements to get in some more scholastic education, probably this

---

[25] J. Gilbert McAllister, "The Archaeology of Porter County," in *Indiana History Bulletin*, X (1932), 1-96; Glenn A. Black, "The Archaeology of Greene County," in *ibid.*, X (1933), 183-346.

[26] W. N. Logan, "Archaeological Investigations in Greene County," in *Proceedings of the Indiana Academy of Science*, XXXVII (1927), 171-74; Coleman to Black, June 19, 1931, "Indiana Historical Bureau, 1931" folder, Black Papers.

Indianapolis *Star*

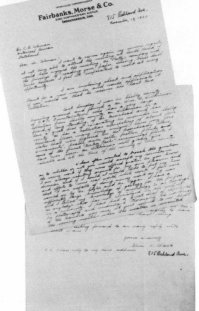

Early supporters of Indiana archaeology

opposite, above, Amos W. Butler,
longtime president of Indiana Academy of Science; J. Arthur MacLean,
director of John Herron Art Institute;
below, Frank M. Setzler, director of the
Society's excavations from 1928 to
1930; E. Y. Guernsey who worked in
the Society's archaeology program
from 1934 to 1939

above, William Ross Teel, chairman
of the Society's archaeological committee, 1926-1940; Warren King
Moorehead, dean of North American
archaeology, who was influential in
shaping the Society's archaeological
program; *right,* Glenn Black offers his
services to the Society, November, 1930

left, Henry C. Shetrone, director of the Ohio State Museum, 1928-1947; *below*, the Ohio State Museum in Columbus, where Black studied in 1931-1932

opposite, above, left to right, Paul Weer, Wilbur D. Peat, E. Y. Guernsey, and Glenn Black at the Nowlin Mound site in the fall of 1934; *below*, Glenn Black at the Nowlin Mound excavation in 1934; WPA workers at Angel site, June 15, 1940

Indianapolis *News*

opposite, The Voegelins and Georg Neumann were members of the "Indiana group" of anthropologists whose research was supported by Eli Lilly; *above*, Carl F. Voegelin, chairman of the Indiana University department of anthropology, 1947-1966; Erminie Wheeler-Voegelin, professor of history at Indiana University, 1956-1969; *below*, Georg Neumann, physical anthropologist, member of the Indiana University anthropology department, 1942-1971; Professor James H. Kellar, director of the Glenn A. Black Laboratory of Archaeology, Indiana University, and Society archaeologist

right, Glenn A. Black and Eli Lilly, October, 1962, at Angel Mounds; *below*, Glenn A. Black Laboratory of Archaeology, Indiana University

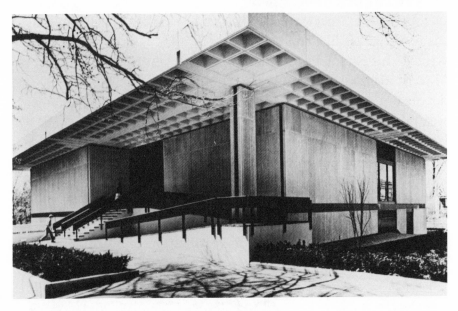

winter, so that we can at least say he has been trained under Shetrone, or "so-and-so." This Black is willing to do and I still have hopes of making a good man out of him. He surely has diligence and enthusiasm, which is a large part of the picture.[27]

Shetrone was apparently somewhat skeptical about accepting Black as a student and requested a description of Black's schooling and previous training in archaeology. Black responded that "my schooling has been rather limited to libraries and books." He listed the numerous archaeological books he had read in his self-education and pointed out that he had made more than three thousand sketches of artifacts "both uncommon and unique and feel sure that it is impossible to stump me on any archaeological relic." More modestly he added, "I have done my best to overcome an unavoidable handicap and if I have it will be most gratifying." Shetrone was satisfied and asked Black to bring along his sketches when he came to Columbus.[28]

Black studied at the Ohio State Museum in Columbus from October, 1931, through May, 1932. Lilly took him to Columbus to get settled in, like a parent taking a child off to college. Black wrote to his patron of his intentions for his time in Columbus, "I want to make myself as useful to the Museum as I can and devote my time to an attempt to absorb every bit of information possible." At the time he declared these intentions Black was a newlywed. He had just married Ida May Hazard, a young woman he had known for some time and whom he had planned to marry the previous summer. Perhaps fearing Lilly's disapproval, Black did not warn him of his planned marriage, and Lilly learned of it through the announcement in an Indianapolis newspaper. Lilly wrote warm congratulations to his protégé, and

---

[27] Dorothy Riker interview, January, 1980; Lilly to Moorehead, August 15, 1931, in "Moorehead" folder, Lilly Papers.

[28] Black to Lilly, September 13, 1931, Lilly Papers.

a somewhat embarrassed Black explained that "Mrs. Black is a very charming girl, pardon the ego, interested in archaeology to the fullest therefore in perfect sympathy with both you and I [sic] and has our interests at heart." Newlywed or no, Black worked extremely effectively during his nearly eight months in Columbus, both in the Museum and in fieldwork, and Lilly received enthusiastic reports from archaeologists who had an opportunity to know Black. Black visited Ann Arbor in the spring of 1933, and Carl Guthe observed that the apprentice "has been making extremely good use of his visit at the Ohio State Museum. . . . I am much impressed with his possibilities and I am anxious to render him every assistance. . . ." Shetrone's report to Coleman, Teel, and Coulter in May praised Black simply by saying he would be glad to have Black as a member of the museum staff.[29]

By March, 1932, Lilly had arranged to carry out his archaeological plans through contributions to the Indiana Historical Society. As Lilly explained it to Black, "that is about the only way I can get credit on my income tax." In his usual way, Lilly requested that the Society give no publicity to his contributions. At the same time, apparently, the Society appointed Black its "permanent" archaeologist. (The Bureau continued to contribute importantly to the work by publishing the lengthy reports of archaeological findings.)[30]

For the next thirty-two years Glenn Black was employed by the Indiana Historical Society through contributions from Eli Lilly. His career was a source of pride to Lilly and to the So-

---

[29] Black to Lilly, October 23, 28, 30, 1931, Lilly Papers; Guthe quoted in Lilly to Black, April 13, 1932, Black Papers; Shetrone quoted in Lilly to Black, May 31, 1932, *ibid.*

[30] Lilly to Black, March 9, 1932, Lilly Papers; Coleman memorandum to John G. Rauch, March 14, 1932, "Archaeology 1928-1936" folder, IHS Papers; *Proceedings of the Indiana History Conference, 1932*, p. 370.

ciety, though his success did not immediately persuade those who doubted his qualifications. Years later Black still remembered with some anger that in the early days Coleman had refused to publish certain conclusions Black had drawn in his reports, findings that were subsequently published first by James Griffin of the University of Michigan and credited to him.[31]

The publication in 1936 of excavations Black had undertaken of Nowlin Mound, a structurally complex, large burial mound in Dearborn County, in 1934 and 1935 brought his first national attention. As recently as 1971 Professor James Kellar of Indiana University described the report as "a landmark in the history of the development of excavational techniques, and there is probably no more precise description of mound architectonics in print. It is," he added, "required reading for any student contemplating mound excavation in the eastern United States."[32]

In November, 1935, Black was offered the position of curator of archaeology at the Ohio State Museum, one of the most prestigious research centers in the country. Shetrone made the offer through Eli Lilly, since he recognized that Lilly had a reasonable claim on Black's services. Lilly was extremely pleased for Black, and he told his protégé that Black should choose only on the basis of his own interests. However, Lilly pointed out that he did intend to continue to support archaeology in Indiana and that there would be opportunities for Black to continue to do good work for the Society. A flattered Glenn Black thanked Shetrone for the honor, but rejected the offer. "We are so young, archaeologically, in Indiana," he explained,

> and we have so much before us that I am reluctant to leave the task barely started. Our setup here is ideal and so long as our country does

---

[31] Black to Lilly, August 7, 1944, Black Papers.

[32] Glenn A. Black, "Excavation of Nowlin Mound," in *Indiana History Bulletin*, XIII (1936), 201-342; Kellar, "Glenn A. Black," in dedication booklet, Glenn A. Black Laboratory of Archaeology, Indiana University, 1971.

not digress too far from the orthodox and become too Socialistic, Mr. Lilly intends to carry on the work in Indiana. We have so much mapped out to do that, frankly, I do not feel that the possibilities for interesting and worthy research are any greater in Ohio than in Indiana.[33]

Foremost among the plans Black had in mind was the excavation of the Angel site in Vanderburgh County. The site was a large one, covering more than four hundred acres, of which 191 acres would ultimately be surveyed as part of the archaeological area, and including eleven mounds. Several of these were large, truncated earth mounds and one was described as "prodigious." There was also evidence of a stockade that had surrounded the village site on three sides. Here then were the remains of a large aboriginal village unlike anything else in Indiana and, though very like sites reported in the Southeast, farther north and west than such sites were expected to be found.[34]

Moorehead had considered the site "of the greatest importance" in 1931 and had urged Lilly to purchase the land. Lilly was willing to consider this "if the price were not exorbitant." Guernsey apparently began negotiations in June, 1931, to purchase the area but nothing was accomplished. Lilly lost interest in the project briefly, grumbling in May, 1932, about "the present socialistic trend of the Government in taking away everyone's money by income and inheritance taxes," but this uncharacteristic mood passed swiftly. By August, Lilly was proposing to Coleman and to a dazzled Glenn Black that he, Lilly, would attempt to purchase the site on behalf of the Indiana His-

---

[33] Shetrone to Lilly, November 29, 1935, Black Papers; Black to Shetrone, December 27, 1935, *ibid.* Lilly did write to Shetrone requesting that if Black decided to go to Ohio the Society be allowed to borrow him a few times a year. Lilly to Shetrone, December 3, 1935, *ibid.*

[34] Black, *Angel Site: An Archaeological, Historical, And Ethnological Study* (2 volumes. Indianapolis: Indiana Historical Society, 1967), I, 41; Kellar, "Glenn A. Black," in Black Laboratory dedication booklet.

torical Society. The plan, outlined by Lilly in a memo recording his conversation with Coleman, was to purchase the mounds "through kind and interested friends," provided that they could be bought for a reasonable price. Lilly urged that the gift to the Society would come from a number of interested people, reflecting wide interest and support, and did not plan himself to bear the greatest part of the financial burden. The Society's name would be used in negotiations, in hopes that the asking prices would not be increased by owners. The whole project was to be managed by the Society's archaeology section; they could investigate the site for two or three years then give it to the state or to the nation as a park. Lilly stipulated that there must be "absolutely no personal publicity for me in this matter. . . ."[35]

The project to purchase the land dragged on for many years. The stumbling block was always the lack of interest by anyone other than Lilly in contributing to the purchase and Lilly's own strong sense that others, especially members of the Evansville community, should contribute.[36]

In 1938 the question finally became an urgent one, since the site was in imminent danger of being incorporated by the city of Evansville. In the summer a farsighted Evansville realtor was able to secure options on the most important properties, and the Society undertook an intensive campaign to raise funds to save the mounds. Glenn Black worked tirelessly for months, writing letters and talking personally to everyone who might be expected to help him: archaeologists, the state park department, Evansville officials and wealthy citizens, newspapers, the Chamber of Commerce, the American Philosophical Society, even the American Legion. Complimentary copies of Lilly's *Prehistoric*

[35] Moorehead to Lilly, May 20, 1931, Lilly to Moorehead, June 12, 1931, May 26, 1932, Lilly to Coleman, August 12, 1932, Lilly to Black, August 17, 1932, Black to Lilly, August 23, 1932, Lilly Papers.

[36] Black to Lilly, August 22, 29, 1935, Lilly to Black, August 27, 1935, Black to Lilly, January 7, November 15, 1936, *ibid.*

Antiquities of Indiana were mailed to every likely prospective contributor, and Coleman and Guernsey joined Black in making the rounds of wealthy Evansvillians. Eli Lilly donated $11,000 to the Society's museum fund, to be "borrowed" to take up the two options that expired in July.[37]

By October it was clear that the effort to secure multiple patrons had failed. "The Angel mound proposition is not dead," Coleman wrote to Guernsey, "but to a regrettable extent is falling back almost entirely upon Mr. Lilly. We have only succeeded in getting promises for $600 from others." When most of the options were about to expire on October 15, Eli Lilly contributed another $57,000 to the Society for their purchase. Of the $71,956.93 purchase price for Angel mounds, Lilly personally contributed $68,000 in 1938, the balance coming from the archaeology fund, to which he had contributed earlier; only $772.00 was raised from other sources. An Evansville newspaperman wrote to Glenn Black on November 1 that, "despite appearances," some people in Evansville were grateful for the Society's action in saving the site and speculated that the city might even repay the Society some day.[38]

No doubt Lilly and the Society took some comfort in the fact that the federal government, at least, was willing to invest in Angel site by approving its proposed excavation as a Works Progress Administration project. Black submitted the application in August; it was approved by WPA in November; and in April, 1939, workers arrived on the site. The Society and the Bureau were cosponsors, agreeing to prepare a scientific report of the results, to be deposited in the Smithsonian, and to place

---

[37] Black to Lilly, July 1, 1938, *ibid.*; "Angel Mounds—General Correspondence 1938-1949" folder, IHS Papers; Minutes of IHS, July 1, 1938.

[38] Coleman to Guernsey, October 5, 1938, "Archaeology 1937-1944" folder, IHS Papers; *Proceedings of the Indiana History Conference, 1938*, p. 23; J. Ben Lieberman, Evansville *Courier*, to Black, November 1, 1938, "Archaeology 1937-1944" folder, IHS Papers.

all the materials recovered from the site with the Indiana Historical Society for preservation and public use. The Society agreed to bear the sponsor's share of the cost, estimated at about 12 percent of the total. Black would later credit Coleman with significant assistance in planning and carrying out the project. (It is tempting to speculate that the Democrat Coleman was an important factor in persuading the Republicans Lilly and Black to use the New Deal program to promote Indiana archaeology, but the author has not seen direct evidence of this.) It was a large project; in August, 1939, Coleman described it as the second largest archaeological project then in operation in the United States.[39]

The WPA project at Angel site lasted thirty-seven months and employed 277 men, none of whom had any previous experience in archaeology. Together Black and his WPA work force surveyed and contoured approximately 193 acres and excavated about 120,000 square feet. They recovered and processed more than 2.3 million archaeological items. It was archaeological research on a grand scale, a kind of extensive public work that archaeologists had rarely, if ever, seen before the WPA program applied it to their own field. The result was an extensive and unusual excavation of a large village site, concentrating less on burial mounds than had been done with similar sites and more on areas of common daily aboriginal life. Black was in search of "the cultural matrix of which the mound's content was only a small part," and this goal required the excavation of "large habitation areas so that recurring patterns and deviations therefrom could be determined."[40]

---

[39] Black, *Angel Site*, I, 20-21; copy, Black to Lilly, September 15, 1938, Lilly Papers; Coleman to John K. Jennings, State WPA Co-ordinator, August 4, 1939, "Angel Mounds 1938-1947" folder, IHS Papers.

[40] Black, *Angel Site*, I, 22, 25, 26; James E. Fitting (ed.), *The Development of North American Archaeology* (Garden City, N.Y.: Anchor Books, 1973), pp. 98, 141; Kellar, "Glenn A. Black," in Black Laboratory dedication booklet.

The excavation essentially was completed in 1942, and at this point, according to the original plan, the Society should have turned the site over to the state for a park and gone on to other projects. Instead Glenn Black, who had moved to a house on the site in 1939, remained on it, both in a physical and professional sense, until his death in 1964. Why did he stay, and was it a productive use of his time?

In fact the mobilization for World War II delayed serious consideration of turning the site over to the state until 1945, but in June of that year Eli Lilly, on behalf of the Society, offered to give the site to the state to be administered by the conservation department. The deed was actually transferred from the Society to the state in December, 1946. The agreement was that the state would fence the site and develop it as an interpretive center. About a week after the deed was transferred, there was a complete shakeup in the conservation department, and the new leaders did not accept the agreement made by their predecessors. The Society retained rights to explore the site, however, and also retained ownership of artifacts acquired by excavation. Black remained on the site as custodian, angry for nearly twenty years that the state did not develop the site as he believed was promised.[41]

In a sense Black then was stuck at Angel site, feeling himself to be its natural protector and the site to be in danger of destruction by neglect. But he made the most of the years at Newburgh. Beginning in 1945 Black organized an archaeological field school at the site in co-operation with Indiana University and the Society. He ran the school every summer through 1962, using the students to excavate various areas, teaching field techniques at the same time. His twenty-six years at the site gave him an integrated knowledge of Angel site's moment in time; it en-

---

[41] Lilly to Governor Ralph Gates, June 8, 1945, Minutes of IHS; Black to Lilly, December 2, 1946, Black Papers; Indianapolis *News*, November 22, 1945.

abled him to write "An Archaeological, Historical, and Ethnological Study."[42]

Among the many plans Lilly and Black shared from the beginning of their collaboration in the early 1930s, the excavation of Angel Mounds and solving the riddle of the Walam
Olum were the most important. The former turned into a life-
time work for Glenn Black; the latter generated Eli Lilly's
support of an important group of researchers working on a
battery of questions and approaches raised by Lilly and
Black.

In mid-September, 1932, Lilly wrote to Carl Guthe for advice
on a major research problem. "Black and I," he announced,
"have a hunch that the Walam Olum may possibly have in it
the key that will open the riddle of the Mound Builders." *Walam
Olum* was the name of a book published in 1833 by Constantine Rafinesque, an American naturalist of mixed reputation. It
purported to be a translation of the tribal legends of the Lenni
Lenape or Delaware Indians, which, Rafinesque said, had been
recorded by pictographs drawn on sticks and bundled together
in a certain order. He claimed that he acquired the sticks in
1822 from a man identified only as the late Dr. Ward of Indiana,
who was said to have acquired them in 1820, and that in 1822
he had obtained the Delaware text for the pictographs from
someone else, not identified at all. Rafinesque studied the Delaware language in Philadelphia between 1825 and 1833, publishing an English translation of the text in 1833. Since no one has
found any record that the sticks in question were recorded as
having been seen by anyone other than Rafinesque—though he
claimed that the Moravians John G. E. Heckewelder and George
H. Loskiel had seen them—, the authenticity of Rafinesque's
manuscript has sometimes been doubted. Based on internal evidence, however, most students accepted Daniel G. Brinton's

---

[42] Kellar, "Glenn A. Black," in Black Laboratory dedication booklet.

estimate that the work was "a genuine native production," though not in Rafinesque's version either very old or pure in linguistic form.[43]

With all its flaws the work offered intriguing clues to the remote past of historic Indiana, and both Lilly and Black hoped it would produce a sort of missing link between the mound building aboriginals and the historic tribes. This romantic notion inspired a wide variety of hardheaded attacks on various problems of North American prehistory that had repercussions far beyond the original problem of the Walam Olum.

Lilly's letter to Guthe in September, 1932, presenting the first of these strategies, suggested establishing a fellowship in Indian languages in order to study the time perspective of the various tribes mentioned in the Walam Olum. From this proposal came the Indiana Fellowship in Anthropology at Yale, held sequentially by Carl and Erminie Voegelin in 1933 and 1934, later to become the pioneers in anthropology at Indiana University. Similarly fellowships were established in Aboriginal North American Ceramics at the University of Michigan (James B. Griffin, 1933); in physical anthropology of the Fort Ancient populations at the University of Michigan (Georg Neumann, 1937-1940); and in tree ring research or dendrochronology at the University of Chicago (Florence Hawley, 1937-1940). In addition to these projects, Glenn Black was attempting, unsuccessfully, to identify early historic Indian sites in northern Indiana (1936, 1937); a lithic laboratory was developed at the Ohio State Museum in 1938; and Paul Weer was locating historical references to early Indian villages of the Walam Olum tribes.[44]

---

[43] Griffin, "A Commentary on an Unusual Research Program in American Anthropology," in Black Laboratory dedication booklet; "Introduction," in *Walam Olum or Red Score: The Migration Legend of the Lenni Lenape or Delaware Indians* (Indianapolis: Indiana Historical Society, 1954), pp. ix-x.

[44] Griffin, "A Commentary on an Unusual Research Program in American Anthropology," in Black Laboratory dedication booklet.

Eli Lilly himself made substantive as well as monetary contributions to the work. His extensive *Bibliography of Indiana Archaeology* was published in 1932, a record of his own rapid and thorough self-education in archaeology. When it was published Lilly was already at work on *Prehistoric Antiquities of Indiana*, an introductory survey of Indiana prehistory. Though he confessed to Glenn Black, to whom he sent draft sections of his work, that "It seems to me they sound a good deal like the third grade and I am just wondering whether I am equal to the task," he knew the kind of book he wanted to write:

> I do not wish to tire out readers because this whole project is designed to get people interested in archaeology who have never been interested before.

In addition, it was Lilly's own attempts to work on Indiana pottery that led directly to the fellowship on the subject at Michigan: as Black told him ruefully in 1931 in response to Lilly's request for sources, "I am afraid you are going to have to be the father of investigation along this line in Indiana."[45]

Lilly was the father of many investigations in North American anthropology. An unselfconscious, intelligent amateur, he could ask the big, imaginative questions with cheerful unpretentiousness and not worry overmuch whether his speculations sometimes sounded preposterous to professionals. More often his inquiries led directly to fruitful scientific studies. He was "fatherly" too in other ways: as a patron he was extraordinary. Griffin doubted "that the patron of any other program of this nature ever participated as fully, shared discouragement with such compassion, or exulted more with each accomplishment."[46]

---

[45] Lilly to Black, August 17, 1932, Black to Lilly, December 13, 1931, Lilly Papers.

[46] Griffin, "A Commentary on an Unusual Research Program in American Anthropology," in Black Laboratory dedication booklet.

Certainly there were many discouragements on the way to the co-operative *Walam Olum* published by the Society in 1954, more than twenty years after the project was conceived. Lilly wondered in 1940 whether what the group was likely to add to knowledge about the document would be worth the trouble, and Glenn Black advised that it should not drag out another six or seven years. A meeting of the "Indiana group" in 1945 on the Walam Olum led both to excavations in New Jersey and another fellowship to study Delaware archaeological culture in the East, which delayed the project another five years.[47]

The resulting publication was an ambitious, provocative co-operative effort, which, according to one reviewer,

> has produced much new material of basic importance for the archaeology, ethnology, and contact history of the eastern United States, far beyond its specific application to this legendary chronicle.[48]

As a by-product of the Walam Olum project, an anthropology department was assembled at Indiana University with Lilly's help. The Society hoped to interest the university in archaeology soon after beginning its own program. Perhaps it rankled Lilly, very much the loyal native son, that it was necessary to go to universities in Illinois, Michigan, and Connecticut, and to the Ohio State Museum for scholars to pursue archaeological topics. In any event, the Society proposed in the summer of 1936 that the university should establish a laboratory to identify prehistoric stone material. By October Ralph Esarey of the geology department (son-in-law of archaeology section member and state geologist W. N. Logan) agreed to work on a stone labora-

---

[47] Lilly to Black, November 11, 1940, Black to Lilly, November 13, 1940, Black Papers.

[48] Quoted in Griffin, "A Commentary on an Unusual Research Program in American Anthropology," in Black Laboratory dedication booklet.

tory for the Society's archaeologists. In 1940 Black and Lilly decided that a study relating plant variations to archaeological features would be useful, and a fellowship was awarded to an Indiana University doctoral candidate in botany, Helen Marsh Zeiner, who did research at Angel mounds from 1940 to 1942.[49]

By 1937 the "Indiana group" was making something of a stir in American scholarly circles, and the inauguration of the Society's *Prehistory Research Series* increased the group's prestige. Glenn Black's election to national office in the Society of American Archaeology in 1939—he served as president in 1941-1942, and held some office all but four years between 1939 and 1957—marked his acceptance in his chosen profession. In May, 1941, the first of Lilly's researchers, the Voegelins, were appointed at Indiana University, he in the history department and she as a university fellow, both with Lilly's support. Black was already expressing interest in teaching an archaeology course "in connection with the Voegelin's classes," and exulted over the visits of Indiana University President Herman B Wells to Angel site in June and October. The Society urged the university to cosponsor the Angel Mounds project in the fall of 1941, asking little in the way of a contribution and couching its request in very flattering terms. ("We naturally look to the University as leader in scientific studies of this sort and want to co-operate in promoting the scientific influence of the University. . . .") This request was apparently refused, but by October, 1941, Lilly reported that Wells was interested in "a museum in the back of his head," and Lilly was considering lending his archaeological collection, i.e., the Society's museum, to the university. By the next spring the plans for an anthropological museum were under way, with

[49] Coleman to William Lowe Bryan, July 30, 1936, "Archaeology 1928-1936" folder, IHS Papers; Ralph Esarey to E. Y. Guernsey, October 6, 1936, "Archaeology 1937-1944" folder, *ibid.*

Georg Neumann brought into the zoology department to develop it.[50]

The war cut into the university's plans for expansion of anthropology—Voegelin, for instance, was shifted for a while to teaching Balkan history and languages—, but by the fall of 1944, under the strong urging of Neumann and Voegelin, Black was asked to teach a course in archaeology at Indiana University. Dean Fernandus Payne described this step as beginning "in a modest way a Department of Ethnology." The university field schools at Angel site began the following summer, under joint sponsorship of the Society and the university. In February, 1947, a department of anthropology was created, and Voegelin was its chairman from 1947 until his appointment as Distinguished Professor in 1966.[51]

Black taught one class a week at I. U. from 1944 to 1960, when he retired to write his report on Angel site. James Kellar, an early student of Black's and his successor as Society archaeologist, described him as a person who was at the same time intense, serious, and warm. He was also a successful classroom lecturer. The room at the Union Building where he stayed over every Thursday to rest from the day's exertions before getting up the next morning to drive back to Newburgh via Indianapolis was invariably a center for students, to whom he dispensed a fatherly concern. In the field school, also, Black was a highly effective teacher to students drawn from all over the country and from abroad. He communicated both his own scrupulous

---

[50] Kellar, "Glenn A. Black," in Black Laboratory dedication booklet; Black to Lilly, May 27, June 23, October 6, 1941, Black Papers; Coleman to Herman B Wells, September 27, 1941, "Archaeology 1937-1944" folder, IHS Papers; Lilly to Black, October 13, 1941, Black Papers.

[51] Griffin, "A Commentary on an Unusual Research Program in American Anthropology," in Black Laboratory dedication booklet; Minutes of IHS, June 8, 1944.

field techniques and his own sense of awe for the past, the latter described by Kellar as "a reverent sense of a site as a human document."[52]

The only professional archaeologist in Indiana until 1960, when Kellar became the first full-time professor of archaeology at Indiana University, Black, a friendly, convivial man, became something of a loner by circumstance. He ran a one-man operation at Angel Mounds for more than twenty years and never found an opportunity to train a successor. He found himself perennially guarding Angel site from people who had no idea what it represented, and he was frequently at odds with the state conservation department, the only subject on which anyone ever saw him lose his temper. But Black was happy in the teacher's role, and his field school attracted students from afar.

Together, a middle-aged drug manufacturer and a more-or-less self-made archaeologist established a remarkable prehistory program in Indiana between 1931 and 1960 through the agency of the Indiana Historical Society. In partial recognition of this Black received an honorary doctorate from Wabash College in 1958. Sadly, Black did not live to see the creation of the interpretive center which he so desired for Angel site; it was built in 1972, and he would perhaps have been annoyed that it was in the end the Lilly Endowment, not the State of Indiana, that funded the project. He did not see the research laboratory built by Eli Lilly in his honor at Indiana University, where the Society's rich archaeological collections can be used, as he wished, for serious research. Nor did he live to complete the detailed archaeological, ethnological, and historical report on Angel site that he began in 1960 and which was published by the Society in 1967.

Lilly's investment in Indiana archaeology was to an important degree an investment in Glenn Black. Their friendship is recorded

---

[52] James Kellar interview, January, 1980.

in their correspondence files, now housed at the Black Laboratory. In their letters one can see two very appealing human beings: the talented, conscientious Black working tirelessly to justify Lilly's confidence in him; and Lilly, deeply proud and fond of his protégé, always encouraging and admiring. Mr. and Mrs. Lilly usually tried to spend a couple of weekends a year—once in the spring and once in the fall—visiting the Blacks at their home at Angel site, and the Blacks usually joined the Lillys for a short time at Lake Wawasee in the hottest part of the summer. Lilly once described their relationship as a *"mutual* admiration society," but a letter he wrote to Black when the latter was having some kind of heart trouble in the winter of 1941-1942 exemplifies it better:

> Dear Glenn
>
> You will agree, I hope, that our close and confidential relationship gives, or should give, me the right to administer a little fatherly advice upon occasion.
>
> To be perfectly frank I don't like a bit these "spells" you are having and want to protest to the best of my ability to your pushing yourself as you seem to be doing. If you keep it up you'll soon be working on some *real* Angel Mounds.
>
> You could just as well as not, insist that the work proceed under a slow enough bell for your assistants to handle the work and run them from your bed if necessary.
>
> And if your doctor says you ought to have a three or six months complete rest it *must* be done, mounds or no mounds—even if it should blow up the whole proposition.
>
> One Glenn Black is worth all the mounds, villages and camp sites in the Mississippi Valley so do listen to reason.
>
> Do be sensible, young fellow, and reassure your old friend that you are doing the very best for yourself—and all of us.
>
> As ever
>
> Eli Lilly

For his part, Black put it simply in 1944 (when considering whether he should accept the position at I.U.):

> Although my principal material interest in life has been, for a good
> many years and the past thirteen in particular, archaeology in Indiana,
> my foremost thought has always been to merit your regard and ap-
> proval in everything I have done. In this I believe I have not labored
> in vain.[53]

Black died of a heart attack in September, 1964. His student
James Kellar, described by Black in a letter to Lilly as "the hard-
est working young man I have ever seen," replaced him as Society archaeologist. The Society's Highway Salvage Program
was carried on by Black's friend and colleague Jack Householder
from 1956 to 1974 until the state began to hire its own archaeologists. Kellar, professor of anthropology at Indiana University
and director of the Glenn A. Black Laboratory of Archaeology,
continues to advise federal agencies and private corporations
about the archaeological significance of proposed building sites
in accordance with historic preservation statutes. Also under his
leadership the focus of the Society's archaeological research interests has shifted from Angel site to the very large Mann site in
nearby Posey County.

The Indiana Historical Society's role in the development of
Indiana archaeology was pivotal. Without the agency of a
learned society, offering leadership and guidance to talented
amateurs as well as a chance to participate substantively, it is
difficult to imagine how either Black or Lilly could have found
an opportunity to make an important contribution to the newly
emerging profession of archaeology. The Society acted as a
crucial intermediary between professional and amateur archaeologists and eventually provided Black with the bridge he
needed to a full professional career.

The focus of archaeological research has shifted quite appro-

---

[53] Lilly to Black, January 14, 1941, [January 7?, 1942], Black to Lilly, May 18,
1944, Black Papers.

priately from historical societies to universities, but the serious amateur, the avocational archaeologist, still has a contribution to make to research in prehistory under the guidance of professional archaeologists. Under the leadership of archaeologist James Kellar the Society honors the legacy of Eli Lilly and Glenn Black by continuing to support research in prehistory and to encourage through the archaeology section the serious collaboration of avocational archaeologists.

IX

Another Beginning – the Society since 1976

John Giles

Gayle Thornbrough
executive secretary

IX

*"[The Eli Lilly bequest] is going to open up all kinds of ave-
nues for the Society."*
Gayle Thornbrough, 1977

In April, 1976, when Gayle Thornbrough took office as executive secretary of the Indiana Historical Society, she inherited a
staff of eleven (six in the library, two in the office, three in publications), a budget of $320,000, and an endowment of roughly
$3.6 million. Her office was in a large room on the fourth floor
of the State Library and Historical Building, partitioned to provide a modicum of privacy, but she and the three editorial
workers with whom she shared the room inevitably were obliged
to overhear one another's telephone conversations. Her business staff was still housed, two corridor lengths away, in the Bureau office. When Thornbrough brought in the Society's first
assistant executive secretary in September, 1976—a brand new
Indiana University Ph.D., Raymond L. Shoemaker, III—he too
was stationed for a while at a desk that was temporarily available in the Bureau. By contrast, in 1979, the Society employed
a regular staff of twenty-five (thirteen in the library, five in the
office, four in publications, one in the Junior Historical Society,
two in the talking books project) and six more on special projects,
with a budget of $920,000 and an endowment of more than $22
million. The Society was housed in ten office rooms and occupied the entire third floor of the 1976 addition to the State Li-

brary and Historical Building, which included a handsome conference room, the Smith Library reading room and stacks, and
an employee lounge and kitchen area.

This great growth in staff, work space, and financial resources
over the past few years was made possible by Eli Lilly. The new
building was funded jointly by the State of Indiana and the
Indiana Historical Society. The ninety-two-year-old patron of
Indiana history and prehistory was present at the building's
dedication in October, 1976; he was in a wheelchair and unchar-
acteristically feeble, but he was there to see the new headquarters, sought for so long and so essential to the Society's future
development, made possible by his gift.

Eli Lilly died a few months later, on January 24, 1977. In his
will he left to the Society 10 percent of his holdings in Eli Lilly
Company, which amounted to 309,904 shares.[1] It was a spectac-
ularly generous gift. Lilly also left to the Society a strong sense
of what kind of an institution he wanted, a view he shared in
broad principles with other trustees and officers of the Society
and which, therefore, is likely to predominate for many years to
come. The substance of that view can be expressed in several
maxims: the Society has an essentially scholarly mission, research and publication; it should undertake projects that make a
lasting contribution; it should avoid owning property; it should
not attempt to compete with or replace historical programs undertaken by governmental agencies but should undertake to do
the kinds of things such agencies are ill-equipped or simply unable to do; it is a not-for-profit public trust with a long-term
overriding responsibility to serve the cause of preserving, col-

---

[1] Other institutions receiving a substantial share of Lilly's holdings included
Butler University, Indianapolis Museum of Art, Earlham College, Wabash
College, Philadelphia College of Pharmacy and Science, Christ Church Episcopal
Cathedral, Indianapolis, and the Children's Museum of Indianapolis.

lecting, and disseminating Indiana history; the Society is a service organization, offering its members an opportunity to support history.

It would be an error to see the Indiana Historical Society, now or at any other time in its history, as the tool or agency of one person. Lilly was an extremely capable capitalist: he invested in projects and people revealing potential for high achievement. The Society in which he chose to invest his time and his money had already demonstrated both tenacity and the ability to attract and hold talented leaders. Lilly wanted to support these civic endeavors, not usurp or overwhelm them. The Society was fortunate that its leadership throughout the forty-seven years of Lilly's continuous interest was composed of men and women of ability and accomplishment, with their own strong senses of civic responsibility. Though Lilly was in a position to make an unusual financial contribution, his fellow officers, board members, and trustees were in every other sense his peers. The Society has been shaped by their collective wisdom.

It is much too early to evaluate the long range impact of the Lilly bequest. Certainly there should be opportunities for the Society to make important new contributions to understanding American history through studies of local, state, and midwestern institutions and persons. The Society has already turned to a wide circle of expert friends to generate and to evaluate projects. Already, as a result, a number of ambitious works are under way.

Among the Society's many responses to its new status was a general reconsideration of its legal bases, the legislative charter of 1831 and the much-amended constitution. A special committee of the Board of Trustees met for more than a year in cooperation with legal counsel engaged specifically to review these considerations. After comparing the Society's legal machinery with that of other not-for-profit organizations, they concluded that the constitution was an unnecessarily cumbersome instrument for day-to-day government and proposed to replace it with amendments to the charter and the enactment of a new code of bylaws. The most important element of the constitution, its statement of purpose, was incorporated into the 1831 charter. Great care was taken to retain that charter, which the committee judged to be a sound basis for the Society's legal existence. The bill to amend the charter was approved by the General Assembly March 1, 1978. The members of the Society repealed the constitution and adopted new bylaws at meetings in November, 1977, and May, 1978. (All of these documents are reprinted in the appendix, pp. 352-65).

In May, 1977, the board of trustees approved a group of new enterprises. First, the Society undertook to expand and/or bolster a number of already existing programs. Among these were two archaeology projects: a survey of the Beanblossom Creek drainage system, designed to help develop a model to predict where archaeological sites can be found by using controlled sampling techniques; and extensive, long-term investigations of the Mann site in Posey County, according to Kellar "the largest prehistoric habitation in Indiana and one of the most complex." In memory of Lilly, a regular customer of the State Library's talking book collections after his sight began to fail, the Society is sponsoring the recording of books in the fields of state and local history. The Indiana Junior Historical Society, a large organization for many years jointly supported by the Society and the Bureau, was provided with a full-time assistant director, thus freeing its director Robert Kirby, to travel more around the state to promote the organization. The Society also increased support of the juniors' summer programs, offering opportunities for more members to participate in camps, workshops, and tours.

Then the board turned to altogether new projects. First, looking around for ways to aid local historical societies and museums, the Society's board added a staff member to act, in cooperation with the Indiana Historical Bureau, as liaison with local organizations and conduct regional workshops. Thomas K. Krasean, field representative, planned and conducted seven workshops. Then, in order to make the combined research resources of the Society's library more accessible to scholars the Society undertook three related projects: the preparation and publication of a guide to the manuscript collections of the Society, an important and ambitious project which depends to a large extent on reducing the backlog of unprocessed manuscripts; awarding fellowships to support dissertations in the field of Indiana and midwestern history; and a symposium for professors of history in Indiana colleges and universities with graduate programs in history to improve their acquaintance with the resources of the Smith Library and the State Library. In the same vein, the Society has supported the preparation by Donald E. Thompson of Wabash College of a checklist of manuscript collections in a wide variety of institutions and in private hands throughout the state.

By March, 1978, the Society's board had approved yet another group of new projects. Of these, two projects were relatively long-term research efforts. The first was a guide to Indiana newspapers, with information about every known newspaper published in the state since 1804, including the location of original and microfilm copies. The project, directed by John W. Miller, whose doctoral dissertation at Purdue University was a study of pioneer Indiana newspapers, was initiated in 1978. The format was designed to follow generally the model of earlier newspaper guide projects in other states. When completed the guide will be an extremely useful research tool. The second long-term effort approved was the preparation of a new state guide book

Eli Lilly, 1885-1977

Indiana Historical Society Board of Trustees

Mrs. John Quincy Adams   Dr. Charles A. Bonsett   David V. Burns

Thomas S. Emison,
chairman

Bert Fenn

Byron P. Hollett

along the basic lines of the Work Projects Administration's *Indiana: A Guide to the Hoosier State* (1941). The new volume, like its predecessor, will include both history and tours. Project director Errol Stevens, whose doctoral dissertation at Indiana University was in the field of Indiana history, expects to provide "a comprehensive guide to Indiana's historical, scenic, and recreational attractions." He began work in 1978.

The Society also is supporting Professor Lance Trusty's history of the Calumet region since 1933, through a grant to the Purdue University Calumet Campus. The work, entitled "The Calumet Region—Workshop of the World," will provide an analysis of important factors since the New Deal in shaping this unique and "non Hoosier" part of Indiana. Trusty hopes to complete the manuscript for publication by the Society in 1981.

To stimulate present-day photographers to make an historic record of our own time and places, the board authorized an annual photography contest. This project is only two years old and is still finding its way, but, it is hoped, will provoke the production of photographs of lasting interest. The board also authorized an effort to collect or copy original old photographs of historic significance to augment the Society library's collection.

In view of the number and scope of new programs and new staff members to run them, the Society initiated a *Newsletter* in 1978, to help members and staff keep track of a sometimes confusing array of activities.

In 1979 the Society and Indiana University together agreed to support a new faculty position at the Bloomington campus, an historian of medicine holding a joint appointment in the Department of History and in the Department of History and Philosophy of Science. The first occupant of this position, Ann G. Carmichael, earned both the Ph. D. and M.D. degrees from Duke University in a special program for history of medicine. Professor Carmichael's appointment began in September, 1979. In addition to teaching, Carmichael began research in the history of medicine in Indiana and served as advisor both for the Smith Library and for the Medical History Committee.

In addition to these new programs the Society committed itself in 1979 to support the ongoing oral history project at Indiana University for six months in 1980 in return for aid in setting up an oral history program for the Society's library. The Society also supports a project to complete the indexing of Indiana county histories, begun under the WPA, whose workers completed indexes for the counties Adams through Marion. In cooperation with the Allen County-Fort Wayne Public Library the Society has undertaken to index the remaining county histories.

The Society also began to support the Genealogy Division of the Indiana State Library in 1979, in recognition of the tremendous services the division performs for many Society members interested in genealogy. The division's hours were extended to include Saturday afternoons from September through May with the Society's support, and the Society also funds an additional staff position in the division.

Clearly, there has been a significant change in the Society's role. From an institution with a small but excellent publications program, a small research library, a vigorous genealogy program, and an unusual archaeology program, the Society has begun to undertake a wide range of activities. The addition of an assistant executive secretary has contributed significant flexibility to the Society's administration in this period of expansion; Shoemaker has been assigned responsibility for programs, special committees and sections, and also has assumed the duties of business manager. Following the advice invited from Lawrence Towner of the Newberry Library, the Society has broadened the range of collecting for its research library and continues to explore for rich new fields to collect.

The values and maxims of the traditional Society, however, are still very much in force. There has been no headlong rush onto unfamiliar grounds. Much of what the Society has undertaken are projects to aid and promote scholarly research: the two guides to manuscript collections, the newspaper guide, the fellowships, the historian of medicine all represent efforts to support research in areas of Indiana history. Many "new" projects are really increased support for well-established programs to which the Society was already committed. Even in its "new" collecting areas the Society is most often returning with new commitment to collecting areas proposed and attempted in years past, like the architectural archives and the photograph collections. Only in its recent excursion into collecting in ethnic and black history has the Society begun new collection programs, though these are by now hardly pioneering efforts.

The Society has displayed stability without rigidity in responding to the new opportunities offered by the Lilly gift. The present leaders feel a great desire to justify the confidence in the Society's future that Eli Lilly demonstrated with his gift.

X

The Indiana Historical Society — A View from a Few Paces Back

John Giles

X

"Today is tomorrow's past."
Historical society axiom

Amerian state historical societies tend to be idiosyncratic institutions; that is, they have not followed a regular pattern. Their developmental histories have been as diverse as their present forms, but there were a few recognizable key factors common to them all: the presence or absence of a leisured group of learned men and women; the willingness or unwillingness of a state legislature to support institutions to preserve history; the presence or absence of one or more highly motivated, long-serving founders or revivers of such societies; and the ability of societies to establish nurturant relationships with important nearby colleges and universities.

In the nineteenth century the older states tended to benefit from the presence of more of these factors than the newer states and, consequently, were more successful in establishing viable state historical societies at an early date. Perhaps it was also not surprising that these early eastern societies, all privately supported, were soon imitated by their eager western neighbors, few of whom succeeded in establishing institutions that would endure for more than a decade. Of these early western efforts, all fraught with difficulties, only the Indiana Historical Society and the Historical and Philosophical Society of Ohio (now the Cincinnati Historical Society) managed to keep an organization

more or less continuously intact from the dates of their founding
(1830 and 1831, respectively) to the present. Much more successful in western states was the strategy adopted by the State
Historical Society of Wisconsin, founded in 1846, of securing
regular state appropriations to support its work. This strategy
eventually was pursued with varying results by nearly all of the
states west of the Alleghenies—though the wealthy California
Historical Society seems altogether to have eschewed the pursuit
of governmental assistance—and most western state societies
succeeded in acquiring regular public support. The Indiana Historical Society, of course, did not.[1]

The historical society movement in the United States has produced a wide variety of institutions described as state historical
societies. Any attempt to place the Indiana Historical Society
clearly within this context is impeded by the fact that the context itself is so varied and confusing.

Even the few generalizations that can be correctly made about
state historical societies serve perhaps as much to obscure important differences as to clarify them. For example, the most
common approach to describing historical societies is to divide
them into categories based on their major sources of financial
support, that is, to divide them into public and private societies.
The usual model taken for the public society is the State Historical Society of Wisconsin; for the private society, the Massachusetts Historical Society. These, however, are rather misleading
examples. Few publicly supported historical societies can emulate the Wisconsin society in annual income, size and quality of
staff, breadth and size of collections, and scope of programs.
Most publicly supported societies are located in western states

---

[1] The information on state historical societies in this chapter comes from Whitehill, *Independent Historical Societies*, and the current AASLH directory of historical societies unless otherwise noted.

(Kansas, Iowa, Missouri, Nebraska, Colorado, South Dakota, Montana, Utah, New Mexico, Nevada, Oregon, and Washington) with relatively small populations, and most have much smaller staffs, smaller budgets, and more restricted programs than Wisconsin's.

As for Massachusetts, that society is simply unique in America and serves as a model only in the sense that its successes are much admired. In fact no modern private historical society follows the Massachusetts Historical Society's example: it is a small, extremely exclusive club composed of men and women who are either learned or wealthy or both; it collects relatively little, basking in the rich glow of an incomparable collection of books and manuscripts relating to early American history assembled for the most part in the eighteenth and nineteenth centuries; it concentrates exclusively on maintaining its library and publishing parts of its rich collections. This is not a design that other private state societies find at all practical for emulation. In fact, the New-York Historical Society, the Historical Society of Pennsylvania, and the Virginia Historical Society have served somewhat more as models for privately supported historical societies than Massachusetts's. They have encouraged relatively larger memberships than Massachusetts's stern 155, though most have continued the requirement of election to membership. They have maintained historical museums as well as libraries and usually have not emphasized publishing as much as their other programs. Many private historical societies receive small regular appropriations from their state governments. Most have emphasized collections in their own state histories, rather than following the broader ambitions of the Massachusetts society. Endowments, physical headquarters, and number and quality of staff vary considerably.

This already complicated portrait of American state historical societies is made yet more complex by the existence of rival state

historical agencies in many states. In states where rather exclusive private historical societies have existed for many years,
broader-based historical organizations have sometimes been
formed to offer a variety of programs to a much wider stratum
of the state's citizens. In New York, for example, the New-York
Historical Society, with a present membership of 1,800 was
joined in 1899 by the New York Historical Association, which
now attracts a membership of nearly 8,000. In still other states
private historical societies have been supplemented and often
challenged by the creation of state agencies mandated to collect,
preserve, and disseminate state history and thus have become
rival collectors. Such state agencies have also often entered the
fields of archaeology, education, museums, and historic sites
preservation. The proliferation of historical agencies in many
states has undoubtedly increased and improved the store of
available historical materials, but it has also raised questions
about the role of the private state historical society and increased
the difficulty of comparing the historical program of one state
with another.

Safe it is, at least, to say that there is no typical state historical
society, not even a typical privately supported state historical society. Who, then, are the Indiana Historical Society's peers? With
whom should this Society compare itself, both in retrospect and
in prospect?

In its regional context at least, the Indiana Historical Society
is like its neighbors only in the sense that all of them differ in
important ways from one another: Ohio's society is a very large
publicly supported organization that has specialized in archaeology and maintaining historic sites; it has a full-time staff of
325 persons and a budget of over $5 million.[2] The Kentucky His-
torical Society is also publicly supported and concentrates on its

---

[2] *The Ohio Historical Society Annual Report Fiscal Year 1979* [n.p., n.d.],
p. 23.

library and publications, though it also maintains museums and historic sites (staff 56, budget $1.3 million).[3] The publicly supported Illinois society is relatively small and essentially operates as an advisory arm of the major state historical agency, the Illinois State Historical Library, whose director is also the society's director. The Illinois State Historical Society has no separate library, does not publish books, but does publish a journal and a junior historian magazine, both edited by members of the library staff (no full-time staff, budget around $70,000).[4] The Historical Society of Michigan, by contrast, is completely independent of the state historical agency, which has traditionally been the most active and productive institution in the field of Michigan history. The society was apparently associated with the Michigan Historical Commission from 1913 to 1963, when the connection was severed, and the society moved eventually from Lansing to Ann Arbor. This society has no library and does not publish books; the organization has concentrated on tours and educational programs but also publishes a popular quarterly magazine (staff 3, budget $200,000).[5]

The Indiana Historical Society does not very closely resemble any of its neighbors, any more than they resemble one another. Its program is considerably narrower than those of the large state-supported societies in Ohio and Kentucky and considerably broader than the programs of Illinois and Michigan. Entirely privately supported, the Indiana society's budget and staff are more than four times larger than those of its only privately supported neighboring society, Michigan's.

Program for program, the comparisons become perhaps some-

---

[3] W. R. Buster, Director of the Kentucky Historical Society, to Lisa Nowak, Indiana Historical Society, February 12, 1980.

[4] "Annual Report," in *Journal of the Illinois State Historical Society*, LXXII (1979), 292, 306.

[5] "Historical Society of Michigan 1977–78 Annual Report," in *Chronicle: The Magazine of the Historical Society of Michigan*, XIV (1979), 13–17.

above, members of the board of
trustees at the April, 1980, meeting:
l. to r., Bert Fenn, Mrs. James P.
Mullin, Richard Ristine, Gayle
Thornbrough, John Windle, Charles
Bonsett, Alan Nolan, Richard Simons,
Byron Hollett, David Burns, Larry
Pitts

Eli Lilly Memorial and Board of
Trustees Room

what more illuminating. In its publication record, the Society is unexcelled by its neighbors. The Society's library is a specialized one and difficult to compare with those of the three neighboring societies that have libraries, but it is fair to say that it is smaller and more exclusively a research library than any of its midwestern peers. In archaeology the Society's work has been excelled only by Ohio. In junior history Indiana has as strong a program as any in the country, offering a fully organized state structure, both on the elementary school and high school levels, and a variety of statewide programs throughout the year. This program is supported in part by the Society. Like Michigan and Illinois, the Indiana society has neither a museum nor a program to preserve historic sites.

Similarly the Society does not closely resemble other prosperous, well-established, privately supported state historical societies in other parts of the country. Unlike the older societies in New York, Pennsylvania, and Massachusetts, the Indiana Historical Society embraces a relatively large, broadly representative membership and generally aspires to even greater numbers. Unlike those other societies, the Indiana Historical Society did not succeed in acquiring a significant permanent library until the twentieth century. The Society's library, consequently, is smaller and more narrowly focused than those of other well-established private state societies. Unlike most other private state societies, the Society has neither a museum nor the "visibility" provided by a separate building for its collections. Unlike the others, the Society maintains a program of archaeological research and in co-operation with the state historical agency supports a statewide junior historical society.

There are a few striking differences between the Indiana Historical Society on the one hand and most other state societies, public and private, on the other. For one, the Society emerged only four years ago as an entirely independent organization after more than fifty years of partial dependence upon the state-supported Indiana Historical Bureau; hence, this very old society is in one sense also very new. Another distinguishing characteristic is the Society's relative freedom from substantial financial obligations. For the most part the Society has deliberately avoided acquiring real property and is housed under a ninety-nine-year lease in a building owned and maintained by the State of Indiana.[6] Its only permanent large program commitment is the library, a relatively small research institution that already owns most of the books and manuscripts the Society set out more than forty years ago to collect in the field of Indiana territorial history. Finally, the Society is distinguished by the size of its endowment, which is among the largest of the private historical societies.[7]

Among privately supported state historical societies then, the Indiana Historical Society is an unusual institution. Unlike most midwestern societies it failed to acquire a significant level of regular state financial support and has remained, sometimes against its will, a privately supported society. The Society's present administrative structure and financial resources are only very recently acquired, and the institution is relatively unencumbered by financial responsibilities. The result is an essentially new, in-

---

[6] The Society owns the forty-acre historic site of Fort Knox II near Vincennes, a gift.

[7] For example, the Massachusetts Historical Society has investments worth a little over $8 million; the New-York Historical Society funds total approximately $12 million; and the Virginia Historical Society's endowment fund appears to be valued at more than $4.5 million. "Meetings and Reports," in *Massachusetts Historical Society Proceedings*, XC (1978), 159; *The New-York Historical Society Annual Report for the Year 1978*, p. 43; "Virginia Historical Society Annual Meeting, January 19, 1979," in *Virginia Magazine of History and Biography*, LXXXVII (1979), 243-44. The Society's endowment funds totaled more than $23.6 million as of September 30, 1979. *Indiana Historical Society Annual Report, 1978-1979*, p. 77.

dependent institution with an opportunity to explore some striking possibilities in support of state and local history in America.

This is a rather dramatic reversal of the Society's fortunes. For
many years the Society was obliged to struggle simply to maintain a bare existence, and then for many more years it was dependent upon a state agency that was itself relatively impoverished. Despite these impediments the Society managed to attract
talented officers and staff and contributed outstanding work in
history and archaeology, at the same time it was building a
unique research library with very limited funds. It is pleasing to
see this tradition of accomplishment under difficult conditions
rewarded with the opportunity to make the most of substantially
greater resources.

The opportunities, which are very great and carry with them
a considerable burden of responsibility, suggest that the Indiana
Historical Society will continue to occupy a distinctive place in
the extremely diverse community of American state historical
societies. Its role should, however, change somewhat in the years
to come, because the Society has the chance to become an ex-
plorer. Since the Society has on the one hand the means to undertake programs other private historical societies have not been
able to attempt, but does not on the other hand have the means
to try every plausible proposal that comes before its directors,
the institution's leaders will be under heavy obligations to re-
think and perhaps to redefine the boundaries of the historical
society's mission.

This is an obligation Society leaders take very seriously. Committees have already been working on different aspects of program and policy planning for some time, soliciting a broad range
of advice and demonstrating a willingness to consider complex
issues thoughtfully and thoroughly. Innovative programs have
already been undertaken—notably the funding of a faculty position in the history of medicine at Indiana University and the

preparation of a new historical guide to Indiana, along the lines of the WPA guide—reflecting the Society's traditional commitment to research and publishing. But the committee's task remains a formidable one. Simply making decisions about what is needed in this state to promote historical knowledge and understanding is difficult; even more complex is deciding how the needs should be met and by which agencies. The question then arises, what should be the newly independent Society's relationships with other agencies? How, in other words, should an independent, responsible historical society operate in a state with a profusion of organizations devoted to one aspect or another of state history? Implicitly the question also arises, what is a state government's basic irreducible responsibility to state and local history? This is an extremely difficult area, made more unwieldy by the virtual impossibility of comparing one state's historical program with that of another, since state budgets are paradigms of rampant individualism. Even the attempt to approximate totals of a state's expenditures on all aspects of history is undermined by the uniqueness of each state's accounting and budgeting procedures. Certainly most observers of historical programs in Indiana have the impression that the Indiana state government traditionally spends significantly less in this area than most of its neighbors. To what extent should a private society concern itself in these issues; to what extent should such an institution step in when government has abdicated its traditional role?

Equally thought provoking are the large questions of whom the state historical society should serve and how best to serve that constituency. These are questions the Society must consciously address if it is to have more than a local significance in the historical society movement. As historical societies have become increasingly staffed by professional historians, they have tended to become less "societies" and more institutions of learning. Historical societies have tended to divide rather sharply between a staff, which "provides" historical materials, and members, who consume a product. This perhaps inevitable division obscures and undermines the general understanding of the historical mission of these societies, a mission which needs to be reviewed and reappraised as a basis for exploring future possibilities.

Historical societies have traditionally played an unusual role in American culture: they have formed a meeting ground upon which amateurs and professionals have acknowledged their common interest in one of a community's most essential and least tangible needs—the need for a coherent past. The participation of responsible nonprofessionals in the work of historical societies testifies to the importance of the historian's function for the larger community. Whereas medical societies, legal associations, library associations, and educational associations have become purely professional bodies, signaling the formation of a guild with monopolistic control over their crafts, professional historians have never been able to establish a monopoly over history. Though the skills needed to research and write history well are no less complex and difficult to acquire than the skills needed for other professions, for many history has seemed too important to be left only to the historians.

Historical societies antedated the emergence of history as a profession by fifty years or more. Hence amateurs and nonhistorians took the initiative in collecting and preserving historical materials. Although the profile of the historian has changed considerably as history has been professionalized, the profile of the active member of historical societies has remained remarkably stable over the years: historical society workers are usually people who feel a high sense of personal responsibility for preserving the records of a community's past—often because of association with either historic events or individuals. This sense of responsibility has endured despite the emergence of experts, like professional historians and archivists, who are committed to many of the same goals.

The basis for this enduring sense of responsibility for history is the recognition, implicit or explicit, that history is a collaboration between the collector/preserver and the researcher/writer, that it is responsible individuals who provide many of the most essential materials for history. Historians, trained and untrained, are dependent upon access to private records; libraries with unique books and manuscripts; and government archives. Professionals can run the libraries and write the books, but it is the private citizen with an historical conscience upon whom all depend for preserving personal records and depositing them where they can be used.[8]

Historical societies also represent one of the most important elements of the historian's public: those who take history seriously in a personal way, those who bring an historic awareness and perspective to their own lives and those of their families and acquaintances. They are themselves historians in the sense of being preservers of the past, individuals who remember and translate their memories into something tangible. Moreover, to a great extent they shape the understanding of history by providing its materials. What is not recorded is forgotten eventually. History is what is recorded and interpreted.

The historical society's traditional recognition of the community's interest in preserving and interpreting its history has been somewhat threatened in the past fifty years by the rise of professionalism in history. Professional historians have tended to believe, as Julian Boyd suggested in his important article "State and Local Historical Societies in the United States," pub-

---

[8] The same impulse to protect the fragile fabric of a community's memory sometimes inspires the historical society member to record his or her own memories of people and events, therewith providing another potentially important record of the past.

lished in 1934, that the sole legitimate function of historical societies is to provide scholars with research material—documents,
catalogs, bibliographies, and guides to manuscript collections,
for example—and that the role of the amateur was henceforward
to keep a respectful distance from the task of writing history.[9] To
a considerable extent societies have accepted this definition of
their role, though some perhaps have been disappointed that no
more has been returned to them by historians in the way of a
usable past. Other societies have downplayed their scholarly
mission and concentrated on popular presentations of state and
local history: historymobiles, pageantry, dramatization, living
history, picture magazines, and the like—often equating super-
ficiality and slanginess with the concept "popular."

The attempt to serve both professional and nonprofessional
constituencies for state and local history and to provide a forum
for exchange and co-operation between the groups is extremely
challenging. The Indiana Historical Society has at times in the
past succeeded dramatically in providing such a forum and will
probably continue to aspire to promote a fruitful collaboration
between imaginative amateurs and professionals, in the tradition of Eli Lilly, for example, and his professional colleagues in
the Society.

But all of this is mere speculation. How the Society will use its
extraordinary new resources is only now being decided. All that
is certain is that this tenacious institution, supported by a relatively small group of responsible men and women throughout
a long and often discouraging history, has emerged as a most
potentially interesting new force in the American historical society movement. With unprecedented opportunities to explore
and to innovate and with thoughtful, responsible leaders care-

---

[9] Julian P. Boyd, "State and Local Historical Societies in the United States," in
American Historical Review, XL (1934), 10–37.

fully re-examining the institution's role, the Society's choices in the years to come will comprise a commentary on the vitality of the historical society idea in the United States. After 150 years it seems clear that the Indiana Historical Society has encountered its most important turning point and is now still more at the beginning than at the end of its career.

APPENDICES

OFFICERS

Officers were elected at annual meetings, held in November or December. The dates reflect the year in which they were elected through the year their successors were elected, unless the office was vacant for a time.

Presidents

Benjamin Parke	1830-1835
Samuel Merrill	1835-1848
Isaac Blackford	1848-1859
John Law	1859-1873
Charles H. Test	1877-1884
William H. English	1886-1896
William Wesley Woollen	1896-1900
Daniel Wait Howe	1900-1920
Charles W. Moores	1920-1923
James A. Woodburn	1923-1930
Evans Woollen	1930-1932
Eli Lilly	1932-1946
William O. Lynch	1946-1949
Anton Scherrer	1949-1951
Mrs. Harry T. Watts	1951-1954
John G. Rauch	1954-1956
John D. Barnhart	1956-1959
Herbert H. Heimlich	1959-1961
Byron K. Trippet	1961-1965
Thomas S. Emison	1965-1973
David V. Burns	1974-

1st Vice-Presidents

Isaac Blackford	1830-1835
Jeremiah Sullivan	1835-1848
George H. Dunn	1848-1854
Aaron B. Line	1859-1886
William Wesley Woollen	1886-1896
John Coburn	1896-1908
Charles W. Moores	1908-1920
James A. Woodburn	1920-1923
Evans Woollen	1924-1930
Richard B. Wetherill	1930-1940
Charles Roll	1940-1941
William O. Lynch	1941-1946
Harry O. Garman	1946-1948
John G. Rauch	1948-1954
Lee Burns	1954-1956

John P. Goodwin	1956-1972
Mrs. John Q. Adams	1972-1974
John T. Windle	1974-

2nd Vice-Presidents

Jesse L. Holman	1830-1835
Charles I. Battell	1835-1842
Charles Dewey	1842-1848
John Law	1848-1859
Rev. George Upfold	1859-1872
John Coburn	1886-1896
Daniel Wait Howe	1896-1900
William E. English	1900-1926
Harlow Lindley	1926-1928
Charles T. Sansberry	1928-1930
Mrs. Harvey Morris	1930-1944
Benjamin D. Hitz	1944-1945
Harry O. Garman	1945-1946
Lee Burns	1946-1954
John D. Barnhart	1954-1956
Herbert H. Heimlich	1956-1959
Lyman S. Ayres	1959-1961
Thomas S. Emison	1961-1965
Mrs. John Q. Adams	1965-1972
	1974-

Third Vice-Presidents

James Scott	1830-1835
Abner T. Ellis	1835-1842
Isaac Blackford	1842-1848
Jeremiah Sullivan	1848-1859
Hamilton Smith	1859-1875
Daniel Wait Howe	1886-1896
William E. English	1896-1900
Bishop D. O'Donaghue	1900-1910
James A. Woodburn	1910-1920
Harlow Lindley	1920-1926
Susan Howe	1926-1927
Charles A. Sansberry	1927-1928
Richard B. Wetherill	1928-1930

Arthur G. Mitten	1930-1938
Wylie Daniels	1938-1941
F. A. Miller	1941-1942
Harry O. Garman	1942-1945
Lee Burns	1945-1946
Ora F. Hall	1946-1947
Helen Elliott	1947-1948
Cornelius O'Brien	1948-1953
John D. Barnhart	1953-1954
Clarence A. Dryden	1954-1961
Mrs. John Q. Adams	1961-1965
John F. Wilhelm	1965-1971
Eugene S. Pulliam	1974-

Recording Secretaries

Bethuel F. Morris	1830-1835
George H. Dunn	1835-1842
William Sheets	1842-1848
Thomas L. Sullivan	1848-1859
John B. Dillon	1859-1879
William H. H. Terrell	1879-1886
Jacob P. Dunn	1886-1924
Christopher B. Coleman	1924-1926

Corresponding Secretaries

John H. Farnham	1830-1835
Isaac Blackford	1835-1842
John Law	1842-1848
Charles W. Cady	1848-1859
John B. Dillon	1859-1879
William H. H. Terrell	1879-1886
William W. Woollen	1886-1896
George S. Cottman	1906-1908
Christopher B. Coleman	1908-1919
Frank B. Wynn	1919-1921
Susan Howe	1924-1926

Secretaries
(Recording and Corresponding
combined after 1926)

Christopher B. Coleman	1926-1945
Howard H. Peckham	1945-1954
Hubert Hawkins	1954-1969

The office of secretary was eliminated by constitutional amendment
in 1969. Duties formerly performed
by secretaries are now performed by
the Executive Secretary, who is appointed by the Board of Trustees.
See under Staff, p. 337.

Treasurers

James Blake	1830-1842
Charles W. Cady	1842-1848
James M. Ray	1848-1881
William De M. Hooper	1886-1894
Charles E. Coffin	1894-1930
John G. Rauch	1930-1945
Evans Woollen, Jr.	1945-1959
Burke Nicholas	1959-1966
Jameson Woollen	1966-1979
Byron P. Hollett	1979-1980
Larry K. Pitts	1980-

Executive Committee

The officers of the Society plus other
elected members comprised the Executive Committee

Samuel Merrill	1830-1835
George H. Dunn	1830-1835
	1842-1848
Isaac Howk	1830-1833
James Whitcomb	1830-1835
	1848-1852
John Law	1830-1835
Henry Coburn	1835-1854
James Farrington	1835-1842
Charles Dewey	1835-1842
James McKinney	1835-1842
James M. Ray	1835-1848
Henry Ward Beecher	1842-1848
Douglass Maguire	1842-1848
James Blake	1848-1859
George W. Mears	1848-1879
John B. Dillon	1848-1859
Calvin Fletcher	1859-1866
John Coburn	1859-1886
Addison L. Roache	1859-1906
Henry S. Lane	1859-1881
John R. Wilson	1886-1907
Addison C. Harris	1886-1916
William De M. Hooper	1886-1894
Jacob P. Dunn	1886-1910

Charles Martindale	1894-1920	Eli Lilly	1946-1963
John H. Holliday	1906-1921	Harry O. Garman	1948-1952
Charles W. Moores	1907-1910	Richard B. Sealock	1948-1949
Eliza G. Browning	1910-1921	John D. Barnhart	1948-1953
George S. Cottman	1910-1916		1959-1963
Mrs. Frank A. Morrison	1916-1925	Herbert Heimlich	1949-1955
Logan Esarey	1916-1921	Mrs. Harry T. Watts	1949-1951
Lee Burns	1920-1945	Lorenz G. Schumm	1951-1959
Evans Woollen	1921-1924	John P. Goodwin	1952-1955
Linnaeus N. Hines	1921-1933	Willis Richardson	1953-1963
Herriott C. Palmer	1921-1925	Lyman S. Ayres	1956-1959
Amos W. Butler	1924-1933	Byron K. Trippet	1959-1961
Mrs. Eva Neal Beck		John F. Wilhelm	1960-1963
(Morris)	1925-1933	Elsie Sweeney	1960-1963
Mrs. Harvey Morris	1925-1931	Thomas S. Emison	1960-1963
Otto M. Knoblock	1929-1935	Mrs. John Q. Adams	1960-1963
Cornelius O'Brien	1933-1948	William E. Wilson	1961-1963
Luther M. Feeger	1933-1936	Mrs. George Blair	1961-1963
Curtis G. Shake	1933-1936		
Albert L. Kohlmeier	1936-1948		
Mrs. W. W. Gaar	1936-1944		
Hal Phelps	1936-1941		
Ora Hall	1941-1946		
Anton Scherrer	1944-1949		
John G. Rauch	1945-1948		
	1955-1963		

For most of its history the Society's executive committee was composed of all other officers in addition to those elected specifically as the executive committee. The committee was expanded and renamed the board of trustees by constitutional amendment in December, 1962.

Board of Trustees

The following persons were specifically elected as Society trustees. All other elected officers are also members of the board.

John G. Rauch	1963-1976	Eugene S. Pulliam	1965-
chairman	1963-1972	Alexander Bracken	1967-1971
Eli Lilly	1963-1977	Herman B Wells	1968-
John D. Barnhart	1963-1968	John L. Ford	1971-1973
Herbert H. Heimlich	1963-1967	Richard O. Ristine	1971-
Willis Richardson	1963-1965	Mrs. James P. Mullin	1972-
Elsie Sweeney	1963-1972	Charles A. Bonsett	1973-
John F. Wilhelm	1963-1965	Thomas S. Emison	1974-
	1970-	chairman	1979-
chairman	1972-1979	Bert Fenn	1976-
William E. Wilson	1963-1971	Alan T. Nolan	1976-
Mrs. George W. Blair	1963-1976	Richard S. Simons	1976-
David V. Burns	1963-	Byron P. Hollett	1977-
Roger D. Branigin	1965-1976	Larry K. Pitts	1979-

LIBRARY COMMITTEE

Lee Burns	1924-1925	Howard H. Bates	1960-1963
	1927-1954	Caroline Dunn	1961-1970
Evans Woollen	1924-1933	Alan T. Nolan	1964-1976
Christopher B. Coleman	1924-1933	Rudolf K. Haerle	1968-
	1938-1944	James P. Mullin	1971-
Amos Butler	1926	Mrs. William T. Ray	1971-1972
Benjamin D. Hitz	1934-1948	John F. Stover	1971-
Perry W. Lesh	1934-1946	Donald E. Thompson	1971-
J. K. Lilly, Jr.	1936-1954	Mrs. Francis Hummons	1973-1974
Frederic D. Rose	1940-1944	Mrs. John C. Miller	1973
Howard H. Peckham	1945-1954	Mrs. Helen Davidson	1974-
W. J. Holliday	1945-1967	J. David Baker	1976-1979
	1971-1972	Bert Fenn	1976
William E. Wilson	1947-1963	Mrs. Conner R. Jester	1976-
	1968-1971	Kenneth P. McCutchan	1976-
Guy Wainwright	1950-1956	Mrs. H. W.	
Lorenz G. Schumm	1955-1959	Rhodehamel, Jr.	1976-
Emma Lou Thornbrough	1955-1967	Theodore L. Steele	1976-
Benjamin D. Hitz, Jr.	1955-1971	Donald T. Zimmer	1976-
Hubert H. Hawkins	1957-1967		

STAFF

Executive Secretary

Hubert H. Hawkins December 1969-
March 1976
Gayle Thornbrough   April 1976-

Assistant Executive Secretary

Raymond Leroy Shoemaker
September 1976-

Assistant Secretary and Treasurer

Lucy M. Elliott   1921-1923

Field Representative

Thomas K. Krasean
November 1977-

Business Office

Cleta Robinson   July 1929-
December 1969*
Alice Johnston   January 1969-
Mary Dick   December 1969-
Emma Lents   February 1977-
Ronald Bone   December 1979-
Carolyn Sue Smith   April 1980-

**Director of Publications
and the Library**

Gayle Thornbrough   1968-

Librarian

Florence Venn   December 1935-
August 1939

* Cleta Robinson was employed
by the Indiana Historical Bureau
for the entire period listed, serving also as Society membership
secretary; from April, 1956, to
December, 1969, she received a
supplementary salary from the
Society.

Caroline Dunn   November 1939-
January 1973
Thomas A. Rumer   January 1979-
(staff since 1973)

Library Staff

Richard C. Smith   May 1936-
April 1941
Gay Russie Ferguson   May 1941-
June 1942
Suzanne White   September 1946-
May 1948
Martha Lois Wilson Willis
October 1948-June 1950
Grace Nixon   January 1949-
January 1958
Eva Draegert   November 1950-
December 1952
Mary E. Studebaker   May 1952-
June 1971
Martha Norman   October 1956-
December 1970
Alice A. Hodson   August 1958-
December 1961
Leona Alig   April 1962-
Joan Gerlach   October 1967-
January 1973
Carolyn Sue Smith   March 1969-
April 1980
Ruth Dorrel   July 1969-
February 1971
Edna Murphy   March 1970-
March 1971
Neda Caperton   June 1971-
February 1974
Edna Miller   August 1971-
September 1978
IdaMae Good Miller
February 1973-
Thomas A. Rumer   August 1973-
Cynthia Todd   July 1974-July 1976
Karen Mowery   January 1977-
May 1978
Jeffrey Gunderson   July 1977-
Pamela Najar   September 1977-
Eric Pumroy   February 1978-

Daniel Kiernan	April 1978-	Lisa Nowak	July 1977-August 1980
Ramona Duncan	June 1978-	Amy Slotten	July 1980-
Linda Carlson Sharp	August 1978-		
Timothy Peterson	December 1978-	**Archaeology**	
Leigh Darbee	May 1979-	Glenn A. Black	March 1932-September 1964
Susan Darnell	June 1979-	Elam Y. Guernsey	January 1933-February 1939
James Leachman	December 1979-	William L. Rude	February 1942-September 1959
Connie McBirney	January 1980-		
Barbara A. McCurdy	April 1980-	Edward Blondin	April 1947-October 1950

Archaeology

Glenn A. Black	March 1932-September 1964
Elam Y. Guernsey	January 1933-February 1939
William L. Rude	February 1942-September 1959
Edward Blondin	April 1947-October 1950
Gertrude S. Behrick	July 1952-March 1967
James H. Kellar	September 1954-
Jack C. Householder	1956-1977
Richard B. Johnston	August 1961-November 1964
Jim Rilley Lamb	October 1964-December 1965

Editorial

Gayle Thornbrough	June 1937-December 1966
Dorothy L. Riker	April 1956-December 1979
Terry Joan Dean	November 1968-May 1970
Paula Corpuz	June 1970-
Lana Ruegamer	October 1975-

SPECIAL PROJECTS

Newspaper Bibliography Project

John W. Miller	June 1978-
Patricia Luken	August 1978-
Paul Brockman	September 1978-
Alicia Rasley	June 1980-

Indiana Guide Project

Errol Stevens	August 1978-
Deirdre Spencer	September 1978-
MaryJo Wagner	September 1978-June 1979
Robert Taylor	February 1979-
Mary Ann Ponder	February 1980-

Indiana History Project—Talking Books

Carol Horrell	May 1979-
Vivian Bokash	August 1979-

County History Indexes

Ruth Dorrel	November 1978-

Indiana Manuscript Checklist Project

Donald E. Thompson	November 1978-

Indiana State Library Genealogy Division

Robert Strange	November 1979-

Indiana Junior Historical Society

Debbie Fausset	June 1977-

Indiana Newspaper Microfilming Project

John W. Miller	April 1980-
Dennis Hardin	May 1980-
Pat Gillogly	June 1980-
Terry Cosby	June 1980-

PUBLICATIONS OF THE INDIANA HISTORICAL SOCIETY

Publications Series

Volume I

1. *Proceedings of the Indiana Historical Society, 1830-1886* (1897)
2. *Northwest Territory: Letter Of Nathan Dane Concerning The Ordinance Of 1787 and Patrick Henry's Secret Letter Of Instruction To George Rogers Clark* (1897)
3. *The Uses Of History*, by Pres. Andrew Wylie, D. D. (1897)
4. *The National Decline of the Miami Indians*, by John B. Dillon (Delivered before the Society May 23, 1848) (1897)
5. *Early History of Indianapolis and Central Indiana*, by Nathaniel Bolton [1853] (1897)
6. *Joseph G. Marshall*, by John L. Campbell [1873] (1897)
7. *Judge John Law*, by Charles Denby [1873] (1897)
8. *Archaeology*, by Prof. E. T. Cox [1877] (1897)
9. *The Early Settlement of the Miami Country*, by Dr. Ezra Ferris (1897)

Volume II

1. *The Laws and Courts of Northwest and Indiana Territories*, by Daniel Wait Howe (1886)
2. *Life and Services of John B. Dillon*, by Gen. John Coburn, With a Sketch by Judge Horace P. Biddle (1886)
3. *The Acquisition of Louisiana*, by Judge Thomas M. Cooley (1887)
4. *Loughery's Defeat and Pigeon Roost Massacre, with Introductory sketch*, by Charles Martindale (1888)
5. *A Descriptive Catalogue of the Official Publications of the Territory and State of Indiana from 1800 to 1890*, by Daniel Waite [sic] Howe (1890)
6. *The Rank of Charles Osborn as an Anti-Slavery Pioneer*, by George W. Julian (1891)
7. *The Man in History, An Oration for the Columbian Year*, by John Clark Ridpath (1893)
8. *Ouiatanon, A Study in Indiana History*, by Oscar J. Craig (1893)
9. *Reminiscences of a Journey to Indianapolis in the Year 1836*, by C. P. Ferguson, and *Life of Ziba Foote*, by Samuel Morrison (1893)
10. *"Old Settlers,"* by Robert B. Duncan (1894)
11. *Documents Relating to the French Settlements on the Wabash*, by Jacob Piatt Dunn (1894)
12. *Slavery Petitions and Papers*, by Jacob Piatt Dunn (1894)

Volume III

1. *A History of Early Indianapolis Masonry and of Center Lodge*, by Will E. English (1895)
2. *Sieur de Vincennes, the Founder of Indiana's Oldest Town*, by Edmond Mallet (1897)

3. *Executive Journal of Indiana Territory, 1800-1816,* edited and annotated by William Wesley Woollen, Daniel Wait Howe, and Jacob Piatt Dunn (1900)
4. *The Mission to the Ouabache,* by Jacob Piatt Dunn (1902)
5. *Fifty Years in Pharmacy,* by George W. Sloan (1903)
6. *Caleb Mills and the Indiana School System,* by Charles W. Moores (1905)

Volume IV

1. *Diary of William Owen from November 10, 1824, to April 20, 1825,* edited by Joel W. Hiatt (1906). Reprinted in 1973 by Augustus M. Kelley Publishers
2. *The Word "Hoosier,"* by Jacob Piatt Dunn, and *John Finley,* by Mrs. Sarah A. Wrigley (His Daughter) (1907)
3. *William Henry Harrison's Administration of Indiana Territory,* by Homer J. Webster (1907)
4. *Making a Capital in the Wilderness,* by Daniel Wait Howe (1908)
5. *Names of Persons Enumerated in Marion County, Indiana, at the Fifth Census, Eighteen Hundred and Thirty* (1908)
6. *Some Elements of Indiana's Population; or Roads West and Their Early Travelers,* by W. E. Henry (1908)
7. *Lockerbie's Assessment List of Indianapolis, 1835,* edited by Eliza G. Browning (1909)
8. *The Scotch-Irish Presbyterians in Monroe County, Indiana,* by James Albert Woodburn (1910)
9. *Indianapolis and the Civil War,* by John H. Holliday (1911). Reprinted by the Society of Indiana Pioneers (1972)

Volume V

1. *Lincoln's Body Guard, the Union Light Guard of Ohio, with Some Personal Recollections of Abraham Lincoln,* by Robert W. McBride (1911)
2. *Internal Improvements in Early Indiana,* by Logan Esarey (1912)
3. *The Sultana Disaster,* by Joseph Taylor Elliott (1913)
4. *An Indiana Village: New Harmony,* by John H. Holliday (1914)
5. *The Pioneers of Morgan County: Memoirs of Noah J. Major,* edited by Logan Esarey (1912)
6. *Life and Military Services of Brevet-Major General Robert S. Foster,* by Charles W. Smith (1915)

Volume VI

1. *Proceedings of the Tenth Annual Meeting of the Ohio Valley Historical Association, Held at Indianapolis, Indiana, October 4 and 5, 1916, In Connection with the Indiana State Centennial Celebration,* edited by Harlow Lindley (1917)
2. *Journal of Thomas Dean, A Voyage to Indiana in 1817,* edited by John Candee Dean (1918)
3. *Early Indiana Trails and Surveys,* by George R. Wilson (1919). Reprinted in 1972 by the Society of Indiana Pioneers.
4. *Minutes of the Society, 1886-1918* (1919)

Volume VII

1. *Sieur de Vincennes Identified*, by Pierre-Georges Roy [1918?]
2. *Morgan's Raid in Indiana*, by Louis B. Ewbank [1918?]
3. *Reminiscences of the Early Marion County Bar*, by William Watson Woollen [1919?]
4. *The National Road in Indiana*, by Lee Burns (1919)
5. *Early Indianapolis*, by Mrs. Laura Fletcher Hodges [1920?]
6. *One Hundred Years in Public Health in Indiana*, by Dr. W. F. King (1921)
7. *Fort Wayne in 1790*, by M. M. Quaife (1921)
8. *Washington County Giants*, by Harvey Morris (1921)
9. *The Science of Columbus*, by Elizabeth Miller (Mrs. Oren S. Hack) (1921)
10. *Abraham Lincoln, Lawyer*, by Charles W. Moores (1922)

Volume VIII

1. *Judge James Lockhart*, by George R. Wilson (1923)
2. *Indiana's First War*, translated by Caroline and Eleanor Dunn (1924)
3. *The Environment of Abraham Lincoln in Indiana, with an Account of the DeBruler Family*, by John E. Iglehart and Eugenia Ehrmann (1925)
4. *Early Navigation on the St. Joseph River*, by Otto M. Knoblock (1925)
5. *The Journey of Lewis David Von Schweinitz to Goshen, Bartholomew County, in 1831*, translated by Adolf Gerber (1927)
6. *The Northern Boundary of Indiana*, by Mrs. Frank J. Sheehan (1928)
7. *Evansville's Channels of Trade and the Secession Movement, 1850-1865*, by Daniel W. Snepp (1928)
8. *Indiana Coverlets and Coverlet Weavers*, by Kate Milner Rabb (1928)
9. *Life in Old Vincennes*, by Lee Burns (1929)

Volume IX

Lucius B. Swift: A Biography, by William Dudley Foulke (1930)

Volume X

1. *Centennial Handbook, Indiana Historical Society, 1830-1930*, edited by Christopher B. Coleman (1930)
2. *Our Pioneer Historical Societies*, by Evarts B. Greene (1931)
3. *The Political Career of Jesse D. Bright*, by Charles B. Murphy (1931)
4. *Unedited Letters of Jonathan Jennings*, with notes by Dorothy Riker (1932)
5. *The Pokagons*, by Cecilia Bain Buechner (1933)

Volume XI

1. *New Harmony: An Adventure in Happiness, Papers of Thomas and Sarah Pears*, edited by Thomas Clinton Pears, Jr. (1933). Reprinted in 1973 by Augustus M. Kelley, Publishers
2. *A History of Spiceland Academy, 1826 to 1921*, by Sadie Bacon Hatcher (1934)
3. *Early Architects and Builders of Indiana*, by Lee Burns (1935)
4. *The Schramm Letters, Written by Jacob Schramm and Members of His Fam-*

ily from Indiana to Germany in the Year 1836, translated and edited by
Emma S. Vonnegut (1935). Reprinted 1975.

5. *Indiana Imprints, 1804-1849. A Supplement to Mary Alden Walker's
"Beginnings of Printing in the State of Indiana, published in 1934,"* by
Douglas C. McMurtrie (1937)

Volume XII

Sons of the Wilderness, John and William Conner, by Charles N. Thompson
(1937)

Volume XIII

1. *The Village at the End of the Road. A Chapter in Early Indiana Railroad
History,* by Wylie J. Daniels (1938)
2. *The Contribution of the Society of Friends to Education in Indiana,* by Ethel
Hittle McDaniel (1939)
3. *Camp Morton, Indianapolis, 1861-1865, Indianapolis Prison Camp,* by
Hattie Lou Winslow and Joseph R. H. Moore (1940)

Volume XIV

1. *The Trail of Death, Letters of Benjamin Marie Petit,* by Irving McKee (1941)
2. *The Diaries of Donald Macdonald, 1824-1826,* with an introduction by
Caroline Dale Snedeker (1942). Reprinted in 1973 by Augustus M. Kelley,
Publishers
3. *Portraits and Painters of the Governors of Indiana, 1800-1943,* by Wilbur D.
Peat (1944).

Volume XV

1. *Pioneer Sketches of the Upper Whitewater Valley, Quaker Stronghold of
the West,* by Bernhard Knollenberg (1945)
2. *The Buffalo Trace,* by George R. Wilson and Gayle Thornbrough (1946)
3. *Education and Reform at New Harmony: Correspondence of William Maclure
And Marie Duclos Fretageot, 1820-1833,* edited by Arthur E. Bestor, Jr.
(1948). Reprinted in 1973 by Augustus M. Kelley, Publishers
4. *The Vincennes Donation Lands,* by Leonard Lux (1949)

Volume XVI

1. *A Friendly Mission: John Candler's Letters from America, 1853-1854,* [edited
by Gayle Thornbrough] (1951)
2. *A Home in the Woods: Oliver Johnson's Reminiscences of Early Marion
County,* as related by Howard Johnson (1951). Reprinted by the Society
in 1971.
3. *From Greene Ville to Fallen Timbers, A Journal of the Wayne Campaign
July 28-September 14, 1794,* edited by Dwight L. Smith (1952)

Volume XVII

*Planting Corn Belt Culture: The Impress of the Upland Southerner and
Yankee in the Old Northwest,* by Richard Lyle Power (1953)

Volume XVIII

1. *The Indiana Gazetteer or Topographical Dictionary, by John Scott.
   Reprinted from the Original Edition, 1826,* edited by Gayle Thornbrough
   (1954)
2. *Ouiatanon Documents,* translated and edited by Frances Krauskopf (1955)
3. *I, Alone, Remember,* by Lucile Carr Marshall (1956)
4. *The Circle, "The Center of Our Universe,"* by Ernestine Bradford Rose
   (1957)

Volume XIX

*Outpost on the Wabash, 1787-1791. Letters of Brigadier General Josiah
Harmar and Major John Francis Hamtramck, and other letters and documents selected from the Harmar Papers in the William L. Clements Library,*
edited by Gayle Thornbrough (1957)

Volume XX

1. *The Bennet Family,* by Mintie Allen Royse (1958)
2. *Leah Jackson Wolford's The Play-Party in Indiana,* edited and revised by
   W. Edson Richmond and William Tillson (1959)
3. *English's Opera House. A paper read before the Indianapolis Literary Club,
   March 5, 1951,* by William George Sullivan (1960)

Volume XXI

Letter Book of the Indian Agency at Fort Wayne, 1809-1815, edited by Gayle
Thornbrough (1961)

Volume XXII

Correspondence of John Badollet and Albert Gallatin, 1804-1836, edited by
Gayle Thornbrough (1963)

Volume XXIII

1. *To Oregon in 1852, Letter of Dr. Thomas White, La Grange County,
   Indiana, Emigrant,* edited by Oscar O. Winther and Gayle Thornbrough
   (1964)
2. *Harmonist Construction, Principally Found in the Two-Story Houses Built
   in Harmonie, Indiana, 1814-1824,* by Don Blair (1964)
3. *The Search for Henry Cross, An Adventure in Biography and Americana,* by
   Douglas W. Hartley (1966)
4. *To Holland and to New Harmony, Robert Dale Owen's Travel Journal,
   1825-1826,* edited by Josephine M. Elliott (1969)

Volume XXIV

At the Headwaters of the Maumee. A History of the forts of Fort Wayne, by
Paul Woehrmann (1971)

Volume XXV

1. *Furniture Makers of Indiana, 1793 to 1850*, by Betty Lawson Walters (1972)
2. *Personal Recollections of Harrison Burns as written in 1907* (1975)
3. *To The West in 1894: Travel Journal of Dr. James Douglass English of Worthington, Indiana* (1977) [edited by Gayle Thornbrough]
4. *Robert Dale Owen's Travel Journal 1827*, edited by Josephine M. Elliott (1977)

Volume XXVI

1. *Sweet Memories of 'Old Indianie,'* by Sarah Brown DeBra (1979)

Special Publications

Prehistoric Antiquities of Indiana, by Eli Lilly (1937)
The Journals and Indian Paintings of George Winter, 1837-1839 (1948)
The Old Northwest: Pioneer Period, 1815-1840, by R. Carlyle Buley (1950). Awarded the Pulitzer Prize in History, 1951
Walum Olum or Red Score: The Migration Legend of the Lenni Lenape or Delaware Indians . . . by Glenn A. Black, Eli Lilly, Georg K. Neumann, Joe E. Pierce, C. G. Voegelin, Erminie W. Voegelin, and Paul Weer (1954)
Eliza A. Blaker: Her Life and Work, by Emma Lou Thornbrough (1956)
Lincoln's Youth: Indiana Years, Seven to Twenty-one, 1816-1830, by Louis A. Warren (1959). Reprinted by Appleton-Century-Crofts in 1959
Schliemann in Indiana, edited by Eli Lilly (1961)
Indiana Houses of the Nineteenth Century, by Wilbur D. Peat (1962). Reprinted by the Society in 1969
Indianapolis in the "Gay Nineties": High School Diaries of Claude G. Bowers, edited by Holman Hamilton and Gayle Thornbrough (1964)
Indianapolis from Our Old Corner, by Charlotte Cathcart (1965)
The House of the Singing Winds: The Life and Work of T. C. Steele, by Selma N. Steele, Theodore L. Steele, and Wilbur D. Peat (1966)
Sketch of Lake Wawasee, by Scott A. Edgell (1967)
Angel Site: An Archaeological, Historical and Ethnological Study, by Glenn A. Black (1967)
Maps of Indiana Counties in 1876, Together with the Plat of Indianapolis and a Sampling of Illustrations. Reprinted from *Illustrated Historical Atlas of the State of Indiana* (1968)
From Then 'Til Now, History of McCutchanville, by Kenneth P. McCutchan. Illustrated by Jerry N. Baum (1969)
From Paddle Wheels to Propellers: The Howard Ship Yards of Jeffersonville in the Story of Steam Navigation on the Western Rivers, by Charles Preston Fishbaugh (1970)
The Diary of Calvin Fletcher
 Volume I: *1817-1838*, edited by Gayle Thornbrough (1972)
 Volume II: *1838-1843*, edited by Gayle Thornbrough and Dorothy Riker (1973)

Volume III: *1844-1847*, edited by Gayle Thornbrough and Dorothy Riker (1974)

Volume IV: *1848-1852*, edited by Gayle Thornbrough, Dorothy Riker, and Paula Corpuz (1975)

Volume V: *1853-1856*, edited by Gayle Thornbrough, Dorothy Riker, and Paula Corpuz (1977)

Volume VI: *1857-1860*, edited by Gayle Thornbrough, Dorothy Riker, and Paula Corpuz (1978)

Volume VII: *1861-1862*, edited by Gayle Thornbrough, Dorothy Riker, and Paula Corpuz (1980)

Henry Ward Beecher: The Indiana Years, 1837-1847, by Jane Shaeffer Elsmere (1973)

An Introduction to the Prehistory of Indiana, by James H. Kellar (1973)

The Secret Orders & ". . . great things have been Done by a few Men. . . ." Letters of Patrick Henry and George Rogers Clark Issued in Facsimile by the Indiana Historical Society as a Contribution to the Observance of the Bicentennial of the American Revolution (1974)

A Documentary History of the Indiana Decade of the Harmony Society 1814-1824

Volume I: *1814-1819*, compiled and edited by Karl J. R. Arndt (1975)

Volume II: *1820-1824*, compiled and edited by Karl J. R. Arndt (1978)

Oscar Carleton McCulloch, 1843-1891: Preacher and Practitioner of Applied Christianity, by Genevieve C. Weeks (1976)

The Chronicle of the Overbeck Pottery, by Kathleen R. Postle (1978)

Alloys and Automobiles: The Life of Elwood Haynes, by Ralph D. Gray (1979)

Portraits and Painters of the Governors of Indiana, 1800-1978, by Wilbur D. Peat, revised, edited, and new entries by Diane Gail Lazarus, biographies of the governors by Lana Ruegamer (1979)

Local History Today: Papers at Four Regional Workshops for Local Historical Organizations in Indiana, June, 1978–April, 1979 (1979)

"Midwestern Transformation: From Traditional Pioneers to Modern Society," by Richard Jensen; "After the Bicentennial and *Roots:* What Next? Local History at the Crossroads," by Robert M. Sutton; "Local History: A Mainspring for National History," by Thomas D. Clark; "Above Ground Archaeology: Discovering a Community's History through Local Artifacts," by Thomas J. Schlereth

Local History Today: Papers Presented at Three 1979 Regional Workshops for Local Historical Organizations in Indiana (1980)

"Some Impressions of the Nonacademic Local Historians and Their Writings," by David J. Russo; "Writing Local History: The Challenge, The Responsibilities, The Pleasure," by Dorothy Weyer Creigh; "Humanities and the Study of Local History," by Roger Fortin; "Using County Records in Writing Your Community's History," by John J. Newman; "Indiana's Historical Services, and Beyond," by Pamela J. Bennett

Bibliographies

A Bibliography of James Whitcomb Riley, by Anthony J. Russo and Dorothy R. Russo (1944)

A Bibliography of George Ade, 1866-1944, by Dorothy Ritter Russo (1947)

A Bibliography of Booth Tarkington, 1869-1946, by Dorothy Ritter Russo and Thelma L. Sullivan (1949)

Bibliographical Studies of Seven Authors of Crawfordsville, Indiana: Lew and Susan Wallace, Maurice and Will Thompson, Mary Hannah and Caroline Virginia Krout, and Meredith Nicholson, by Dorothy Ritter Russo and Thelma L. Sullivan (1952)

Lecture Series

1969-1970 *Redcoats and Red Men*

"The Development of American Military Confidence," by Howard Peckham; "The Transformation of Republican Thought, 1763-1887," by James Morton Smith; "Some Recent Interpretations of Jeffersonian America," by Harry L. Coles

1970-1971 *American Indian Policy*

"The Image of the Indian in Pre-Civil War America," by Francis Paul Prucha; "Indian Policy After the Civil War: The Reservation Experience," by William T. Hagan; "Toward Freedom: The American Indian in the Twentieth Century," by Alvin M. Josephy, Jr.

1971-1972 *History and the Role of the City in American Life*

"The City as a Melting Pot," by Arthur Mann; "Four Stages of Cultural Growth: The American City," by Neil Harris; "An Urban Historian's Agenda for the Profession," by Sam Bass Warner, Jr.

1972-1973 *1876, the Centennial Year*

"Engines, Marbles, and Canvases: The Centennial Exposition of 1876," by Lillian B. Miller; "Seed Time of Modern Conflict: American Society at the Centennial," by Walter T. K. Nugent; "Art and Culture in the Centennial Summer of 1876," by H. Wayne Morgan

1973-1974 *Human and Cultural Development*

"Man, Evolution, and Society," by J. T. Robinson; "Prehistoric Urban Evolution in North America," by Melvin L. Fowler; "The Country Life Is to Be Preferred: A Brief Review of Theories on the Origins of Civilization in the Old World," by Brian M. Fagan

1976-1977 *The History of Education in the Middle West*

"Uncommon Schools: Christian Colleges and Social Idealism in Midwestern America, 1820-1950," by Timothy L. Smith; "Education in Utopia: The New Harmony Experience," by Donald E. Pitzer

Proceedings of the Robert Owen Bicentennial Conference

Robert Owen's American Legacy, edited by Donald E. Pitzer (1972)

"Robert Owen's New Harmony: An American Heritage," by Roger D. Branigin; "Introduction to Premiere Documentary Film 'New Harmony: An Example and a Beacon'," by Herman B Wells; "Robert Owen's Quest for the New Moral World in America," by John F. C. Harrison; "Robert Owen and the Millennialist Tradition," by Robert G. Clouse; "Robert Owen in American Thought," by Merle Curti; "Robert Owen and Philosophy," by Robert Ginsberg

Proceedings of Indiana American Revolution Bicentennial Symposia

Contest for Empire, 1500-1775, edited by John B. Elliott (1975)
"Agents of Empire in Colonial America," by George M. Waller; "The Impact of the European Presence on Indian Culture," by James A. Brown; "Spanish Indian Policy and the Struggle for Empire in the Southeast, 1513-1776," by John J. TePaske; "The 'Rising French Empire' in the Ohio Valley and Old Northwest: The 'Dreaded Juncture of the French Settlements in Canada with those of Louisiana'," by George A. Rawlyk; "Britain and the Ohio Valley, 1760-1775: The Search for Alternatives in a Revolutionary Era," by Jack M. Sosin; "The Advance of the Anglo-American Frontier, 1700-1783," by Thomas D. Clark

The French, The Indians, and George Rogers Clark in the Illinois Country (1977)
"French Settlers and Settlements in the Illinois Country in the Eighteenth Century," by John Francis McDermott; "George Rogers Clark and Indian America, 1778-1780," by George C. Chalou; "Target Detroit: Overview of the American Revolution West of the Appalachians," by George M. Waller; "Studying George Rogers Clark's Illinois Campaign with Maps," by John H. Long; "The Old Northwest and the Peace Negotiations," by Dwight L. Smith

This Land of Ours: The Acquisition and Disposition of the Public Domain (1978)
"Perceptions and Illustrations of the American Landscape in the Ohio Valley and the Midwest," by Hildegard Binder Johnson; "The Land Office Business in Indiana," by Malcolm J. Rohrbough; "Changing Images of the Public Domain: Historians and the Shaping of Midwest Frontiers," by Reginald Horsman; "The Land Cession Treaty: A Valid Instrument of Transfer of Indian Title," by Dwight L. Smith; "The Nationalizing Influence of the Public Lands: Indiana," by Paul W. Gates

Publications by Society Sections

Family History and Genealogy

Hoosier Genealogist
quarterly publication, 1961-
guest editors, January 1961–December 1961
edited by Nell W. Reeser, January 1962–April 1965
       Dorothy L. Riker, May 1965–September 1978
       Rebah Fraustein, December 1978–

Genealogy
issued eight times per year, 1973-
compiled by Willard Heiss

Abstracts of the Record of the Society of Friends in Indiana, edited by Willard Heiss
Part I (1962); Part II (1965); Part III (1970); Part IV (1973); Part V (1974); Part VI (1975); Index (1977)

1820 Federal Census for Indiana (1966)

1840 Federal Population Census, Indiana (1975)

Early Marriages of Wayne County, Indiana, 1811-1822, by Irene M. Strieby. Reprinted from the *Indiana Magazine of History* (1965)

Clark County, Indiana: Abstracts of Wills and Executors' Records, 1801-1833, Marriage Records, 1807-1824, compiled by Dorothy Riker (1969)

Indiana Source Book: Genealogical Material from THE HOOSIER GENEAL-OGIST, 1961-1966, Volume One, edited by Willard Heiss (1977)

Genealogical Use of Catholic Records in North America, by Monsignor John J. Doyle (1978)

Genealogical Sources: Reprinted From The Genealogy Section INDIANA MAGAZINE OF HISTORY, compiled by Dorothy Riker (1979)

Admission Records Indianapolis Asylum for Friendless Colored Children, 1871-1900, transcribed and arranged by Jean E. Spears and Dorothy Paul (1978)

Medical History

Medical History Quarterly, July 1974–
compiled by Dr. Charles Bonsett

Military History

Military History Journal, January 1976–
compiled by Richard Clutter

Prehistory Research Series

Volume I   July 1937–August 1940

1. *Preliminary Notes on the Iroquoian Family*, by Paul Weer (July 1937)
2. *Jacob Piatt Dunn: His Miami Language Studies and Indian Manuscript Collection*, by Caroline Dunn (December 1937)
3. *Shawnee Stems and the Jacob P. Dunn Miami Dictionary, Part I, Stems in p-*, by C. F. Voegelin
4. *Preliminary Notes on the Caddoan Family*, by Paul Weer (March 1938)
5. *Shawnee Stems and the Jacob P. Dunn Miami Dictionary, Part II, Stems in t- and č-*, by C. F. Voegelin (June 1938)
6. *Hidatsa Texts, collected by Robert H. Lowie, with Grammatical Notes and Phonograph Transcriptions*, by Zellig Harris and C. F. Voegelin (May 1939)
7. *Preliminary Notes on the Muskhogean Family*, by Paul Weer (August 1939)
8. *Shawnee Stems and the Jacob P. Dunn Miami Dictionary, Part III, Stems in k- and š-, and θ*, with appendix, *Non-Initial Elements*, by C. F. Voegelin (October 1939)
9. *Shawnee Stems and the Jacob P. Dunn Miami Dictionary, Part IV, Stems in l-, m-, and n-*, by C. F. Voegelin, with appendix, *Gestalt Technique in Stem Composition*, by B. L. Whorf (April 1940)
10. *Shawnee Stems and the Jacob P. Dunn Miami Dictionary, Part V, Stems in w- and h- vowel*, by C. F. Voegelin, with *Index to Parts I-V* (August 1940)

Volume II   March 1941–December 1944

1. *McCain Site, Dubois County, Indiana*, by Rex K. Miller (March 1941)
2. *The Goodall Focus. An Analysis of Ten Hopewellian Components in*

Michigan and Indiana, by George I. Quimby, Jr. (October 1941)

3. *Additional Hopewell Material from Illinois,* by James B. Griffin (December 1941)

4. *Mortuary Customs of the Shawnee and Other Eastern Tribes,* by Erminie Wheeler Voegelin (March 1944)

5. *Angel Site, Vanderburgh County, Indiana: An Introduction,* by Glenn A. Black (December 1944)

Volume III

1. *Delaware Culture Chronology,* by Vernon Kinietz (April 1946)

2. *The Bell-Philhower Site, Sussex County, New Jersey,* by William A. Ritchie (October 1946)

3. *The Atlatl In North America,* by James H. Kellar (June 1955)

4. *The C. L. Lewis Stone Mound and the Stone Mound Problem,* by James H. Kellar (June 1960)

Volume IV

1. *Two Graves in Warrick County, Indiana, New Angel Site,* by Richard B. Johnston and Glenn A. Black (August 1962)

2. *Proton Magnetometry And Its Application To Archaeology: An Evaluation at Angel Site,* by Richard B. Johnston (April 1964)

3. *Fluted Points And Late-Pleistocene Geochronology In Indiana,* by John T Dorwin (December 1966)

4. *The Bowen Site: An Archaeological Study of Culture In The Late Prehistory of Central Indiana,* by John T Dorwin (October 1971)

Volume V

1. *The Late Prehistoric Occupation of Northwestern Indiana: A Study of the Upper Mississippi Cultures of the Kankakee Valley,* by Charles H. Faulkner (1972)

2. *The Hopewellian Interaction Sphere: The Evidence For Interregional Trade and Structural Complexity,* by Mark F. Seeman (1979)

Joint Publications

In co-operation with the Indiana Historical Bureau the Society has issued a paper-covered edition of the following titles.

Readings in Indiana History, compiled by Gayle Thornbrough and Dorothy Riker (1956)

Indiana in the War of the Rebellion. Report of the Adjutant General. A Reprint of Volume I of the Eight-Volume Report Prepared by W. H. H. Terrell and Published in 1869, edited by Gayle Thornbrough and Dorothy Riker (1960)

A History of Indiana Literature, by Arthur W. Shumàker (1962)

The History of Indiana

HONORARY MEMBERS

1831

Nathan Dane, Massachusetts
Joseph Story, Massachusetts
Daniel A. White, Massachusetts
Edward Everett, Massachusetts
Thomas L. Winthrop, Massachusetts
Orville Dewey, Massachusetts
Jared Sparks, Massachusetts
John Quincy Adams, Massachusetts
Francis C. Gray, Massachusetts
Nathan Cyril, Ohio
Timothy Flint, Ohio
Samuel Gilman, South Carolina
Rowland Heylin, Pennsylvania
William Gibbes Hunt, Tennessee
James Kent, New York
Edward Livingston, Louisiana

1887

General Charles W. Darling,
Utica, New York

1891

Hon. Thomas M. Cooley,
Ann Arbor, Michigan
Hon. George W. Julian, Irvington
J. H. B. Nowland, Indianapolis

1898

Governor James A. Mount

1900

Hon. William Copley Winslow,
Boston

1906

David Starr Jordan,
Leland Stanford University
David Turpie, Indianapolis
Thomas A. Goodwin, Indianapolis
M. L. Bundy, New Castle, Indiana
Oscar J. Craig, Missoula, Montana
William H. Mace,
Syracuse, New York
Enoch A. Bryan,
Pullman, Washington

1906

A. C. Shortridge, Indianapolis

1907

Benjamin F. Parker,
New Castle, Indiana
Prof. Homer J. Webster,
Alliance, Ohio

1917

George S. Cottman, Indianapolis

1920

Daniel Wait Howe
Charity Dye

1924

Jack Higgins, Wabash City, Indiana

1925

Evaline M. (Mrs. John H.) Holliday
Elizabeth N. (Mrs. Charles) Moores

1927

Senator Albert J. Beveridge

1931

Charles E. Coffin

1937

Claude G. Bowers
Enoch A. Bryan
Mrs. Jacob P. Dunn
William H. Mace

1947

Charles A. Beard
Mary R. Beard

1948

Prof. Wendell Holmes Stephenson

1954

William O. Lynch

CHARTER

Chapter XXXIV.

An Act to incorporate the Indiana Historical Society.
[Approved, January 10, 1831.]

Sec. 1. *Be it enacted by the General Assembly of the state of Indiana*, That Benjamin Parke, John H. Farnham, Bethuel F. Morris and James Blake, with their associates, are hereby created and constituted, a body politic and corporate, by the name and style of the "Indiana Historical Society," and by such name may have perpetual succession, hold, purchase, receive, enjoy and transfer any property, real and personal, have and use a common seal, sue and be sued, plead and be impleaded, defend and be defended in all courts of judicature whatever.

Sec. 2. There shall be an annual meeting of the members of said society, at the time and place appointed by their constitution; at which time and place the officers of said society named in said constitution, shall be elected, who shall continue in office until the next annual meeting, and until their successors are elected. The members of said society, at such meeting, may alter and amend their constitution, change the time of the annual meeting, and frame such laws for the government of said society, as they shall think proper, the same not being inconsistent with the laws and constitution of this state.

Sec. 3. The officers of said society may make such rules for their own government, and for carrying into effect the objects of the society, not inconsistent with its constitution, as they shall think proper; all which, together with their receipts and disbursements, shall be reported to the annual meetings of the society.

Sec. 4. The secretary of state shall deliver to the officers of said society one copy of the laws of this state, and one copy of the journals of the senate and house of representatives, which may hereafter be published, and also copies of the laws and journals of former years, where more than five copies of the same for any one year remain in his office. The secretary shall also deliver to the officers of said society, all books and other articles which have been or may be transmitted to his office for the use of said society.

CHARTER

[s. 139. Approved March 1, 1978.]
(with amendments from Public Law No. 152)

Sec. 1.   *Be it enacted by the General Assembly of the state of Indiana*, That Benjamin Parke, John H. Farnham, Bethuel F. Morris and James Blake, with their associates, are hereby created and constituted, a body politic and corporate, by the name and style of the "Indiana Historical Society," and by such name may have perpetual succession, hold, purchase, receive, enjoy and transfer any property, real and personal, have and use a common seal, sue and be sued, plead and be impleaded, defend and be defended in all courts of judicature whatever.

Sec. 1.5.   The objects of the society shall be: the collection and preservation of all materials calculated to shed light on the natural, civil, and political history of Indiana; the publication and circulation of historical documents; the promotion of useful knowledge; and the friendly and profitable intercourse of such citizens as are disposed to promote these ends.

Sec. 2.   There shall be an annual meeting of the members of the society at a time and place to be specified in the bylaws. At each annual meeting one-third (⅓) of the members of the governing body shall be elected by the members of the society in a manner and for terms to be specified in the bylaws. The number of members of the governing body shall be fixed by the bylaws. The members of the society, at the annual meeting, may adopt such resolutions for the government of the society, as they think proper, and as are not inconsistent with this charter and with the laws and constitution of this state.

Sec. 3. The governing body of the society may make such bylaws as it thinks proper for the government of the society and for carrying into effect the objects of the society, not inconsistent with this charter or with any resolution that is adopted at an annual meeting of the members of the society; all which, together with their receipts and disbursements, shall be reported to the annual meeting of the society.

Sec. 4. The legislative council shall deliver to the society one copy of the laws of this state, and one copy of the journals of the senate and house of representatives, which may hereafter be published, and also copies of the laws and journals of former years, where more than five copies of the same for any one year remain. The secretary of state shall deliver to the society, all books and other articles that have been or may be transmitted to his office for the use of the society.

Sec. 5. Because an emergency exists, this act takes effect on its passage.

CODE OF BYLAWS

(adopted by the members of the Indiana Historical Society
at meetings in November, 1977, and May, 1978)

Article 1
Identification

Section 1.01. *Name.* The name of the corporation (the "Society") shall be as provided in the legislative charter.

Section 1.02. *Principal Office.* The post office address of the principal office of the Society is 315 West Ohio Street, Indianapolis, Marion County, Indiana 46202.

Section 1.03. *Seal.* The seal of the Society shall be circular in form and mounted upon a metal die, suitable for impressing upon paper. About the periphery of the seal shall appear the words "Indiana Historical Society" and the year "1830." In the center of the seal shall appear the word "Seal" and the design of the original state capitol building at Corydon, Indiana.

Article 2
Membership and Dues

Section 2.01. *Membership.* A person desiring a membership in the Society shall submit a written application in a form approved by the board of trustees. Anyone shall be eligible to apply for membership; the board of trustees shall have final authority to elect members in the Society. Membership may be terminated by the board of trustees for cause. A person shall cease to be a member for failure to pay dues upon such terms as the board may, from time to time, specify.

Section 2.02. *Classes of Membership.* The classes of membership shall include annual, sustaining, contributing, life, and such other memberships as the board of trustees shall from time to time establish.

Section 2.03. *Dues.* Members of the Society with an annual, contributing, or sustaining membership shall pay dues each year on or before January 30 in an amount specified by the board of trustees. Failure to pay dues shall subject a person to suspension or expulsion. A life member shall only be required to make a single payment in an amount specified by the board of trustees.

Article 3
Meetings of the Membership

Section 3.01. *Annual Meetings.* An annual meeting of the members shall be held at a time and place as the board of trustees may determine. Failure to hold an annual meeting shall not work a forfeiture or dissolution of the Society.

Section 3.02. *Special Meetings.* A special meeting of the Society may be called at any time by the president, or, in the case of his death, absence, or disability, by any three trustees. A special meeting of the Society shall also be called at any time on the written request of thirty (30) members addressed to the president.

Section 3.03. *Place of Meetings.* All meetings of the membership of the Society shall be held at a place, within Indiana, as may be specified in the notice of the meeting. If no place is specified, then the meeting shall be held at the principal office of the Society.

Section 3.04. *Notice of Meetings.* A notice of a meeting will be provided at least ten (10) days in advance in a form and manner determined by the board.

Section 3.05. *Voting Rights.* Every member shall be entitled to one vote.

Section 3.06. *Voting by Proxy.* Voting may be in person, by proxy, or by mail as the board may specify.

SECTION 3.07. *Quorum.* Six members present in person at any meeting of the membership shall constitute a quorum for the transaction of business.

SECTION 3.08. *Voting List.* The executive secretary of the Society shall keep a complete and accurate list of all members entitled to vote at the principal office of the Society. The list may be inspected by a member at any reasonable time.

Article 4
The Board of Trustees

SECTION 4.01. *Governing Body.* The governing body of the Society shall be a board of fifteen trustees. At each annual meeting, the members shall elect five trustees, each to serve a three year term.

SECTION 4.02. *Meetings of Trustees.* Meetings of the trustees shall be held not less than annually and may be held upon the call of the chairman or upon the call of three or more trustees at any place within the state of Indiana upon 48 hours notice. The notice shall specify the time, place, and general purpose of the meeting and shall be given to each trustee personally, by mail, or by telephone. Notice of a meeting may be waived, and attendance at a meeting shall excuse the requirement of notice.

SECTION 4.03. *Quorum of Trustees.* Eight trustees shall constitute a quorum for the transaction of business at any meeting.

SECTION 4.04. *Resignation.* A trustee may resign by notifying the chairman of the board.

SECTION 4.05. *Vacancies.* A vacancy in the board of trustees shall be filled by the remaining members of the board. A trustee so selected shall serve the unexpired balance of the term.

Article 5
The Officers of the Society

SECTION 5.01. *Officers.* The officers of the Society shall consist of a chairman of the board of trustees, a president, one or more vice-presidents, a treasurer, and an executive secretary. Two or more offices may be held by the same person, except the offices of president and secretary shall not be held by the same person. The trustees shall elect the officers at their first meeting after the annual meeting of the members of the Society. Each officer shall hold office for a term of one year or until his successor is elected.

SECTION 5.02. *Vacancies.* Whenever a vacancy shall occur in any office, the board of trustees may fill the vacancy, and an officer so elected shall hold office until the next regular election of officers as provided in Section 5.01.

SECTION 5.03. *Chairman of the Board.* The chairman of the board shall preside at all meetings of the board of trustees, shall, in the absence of other provision, appoint the chairman and members of all standing and temporary committees, and shall perform such other duties as the board may prescribe.

SECTION 5.04. *The President.* The president shall preside at all meetings of the membership and shall preside at meetings of the trustees if requested to do so by the chairman and shall discharge all duties that devolve upon a presiding officer and perform such other duties as the trustees may prescribe. He shall be an ex officio member of all standing committees.

SECTION 5.05. *Vice-President.* A vice-president designated by the board of trustees shall perform all duties incumbent on the president during the absence or disability of the president. Vice-presidents shall perform such other duties as the board of trustees may prescribe.

SECTION 5.06. *The Treasurer.* The treasurer shall have

custody of all corporate funds and securities and shall keep or cause to be kept in books belonging to the Society full and accurate accounts of all receipts and disbursements. He shall deposit all money and securities in such depository as may be designated for that purpose by the board of trustees. He shall furnish at meetings of the board of trustees, or whenever requested, a statement of the financial condition of the Society and shall perform such other duties as may be prescribed by the board of trustees. He shall report all receipts and disbursements at the annual meeting of the membership as required by the Society's charter.

SECTION 5.07. *Executive Secretary.* The executive secretary shall be a full-time employee of the Society, shall be its chief administrative officer, and shall have general management of its affairs subject to the discretion and control of the board of trustees. The executive secretary shall be an ex officio member of all standing committees, in charge of correspondence with the membership and with others and shall assist the board of trustees, officers, and committees in the performance of their functions. The executive secretary shall keep custody and care of the corporate seal and minutes of the Society. The executive secretary shall attend all meetings of the membership and of the board of trustees and shall keep or cause to be kept a true and complete record of the proceedings of such meetings in a book provided for the purpose. The executive secretary shall perform such other duties as the board of trustees may prescribe.

SECTION 5.08. *Removal.* Any officer of the Society shall serve only at the pleasure of the board of trustees.

SECTION 5.09. *Resignation.* Any officer or member of a committee may resign at any time. A resignation shall be made in writing and shall take effect at the time specified therein, and, if no time is specified, at the time of its receipt by the president or executive secretary of the Society. The acceptance of a resignation shall not be necessary to make it effective.

Article 6
Committees

SECTION 6.01. *Executive Committee.*   Unless the board shall provide otherwise, the officers of the Society elected by the board shall constitute an executive committee of the Society. The executive secretary of the Society shall serve as secretary of the executive committee. The executive committee shall transact such business of the Society as may require attention between meetings of the board of trustees. All business transacted by the executive committee shall be reported to and be subject to approval by the board of trustees at its next regular meeting.

SECTION 6.02. *Finance Committee.*   The chairman of the board of trustees shall, with the advice of the board of trustees, appoint from among the trustees a chairman and not fewer than two additional members to a standing committee to be designated the finance committee. The finance committee shall review the financial affairs of the Society, determine what financial policies and courses of action are prudent and appropriate, and make recommendations to the board of trustees concerning financial matters, including the management, investment, and use of the Society's assets. In performing these functions, the finance committee shall give due consideration to the need to preserve the Society's assets and to the future and long-range needs of the Society. The finance committee shall hold regular quarterly meetings and such special meetings as may be called by the chairman of the finance committee or a majority of its members. A majority of the finance committee shall constitute a quorum at any meeting of the finance committee. The finance committee shall submit a written report to the board of trustees at least annually.

SECTION 6.03. *Library Committee.*   The chairman of the board of trustees shall, with the advice of the board of trustees, appoint a standing committee not to exceed 15 persons in number to be designated as the library committee. Each appointment shall be for a three year term. The library committee shall select its own officers and determine its own quorum and procedure. Vacancies on the library committee shall be filled by the chairman with the advice of the board of trustees. The library committee shall be responsible for the formulation and execution of a policy for the Society in the acquisition of books, manuscript materials, and artifacts. The library committee shall propose a budget for its operation to the board of trustees each year prior to the board's budget meeting. The library committee shall make a written report of its actions and acquisitions each year to the board of trustees.

SECTION 6.04. *Other Committees.*   The board of trustees may, from time to time, create other standing or temporary committees as it shall determine necessary or desirable for the execution of the Society's mission.

Article 7
Sections

SECTION 7.01. *Authorization of Sections.*   The board of trustees may from time to time authorize the creation of a special section of membership from among the general membership relating to a special interest within the Society's general mission, such as genealogy, military history, or other special interests. The board may discontinue, combine, or change sections previously authorized.

SECTION 7.02. *Section Membership.*   Membership in a section shall be open to all members of the Society upon reasonable terms that the board of trustees or a majority of the section members may specify for all members of the section. Section dues or fees may be established by a section, provided that such dues or fees are approved by the board of trustees.

SECTION 7.03. *Government of Sections.* A section shall be governed by written rules developed by the section, which written rules shall be subject to the approval of the board of trustees. Such rules shall provide for a board or officers and for the periodic election thereof by the members of the section. Such rules shall also identify the representative or representatives authorized to expend the funds budgeted for the section.

SECTION 7.04. *Liaison with Board of Trustees.* The board or officers of a section, as provided by the section's rules, shall select a delegate who shall be entitled to attend each meeting of the board of trustees. A section delegate shall be entitled to be heard on any matter particularly affecting his section but shall not be entitled to vote unless he shall also be an elected trustee.

7.041. Prior to a meeting of the board of trustees, a section delegate may request a place on the agenda of that meeting, which request shall be granted unless the chairman of the board of trustees decides that there is insufficient time available.

7.042. A section delegate shall receive copies of the agenda and minutes of meetings of the board of trustees and copies of other materials prepared for the use of the trustees at such meetings.

SECTION 7.05. *Section Budgets.* A section shall submit to the members of the executive committee a proposed budget for its operation on or before September 1 of each year, for submission of the board of trustees for approval.

7.051.   After a section budget is approved, a section shall be entitled to the expenditure of any money authorized by its budget, as approved by the board of trustees, upon the submission of an appropriate voucher.

7.052.   A section shall be responsible to the board of trustees for a written accounting of its expenditures on request by the board of trustees and in any event promptly after the conclusion of the Society's fiscal year.

SECTION 7.06.   *Section Responsibility.*   The formulation and execution of the policy and activities of a section shall conform to the written rules referred to in Section 7.03. Actions by a section in the name of the Society or on its credit, and publications issued by a section in the name of the Society, shall be subject to the approval of the board of trustees.

Article 8
Budget

An annual budget shall be prepared by the executive secretary of the Society and submitted to the board of trustees for approval prior to the end of each fiscal year.

Article 9
Corporate Books

The books and records of the Society may be kept at such places within the state of Indiana as the board of trustees may from time to time determine.

Article 10
Contracts, Checks, Notes, Etc.

All contracts and agreements authorized by the board of trustees, and all checks, drafts, notes, bonds, bills of exchange, and orders for the payment of money, shall, unless otherwise directed by the board of trustees, or unless otherwise required by law, be signed by any two of the following officers, who are different persons: president, any vice-president, or treasurer. The board of trustees may, however, authorize any one of such officers to sign checks, drafts and orders for the payment of money singly and without the necessity of a countersignature, and may designate employees of the Society, other than those named above, who may, in the name of the Society, execute drafts, checks and orders for the payment of money in its behalf.

Article 11
Indemnification of Trustees

The Society shall indemnify any person (and his successors in interest) who may serve or has served as a trustee or officer of the Society against any expenses, including amounts paid upon judgments, counsel fees, and amounts paid in settlement (before or after suit is commenced), actually and necessarily incurred by him in connection with the defense or settlement of any claim, action, suit, or proceeding asserted against him by reason of his service as a trustee or as an officer, unless he shall have acted in bad faith or willful disregard of the Society's best interests. This indemnification shall be in addition to any other rights to which he may be entitled under any law, agreement, vote of members, or otherwise.

Article 12
Amendments

The power to make, alter, amend, or repeal this code of bylaws is vested in the board of trustees.

A NOTE ON SOURCES

The most important printed sources for this study were *Proceedings of the Indiana Historical Society, 1830-1886* (Indiana Historical Society *Publications*, Volume I, 1897); *Minutes of the Society, 1886-1918* (Indiana Historical Society *Publications*, Volume VI, 1919); *Indiana History Bulletin*, monthly publication of the Indiana Historical Bureau, 1924-1979; *Proceedings of the Indiana History Conference*, annual publication, 1919-1933, thereafter published in the *Bulletin*, 1935-1955; after 1955 annual IHS meeting reports appear in the *Bulletin* through 1969; the *Indiana Historical Society Annual Report* has appeared since 1969.

The most important primary source for the study was the records of the Indiana Historical Society. Most of the old files (1924 to 1955) are presently stored in eight cardboard boxes containing extensive file folders. Much of the correspondence is arranged by county, with correspondence filed chronologically within that file. There are, in addition, library files in the Society library, publication files in the publications division, and a significant portion of current and old files in the Society business office. In addition the Society library holds manuscript minute books: "Minutes of Indiana Historical Society. Book I," 1830-1877; "Minutes of the Indiana Historical Society, 1886 to 1922. Book 2"; "Minutes of Ind. Hist. Soc. Beginning Jan. 1, 1919 (all previous minutes are in print)," 1919; "Minutes of the Indiana Historical Society [including executive committee minutes]," 1919-1929; "Meeting of the Executive Committee of the Indiana Historical Society," 1930-1956; "Library Committee. Indiana Historical Society," 1934-1969.

Other important sources include the Records of the Indiana

Historical Bureau, 42 boxes, and Records of the Indiana Historical Commission, 17 boxes, in the Archives Division, Commission on Public Records, Indiana State Library and Historical Building.

Other collections consulted include the following, with the abbreviations used in the footnotes:

Glenn A. Black Papers, Glenn A. Black Laboratory of Archaeology, Indiana University, Bloomington	Black Papers
Amos Butler Papers, Lilly Library, Indiana University, Bloomington	Butler Papers
George S. Cottman Papers, Indiana Division, Indiana State Library	Cottman Papers
John B. Dillon Papers, Indiana Division, Indiana State Library	Dillon Papers
Lyman Draper Collection, Wisconsin State Historical Society Library, microfilm copy in Indiana Division, Indiana State Library	Draper Papers
William H. English Papers, Joseph Regenstein Library, University of Chicago	English Papers, Chicago
William H. English Papers, Indiana Historical Society Library	English Papers, IHS
Eli Lilly Papers, Glenn A. Black Laboratory of Archaeology, Indiana University, Bloomington	Lilly Papers
Samuel Merrill Papers, Indiana Historical Society Library	Merrill Papers

William Polke Papers, Lilly Library,
    Indiana University, Bloomington

Polke Papers

John Tipton Papers, Indiana Division,
    Indiana State Library

Tipton Papers

James A. Woodburn Papers, Lilly
    Library, Indiana University,
    Bloomington

Woodburn Papers

INDEX

Index